*Margaret Morris*

# Britain and the Second World War

## The Fontana History of War and Society

The purpose of the series is to examine the impact of war on the course of British history. The need for the systematic study of war in the wider political, social and international context has never been greater. Although Britain has won every major war in the nineteenth and twentieth century her power in the world has shrunk. Britain has gone to war in the defence of interests and ideals which the nature and conduct of war proved difficult to uphold. War inflicts grievous injury yet the years of conflict appear to coincide with industrial and social advances. These are some of the problems which each volume, written by an authority in the field, seeks to answer. In thus focusing on the impact of war, the series will complement the more traditional view of the course of British history.

D1612431

The Fontana History
of War and Society

*General Editor:*
Professor J. A. S. Grenville

*In Preparation*
Britain and the Great War 1914-18
*Trevor Wilson*

Britain and the Boer War
*J. A. S. Grenville*

*To Follow*
Britain and the Crimean War
Britain and the Napoleonic Wars

# Britain and the Second World War

Henry Pelling

Collins
The Fontana History of War and Society

©Henry Pelling 1970

Made and Printed in Great Britain by
William Collins Sons & Co. Ltd., Glasgow

CONDITIONS OF SALE:
This book is sold subject to the condition that
it shall not, by way of trade or otherwise, be lent,
re-sold, hired out or otherwise circulated without
the publisher's prior consent in any form of
binding or cover other than that in which it is
published and without a similar condition
including this condition being imposed on the
subsequent purchaser

# Contents

# List of Maps and Diagrams

# Preface

I wish to acknowledge the kind assistance of the following persons who enabled me to use copyright material for which they are responsible: Rt Hon. Julian Amery, MP; Earl Attlee; Dorothy, Countess of Halifax; Admiral William H. Leahy, USN; Mrs Stephen Lloyd (for Neville Chamberlain); Captain S. W. Roskill, DSC, RN (for Lord Hankey); Viscount Samuel. For excerpts from the Lloyd George Papers and from letters of Lord Beaverbrook, I am indebted to Beaverbrook Newspapers and to the First Beaverbrook Foundation. I am also grateful to the Twenty-Seven Foundation for a travel grant to visit the United States in order to study sources there. Finally, the general editor of this series, Professor John A. S. Grenville, and my publisher, Mr Richard Ollard, have done me the kindness of reading the entire work in typescript, and have made valuable suggestions for its improvement. The responsibility for the shortcomings that remain is, of course, entirely mine.

H.M.P.

*St John's College, Cambridge*

*Guide to Footnotes*

All references to Hansard are to the Fifth Series and, unless otherwise stated, to Proceedings in the House of Commons.

*Parliamentary Papers* are indicated by *P.P.* and the year of publication, except in very recent years, when the Command Number is given.

References to W. S. Churchill's *Second World War* are to the First Edition except in the case of volume 1, where the Third Edition is used.

Titles of books which appear in abbreviated form in the footnotes will be found in full in the list of Books for Further Reading.

Detailed references to unpublished sources have not been provided in cases where the papers concerned are clearly catalogued, and the student will have no difficulty in tracing the reference.

Part One

# The Threat of War

# 1.  Introduction

When Britain went to war at the beginning of September 1939, there was a strange mixture of organization and confusion in government behaviour. On the one hand, Parliament was at once asked to pass a bill establishing five new ministries, which it did in one day; the Fleet was efficiently mobilized, as were the Army and Air Force Reserves and the Territorials; Civil Defence was swiftly put on the alert and one and a half million mothers and children were transported out of the expected target areas of enemy air raids. On the other hand, there was widespread puzzlement at the fact that there was no actual declaration of war. Poland had been invaded at many points at dawn on Friday, September 1st; German aircraft were active in bombing Polish towns and airfields; yet throughout that day and throughout Saturday no British ultimatum was sent to Germany, and no announcement of its impending despatch was made. Winston Churchill, still without access to official sources, could not understand what was happening. On the Friday he was invited by Neville Chamberlain, the Prime Minister, to join his War Cabinet, and he agreed to serve; but he heard nothing further that day or on Saturday, and began to wonder, as he wrote to Chamberlain, whether 'entirely different ideas have ruled from those which you expressed to me when you said "the die was cast".'[1] At the House of Commons bewilderment prevailed, and tempers began to rise. Those on the fringes of government heard of a 'stormy' session of the Cabinet, at which it seemed that decisions had been reached; but the Prime Minister's Parliamentary Private Secretary, Lord Dunglass (later known as Sir Alec Douglas-Home) still believed that 'the brand might be

1. Churchill, *Second World War*, i, 362f.

snatched from the burning'.[2] In the evening Chamberlain addressed the Commons, but made no announcement of an ultimatum. As Arthur Greenwood, the acting leader of the Labour Opposition, rose to protest, a prominent Conservative backbencher, Leopold Amery, shouted to him 'Speak for England'.[3] 'I wonder,' said Greenwood, 'how long we are prepared to vacillate at a time when Britain and all that Britain stands for, and human civilization, are in peril.'[4] Later in the evening, the Cabinet reassembled, and at last decided on an ultimatum, which was to expire at 11 next morning (Sunday September 3rd).

After this late-night decision, the tension relaxed. At the Foreign Office Lord Halifax, the Foreign Secretary, 'seemed relieved that we had taken our decision . . . We laughed and joked.'[5] Hugh Dalton, the Opposition spokesman on foreign affairs, who had been waiting in a corridor for news, reacted warmly to the announcement: ' "I do call that good news! Thank God!" he said and walked off.'[6] Next morning—a day of cloudless sunshine—the ultimatum expired at its due time; Chamberlain sadly announced the outbreak of war over the radio; and almost at once the London air raid sirens wailed out their warning for the first time in earnest. Half expecting immediate disaster from the sky, Londoners made their way hastily to the shelters, which were already prepared and assigned. Churchill, who was still at his flat in Pimlico, took with him 'a bottle of brandy and other appropriate medical comforts.'[7] But nothing happened; the 'all clear' blew after ten minutes. It was a false alarm.

What was the reason for this curious hesitation on the

2. Rhodes James, *Chips*, p. 211.
3. But Harold Nicolson (*Diaries*, i, 419) thought it was Boothby.
4. Hansard 351, 282f. (2 Sept., 1939).
5. Kirkpatrick, *Inner Circle*, p. 144.
6. J. Wedgwood, *Memoirs of a Fighting Life* (1941), p. 238. But cf. Dalton, *Fateful Years*, p. 267.
7. Churchill, *op. cit.*, p. 364.

brink of war? It owed not a little to the fact that although Britain and France faced the crisis as allies, their alliance was newly formed, full of misunderstandings, and vague in its political and military arrangements. There was an unwillingness on the part of politicians of both countries to recognize the extent of their mutual dependence. Of the two, historically no doubt Britain was more to blame: her leaders and still more her people hardly felt themselves to be part of Europe; and the twenty-two miles which separated Calais from Dover still seemed to be a barrier that enabled them to take a distant and even disinterested view of affairs on the Continent. To be sure, in the eighteenth and nineteenth centuries a 'blue-water' policy, by which in peacetime the country depended almost entirely on naval power, had operated well enough. Even in the early twentieth century, when agreements of a sort were made with France and Russia, and when an expeditionary force was prepared for a continental war, the commitment was so small and so tentative that it hardly seemed to be a major change of policy. But the First World War itself, with its terrible toll of the nation's young manhood in the trench warfare of Flanders, was a severe shock to all the existing preconceptions of Britain's need for military preparedness.

In the immediate aftermath of the First World War, British politicians were not prepared to face the harsh questions which it had posed for the future conduct of policy. They did not like to consider whether a permanent alliance, or at least a large peacetime army, would not be a better safeguard of the country's safety than reversion to purely traditional methods, coupled with reliance on the League of Nations, whose members were pledged to 'co-operate' and 'consult' in seeking disarmament and a peaceful solution to international problems. A proposal that Britain and the United States should jointly guarantee the frontiers of France was speedily abandoned by the British government when in 1920 the United States withdrew from all its European commitments. Later, by the Treaty of Locarno in 1925, Britain guaranteed the Franco-German frontier: but the fact of German disarmament under the Treaty of Versailles encouraged Britain to revive her old policy of relying almost exclusively for her defence upon the Navy. The Army and the Royal Air Force could be allowed to decline to the level necessary to maintain the Empire against colonial marauders.

Although it was politically unavoidable, there were serious dangers to Britain in the policy of allowing the Army and the Air Force to contract to minuscule size. Modern warfare required complicated weapons and well-trained personnel. Other countries were developing their industrial potential more rapidly than Britain, and they could easily obtain a lead in armament manufacture which Britain would find it difficult to overcome. The solution for this dilemma which commended itself to the British Cabinet was the 'ten-year rule'. This was the formula, annually reconsidered, which in its 1928 form declared

> that it should be assumed for the purpose of framing the estimates of the fighting services that at any given date there will be no major war for ten years.[8]

This formula remained in operation until March 1932; and under its auspices the proportion of the gross national product which was devoted to defence fell as low as $2\frac{1}{2}\%$.

But the abandonment of the formula did not lead to any rapid change of policy. Britain was still in the depths of the economic depression, and the new National Government, consisting mostly of Conservatives, sought to effect a recovery by the most orthodox methods of budgetary stringency. Furthermore, the threat to the peace still seemed very distant. At first the major troublespot was in the Far East, where in 1931 Japan had defied the League and turned Manchuria, part of the old Chinese Empire, into a puppet state of her own. But Britain was not prepared to take any initiative against Japan so long as her own interests in the Far East were not the object of direct

8. Postan, *British War Production*, p. 1.

attack. Then in January 1933 Adolf Hitler, at the head of
the National Socialist or Nazi Party, took power in Germany. He was avowedly committed to the liquidation of
the Versailles settlement. All the same, the French could
be expected to take care of this threat by themselves for
some time to come, for as yet there was no German air
force and only a very small army and navy. Further, the
Rhineland was still demilitarized, so that French troops
could at any time march into Germany. Late in 1933 the
Chiefs of Staff were instructed to draw up a programme
for remedying the worst deficiencies of British armaments,
but they were not expected to do more than this, and they
were told that no provision should be made for measures
of defence required 'exclusively against attack by the
United States, France or Italy', as all these powers were
assumed to be friendly.[9] As late as 1935 the increase in
the defence estimates was little more than 20% above the
lowest figures of the preceding decade.

The year 1935 proved to be a critical one for British
policy. For one thing, it was an election year, as Stanley
Baldwin, who had succeeded Ramsay MacDonald in the
leadership of the National Government, decided to seek a
renewal of its mandate. But in addition to this, it saw a
further challenge to the League of Nations, this time from
Italy, a power supposedly friendly to Britain although
ruled by the Fascist dictator Mussolini. Mussolini was
threatening an invasion of Abyssinia, a country which had
long been regarded as lying within the Italian sphere of
influence, but which Mussolini's own government had
earlier sponsored for membership of the League. People
in Britain suddenly began to take the League seriously:
if Italy could be prevented from invading Abyssinia, it
was possible that a system of collective security would
be created which would keep all the potentially aggressive
powers in restraint, including Germany and Japan; and all
this might well be done without any single power having

9. Italy was removed from this clause in July, 1937. See
Cabinet Minutes.

to spend large sums on rearmament. Such, at any rate, was the reasoning of the Liberal and Labour parties; and the so-called Peace Ballot, organized by members of the League of Nations Union, seemed to show that millions of people agreed with them. Baldwin and his colleagues, who were sceptical about the prospects of collective security through the League, nevertheless felt that they might lose the election if they did not at least undertake to try this policy. Perhaps Baldwin—a Conservative, but a moderate one—was unduly influenced on the question by ex-Liberal and ex-Labour men among his colleagues. At all events, he felt that defence increases by themselves would simply make the government unpopular, and he gave a pledge that 'there will be no great armaments'.[10] In October Italian forces invaded Abyssinia; the League powers, including Britain, imposed limited economic sanctions; and Baldwin called his general election.

The 1935 election provided the government with an easy victory. This was partly because Baldwin had so largely adopted the opposition foreign policy, but it was by no means exclusively because of this: and it may well be that Baldwin could have won the election even on a policy of re-armament. The Labour Party, which was the main opposition party, was still in a very weak position after its split in 1931, when it lost its best-known leaders, and its disaster in the election of that year, when it was reduced to a rump of 46 MPs. Its leader since 1932, the veteran left-winger George Lansbury, was an out-and-out pacifist who would not even accept the policy of collective security through the League; and it was only on the very eve of the election that after a rough passage at the Labour Party Annual Conference he was induced to resign. He was replaced by the mild-mannered and modest deputy leader of the party, Major Clement Attlee, who was virtually unknown to the mass of the voters. Then there was the important fact that in the preceding two years a gradual economic recovery had taken place, and the

10. *The Times,* 1 Nov., 1935.

number of the unemployed had dropped from almost three million to a little over two million. Although this latter figure was still distressingly high, the electors might well recall that it was under the last Labour Government that the great increase in the total had taken place. And so the 1935 election returned to Parliament no less than 431 MPs pledged to support Baldwin's National Government. Of these, 387 were Conservatives. On the Opposition side, there were 154 Labour MPs; an independent Liberal Party of 17; and a dozen more or less isolated independents. While by comparison with 1931 the Labour Party had won over a hundred seats, it was still a long way from returning to power again.

As soon as the election was over it became clear that the limited economic sanctions imposed by the League were quite ineffective. The alternatives were, to impose more effective sanctions, including that on oil, and if necessary to close the Suez Canal; or to back down and try to save something of independent Abyssinia by coming to terms with Mussolini. The British and French Foreign Ministers, Samuel Hoare and Pierre Laval, were soon agreed on the latter course, not because the combined strength of the two powers could not have crushed Mussolini's ambitions, but because they wanted Italy as an ally against the growing pretensions of Germany. But this *realpolitik* did not commend itself to the British public; and when the Hoare-Laval proposals were published in December there was such a storm that Baldwin had to disavow them and force his Foreign Secretary to resign, replacing him with a junior minister, Anthony Eden, who had shown signs of wanting to maintain a firmer line. Nevertheless, nothing was done to strengthen the existing sanctions; in May 1936 the Emperor of Abyssinia was obliged to go into exile; and in June the sanctions against Italy were rescinded.

Meanwhile, just as Hoare and Laval had feared, Hitler had been able to take advantage of the conflict between the other European powers. In March 1936 he sent

German troops to re-occupy the Rhineland, which was demilitarized under the Versailles Treaty. The attitude of the British government to the Versailles Treaty had already been demonstrated by the Anglo-German Naval Agreement of 1935, which indicated Britain's acceptance of an expansion of German naval power well beyond the Versailles limits. But the occupation of the Rhineland also breached the Locarno Treaty of 1925, which had been freely entered into by the German government: and there were at least some French leaders who realized that if they did not react strongly there would be no way, short of a major war, of preventing Germany from dominating Europe. The French Foreign Minister Flandin, who had replaced Laval, was an advocate of a strong policy; and he came to London to demand a simultaneous mobilization of armed forces. But he found no enthusiasm for his proposal in Whitehall. Majority British opinion at all levels appeared to judge the German action in isolation and refused to consider its significance for the future. Was it not 'equitable' that a nation should be free to occupy its own territory with troops, and to build fortifications there? As the Liberal spokesman Lord Lothian put it, the Germans were only going into 'their own back-garden.'[11]

The capacity of British politicians to take such a detached view of the new German challenge was both irritating and alarming to the French. It was partly due to a failure to realize that the English Channel no longer afforded the same degree of protection as it had done in the past. But there were also other factors. Many people in Britain had a feeling of guilt about the Treaty of Versailles, which had subjected Germany to unilateral restrictions upon her military strength, as well as to payment of reparations, the readjustment of European frontiers, and the loss of colonies. If the Nazi regime showed resentment against the western powers, this could readily be explained as the effect of the provisions of Versailles, which in the British

11. Butler, *Lothian*, p. 213.

view were largely due to French intransigence at the conference table. Then again, right-wing opinion in Britain regarded a strong Germany as a valuable bulwark against Russian Communism. Hitler was bitterly anti-Communist, and at the same time frequently spoke of Britain and her Empire in moderate, even friendly, language. Finally, Germany was like Britain a heavily industrialized country, and British businessmen had many contacts with their counterparts in Germany. At a time when men with long years of experience in industry were in the leading posts of British government—in particular, Stanley Baldwin, the Prime Minister, and Neville Chamberlain, his Chancellor of the Exchequer—it is perhaps not surprising that the idea prevailed that Britain could 'do a deal' with Germany in order to keep the peace. Little was as yet known about Nazi concentration camps and the persecution of the Jews; and some of the stories about atrocities could be put down to the inventive propaganda of the extreme Left. Both Baldwin and Chamberlain had been too old to serve in the armed forces in the First World War; but they had been powerfully impressed by the appalling loss of life which had taken place, and were prepared to make many concessions to avoid a repetition of such a tragedy.

All this necessitated a foreign policy that was largely independent of that of the successive French governments of the period. Whereas French policy was profoundly distrustful of the course of events in Germany, and consequently almost entirely negative, British policy was based on the more optimistic notion that the new German régime could gradually be tamed by friendship and concessions. In 1937 British ministers, including Lord Halifax who actually visited Hitler, hinted that Britain's share of the ex-German colonies would be returned in exchange for a general settlement, no doubt including arms limitation. But Hitler was not interested, since to him colonies were of slight importance compared to the revision of Germany's boundaries in Europe.

Meanwhile Conservative critics of the National Government, and in particular Winston Churchill, drew attention to the scale of German re-armament, and demanded action to enable Britain to keep up. Churchill it is true was somewhat of a lone voice, distrusted both by Left and Centre in politics. His support for the intervention in Russia at the end of the First World War had given him the reputation of a warmonger, and his bitter campaign against constitutional advance in India had cut him off from moderate opinion in his own party. Yet his detailed charges about the neglect of British defences, and the dangers of a re-armed Germany, could not but arouse some concern. A present-day historian, Mr A. J. P. Taylor, has pointed out that Churchill's figures for German re-armament were much exaggerated.[12] This is true, but the German lead over Britain was still very large. Even on Mr Taylor's figures, German expenditure on defence in 1936 was running at over £400 million, while the British estimates for the year 1936-7 totalled less than half this sum. Of even greater significance was the fact that German aircraft production far exceeded the British. This was something that even the most pacific of British governments could not afford to ignore. In his last year as Chancellor of the Exchequer Chamberlain busied himself with the details of a re-armament programme, and early in 1937 produced proposals for the expenditure of £1500 million over a five year period. This was a formidable commitment; but it was designed to build up gradually, and there was no escaping the fact that the actual production of the arms would seriously lag behind the German performance.

Nor did the programme take into account the possibility of co-ordinating the defence of Britain with that of France. Although there had been a show of staff consultations between the two powers after the re-occupation of the Rhineland, nothing had been decided as a result.

12. Taylor, *Origins of the Second World War* (Penguin ed., 1964), p. 17.

Significantly, the British government had simply not made up its mind about the role of the British army in any future war. Duff Cooper, the Secretary for War, thought that an Expeditionary Force to serve on the Continent should once again be prepared, as in the years before the First World War. But this aroused strong opposition from Chamberlain, who thought that 'it was not for France to dictate to us the distribution of our forces'.[13] Furthermore, as he put it in a Paper for the Cabinet, 'the political temper of people in this country is strongly opposed to continental ventures';

> They will be strongly suspicious of any preparations made in peacetime with a view to large-scale operations on the Continent, and they will regard such preparations as likely to result in our being entangled in disputes which do not concern us.[14]

The last clause was a hint at the military alliance which France had with Czechoslovakia—an alliance which was also supported by a guarantee from the Soviet Union, but which was not binding in any way on Britain. Chamberlain's Paper produced a reaction of astonishment from Duff Cooper, who replied that he could hardly believe that 'the Cabinet will be prepared to banish such a possibility [i.e. a continental war involving Britain] from their minds.'[15]

But the Cabinet did not veer towards Duff Cooper's standpoint as the German threat developed. On the contrary, Chamberlain's position in the Cabinet was strengthened when he succeeded Baldwin as Prime Minister in the summer of 1937; and one of his first acts was to move Duff Cooper from the War Office to the Admiralty, and to replace him with Leslie Hore-Belisha, who was willing

13. Cabinet Minutes, 16 Dec., 1936.
14. Cabinet Paper 334, Dec., 1936.
15. Cabinet Paper 337, Dec., 1936.

to accept a different version of the army's role. At the end of the year it was laid down that the primary task of the regular army was 'the defence of Imperial commitments, including anti-aircraft defence at home.'[16] There was consequently no need to plan for the production of heavy tanks or the other major items of equipment which were necessary for warfare against the forces of an advanced industrial power.

Thus the re-armament of Britain proceeded slowly and deliberately, and without consideration of the needs of land warfare on a major scale. To be sure, there was some reason to believe that, with their Maginot Line, the French would now have less need of allies to assist them on the ground. And industrial capacity which was not needed for making tanks could be better used, in Chamberlain's view, on speeding up the programme of aircraft manufacture. Without sacrificing her peacetime economy, Britain could not expect to keep up with Germany in every sphere of defence preparations; and so it was best to concentrate on the Navy, always the first charge on British defence expenditure, and on the Air Force, which was so important for the defence of London.

The Chiefs of Staff, who had been pressing for re-armament for years, were naturally pleased to have secured the programme which was authorized in 1937. But in view of the threatening international situation, which indicated that Britain might find herself at war simultaneously with Germany and Italy and Japan, they felt it necessary to point out that they could not imagine, even when the re-armament were complete, that it would be possible for Britain to fight successfully against all three powers at once. They therefore ventured into politics to the extent of saying:

> We cannot . . . exaggerate the importance, from the point of view of Imperial defence, of any political or international action that can be taken to reduce

16. Cabinet Paper 316, Dec., 1937.

the number of our potential enemies or to gain the support of potential allies.[17]

Unfortunately, as Chamberlain observed, there was not much to be looked for from 'potential allies'. France was an 'important friend . . . strong defensively', but 'the French air force was far from satisfactory':

> The power that had the greatest strength was the United States of America, but he would be a rash man who based his considerations on help from that quarter.[18]

The Chiefs of Staff themselves had stated that Russian intervention, owing to the 'purges' in the armed forces and the danger of bringing Japan in on the other side, would be 'an embarrassment rather than a help.'[19] As for the smaller powers, Chamberlain said, they were friendly, but 'he did not think that they would add much to our defensive or offensive strength.'[20]

The obvious conclusion, already in Chamberlain's mind, was that it was essential to 'reduce the number of our potential enemies' by pressing on with a policy of 'appeasement'. The difficulty of the policy, however, was that it evoked no response from the potential enemies. All of them became convinced, after the failure of sanctions and the re-occupation of the Rhineland, that Britain and France had no intention of going to war over any issue that was less than a direct attack on their own territory. Germany and Italy intervened in the Spanish Civil War (1936-9) while paying lip-service to the policy of non-intervention which Britain and France sought to establish. Japan became involved in a full-scale war with China, but this made for worse rather than better relations with

17. Cabinet Paper 296, Dec., 1937.
18. Cabinet Minutes, 8 Dec., 1937.
19. Cabinet Paper 316, Dec., 1937.
20. Cabinet Minutes, 8 Dec., 1937.

Britain, as the Japanese forces badly injured the British ambassador to China in a bombing incident, and also attacked a British gunboat.

Chamberlain dominated his Cabinet more than most Prime Ministers, and although he had had virtually no experience of the conduct of foreign policy, he was quite prepared to override or circumvent his young Foreign Secretary, Anthony Eden, who had been rapidly promoted by Baldwin. Eden believed that any reconciliation with Italy must involve some definite signs of concession on the Italian side, such as the withdrawal of a significant number of troops from Spain. Chamberlain was not so particular, and in February 1938 there was an undignified scene when the two ministers quarrelled in the presence of the Italian ambassador. Eden then resigned from the government, and was replaced by Lord Halifax, who sympathized more warmly with the appeasement policy. Only a few weeks later Hitler formally annexed Austria and forthwith invaded the country, meeting virtually no opposition. Czechoslovakia, a Slav country with a substantial German-speaking population within its borders, was now surrounded on three sides by German forces and was obviously to be the next victim of Hitler's policy of expansion.

After the Austrian coup Chamberlain momentarily showed signs of changing his policy. 'Heaven knows', he wrote privately, 'I don't want to get back to alliances but if Germany continues as she has done lately she may drive us to it.'[21] But on mature consideration he decided against any such course. It was in his view better to let Germany absorb the German-speaking areas of Czechoslovakia than to make any sort of stand on this issue. Hitler, he reminded himself, was only asserting the principle of self-determination of peoples, which had been the ostensible basis of the Versailles settlement. The danger was, however, that France might be drawn into war on behalf of Czechoslovakia because of her treaty of mutual assistance; and

21. Feiling, *Chamberlain*, p. 342.

this in turn might present Britain with the sort of situation which had led her to war in 1914. Chamberlain determined to avoid such developments by pressing the Czechs to make immediate concessions; and he was greatly assisted by the weak attitude of the French, who realized that in the event of war their army could do little to assist the Czechs now that the Rhineland had been remilitarized. Unfortunately for both Britain and France, Hitler did not really want any concessions of German-speaking territory by the Czechs. He wanted war, at any rate against Czechoslovakia. This was demonstrated quite clearly when the Czech government accepted the demands of the leader of the German minority, Henlein, only to find that, on instructions from Berlin, the price of agreement had gone up.

As the tension rose in September 1938 Chamberlain played what he regarded as a trump card—an offer to visit Hitler personally in Germany. For propaganda purposes Hitler could hardly refuse to meet the British Prime Minister, but he heartily disliked being deprived of his opportunity to crush Czechoslovakia by force, which at first he thought could be done without the danger of a general war. Chamberlain, however, without meaning to do so had involved Britain deeply in the search for a peaceful solution of the crisis; and when it seemed, after his first contacts with Hitler, that Germany was about to invade Czechoslovakia without further ado, his Cabinet colleagues obliged him to take a stronger line: the British fleet was mobilized, trenches were dug in the London parks and there was a distribution of gas-masks to the civil population. At the same time a solemn warning of the danger of general war was given to the German leader. At this point Hitler modified his attitude somewhat, and agreed to a suggestion, put forward by Mussolini, that a conference should be held on the subject, to be attended by Britain, France, Germany and Italy. Both Czechoslovakia herself, the unhappy victim of Hitler's claims, and Russia, her other ally, were denied membership of the conference. But Chamberlain accepted the idea with alacrity.

It was by all accounts with considerable reluctance that Hitler abandoned his planned offensive against the Czechs, in return for the concession, at the four-power conference which was held at Munich, of virtually all he demanded. But the fact was that Chamberlain, the tall, thin, elderly civilian with the umbrella, was warmly greeted by the German population; and all Hitler's advisers, both political and military, and also Mussolini, were urging the German dictator to accept what was already a bloodless victory. All the same, his behaviour was unusual: he 'was obviously in a black mood, furious with the whole business . . . [He] did not disguise the effort he was making to take part in the conventional courtesies which closed the proceedings.'[22] This was not the behaviour of a man who felt he had won a great success—although, to be sure, a great defeat had been inflicted on both Britain and France. The fortifications on the Czech border were handed over to Germany, and the remainder of the country lay open to occupation. Russia was ignored; and the small powers of the Balkans realized that they must accept a virtual German suzerainty.

As for Chamberlain, he behaved as if the victory had been his, and was received in that fashion by the great bulk of people in London on his return from Munich. Acknowledging the cheers of the crowd at No. 10 Downing Street, he went so far as to speak of the Munich agreement as 'peace with honour . . . peace in our time.' In fact, it was peace with dishonour, peace at the expense of France's only continental ally. It has been argued that Munich served a useful purpose because it convinced Britain's overseas Dominions that Britain and France would go far along the road of concession in order to save the peace; and so it won their support, in varying degrees, when war actually broke out. There is some truth in this: and in particular it is doubtful if South Africa, which

22. Kirkpatrick, *op. cit.*, p. 128.

joined in the war in 1939, would have done so in 1938. But none of the Dominions had standing armies, and their military contributions were bound in the short run to be small.

The other main justification which has been made for the Munich agreement is that it gave Britain and France a few more months in which to re-arm. It is questionable, however, whether the extra months were more to the advantage of Britain and France than to that of Germany. The French Army and air force were, if anything, wasting assets; and the German tanks which were to win the battle of France in 1940 were only issued to units just before the battle. Furthermore, the Czech army and fortifications, which were formidable, were lost to the western powers, as was the possibility, however imponderable, of Russian intervention on their side. The main advantage which the western powers gained from the delay was in the improvement of British air defences: in the installation of radar and in the supply of modern types of fighter aircraft—the Hurricane and the Spitfire—in numbers sufficient to blunt a German air offensive. But it is unlikely that there would have been a dangerous air offensive against Britain until the French armies had collapsed.

Of course, the calculations made at the time were based on inaccurate information about the relative strengths of the powers concerned. We now know that in the course of 1938 the proportion of the German national product that was devoted to defence was of the order of 16%, whereas the corresponding proportion in Britain's case was only 7.9%.[23] British and French expenditure combined was little more than half that of Germany. But it was believed in Britain in 1938 that Germany's strength was very much greater than even these figures suggest. The dangers of air attack on London were especially exaggerated. It was thought possible that the German Air Force could drop 700 tons of bombs on London every day in the first fortnight of war: and it was assumed (on the rather

23. H. Hillmann in RIIA, *World in March 1939*, p. 456.

dubious evidence of air raids on London in the First World War, and of those on Barcelona in the Spanish Civil War) that there would be fifty to seventy-two casualties per ton of bombs, one-third of which would be immediately fatal. At this rate, up to 211,000 civilians would be killed and 422,000 injured after two weeks of war. In reality Germany had no plans for strategic bombing; the number of air raid deaths in London throughout six years of war was less than 30,000; and the rate of deaths per ton of bombs was less than three.[24]

It is not surprising, therefore, that Chamberlain decided after Munich that he must press on with the armament programme, while at the same time continuing the policy of appeasement. The production of aircraft, and particularly of fighter aircraft, was accelerated; and military talks were initiated with the French, which were bound to lead to a French demand for land forces to counterbalance the loss of the Czech divisions. A small family air raid shelter, known after the minister in charge as the 'Anderson', was rapidly put into production: one and a half million of them had been delivered free by the outbreak of war. As for appeasement, Chamberlain concentrated his efforts for the time being on Italy, and visited Rome in January 1939 for talks with Mussolini. He returned empty-handed, but nevertheless convinced that 'the journey has definitely strengthened the chances of peace'.[25] This wishful thinking communicated itself to his colleagues. Early in March Sir Samuel Hoare, who was now Home Secretary, claimed that the spirit of co-operation between the powers which was revealed at Munich indicated that Europe could 'look forward to a golden age of prosperity'.[26]

The optimism in Whitehall and among Chamberlain's supporters in the country was rudely dashed by the German occupation of the rump of Czechoslovakia on March 15th, 1939. Now for the first time large numbers

24. Titmuss, Social Policy, pp. 6, 14, 560.
25. Feiling, op. cit., p. 393.
26. Templewood, Nine Troubled Years, p. 328.

of people not of German stock were being incorporated in the Reich. At all levels in Britain there was an immediate revulsion of feeling against Germany, and many who had previously thought that appeasement might work abandoned the hope altogether. The inevitability of war within a few months was accepted; and in response to pleas from the French Cabinet it was decided to double the size of the Territorial Army, and then to introduce conscription and to make definite plans for the despatch of an expeditionary force to France on the outbreak of war. At the same time, there was a drastic change in foreign policy. Rumours of an impending German attack on Rumania led the government to hasty consultation with the French and to the two governments' joint guarantee of the independence of Rumania and also Poland, which was regarded as a useful ally. Considering that the western powers could do no more for Poland than they could for Czechoslovakia, this seemed a rash commitment; but the advice of the military experts was to the effect that Poland had a stronger army than Russia, and that Germany might draw back from a two-front war.[27] Such an absurd overestimate of Polish strength was probably due to reliance on purely military advice, without taking account of the country's relative industrial capacity, which is so important for equipping and maintaining an efficient army and air force. At all events, from the spring of 1939 Britain was committed to a continental policy of alliance, of the type that Chamberlain had for so long struggled to avoid.

The late spring and early summer of 1939 was a period full of tension, in which the western powers waited for Hitler finally to throw down the gauntlet, and both sides manoeuvred for the support of Russia. To the outer world, it looked as if there could be no reconciliation between Communism and Nazism—two ideologies which were so bitterly opposed. But Stalin, the Russian dictator, had already given Hitler a hint of his intentions when in a

27. *Ibid.*, p. 344.

public speech he had declared that Russia did not want to be drawn into a war to 'pull the chestnuts out of the fire' for other countries. Since Britain and France were committed to the defence of Poland and Rumania and in general to the independence of small nations, it was clear that Hitler could outbid them by offering Russia territorial gaints at the expense of Poland and her other neighbours. On August 22nd Hitler and Stalin suddenly announced that they were signing a non-aggression pact. In a secret annex they agreed to a mutual division of Eastern Europe.

Hitler could now give instructions for the invasion of Poland, for which planning had been completed. The date chosen for the attack was September 1st. Various frontier incidents were manufactured for purposes of propaganda. At the same time, attempts were made to suggest that the Polish government had refused to accept any re-adjustment of the status of Danzig, the Polish treaty-port, and the Polish Corridor through East Prussia, where part of the population was German. The British government had urged the Poles to negotiate on these questions, but they refused to do so under duress; and Hitler had no intention of delaying his invasion plans. At dawn on the appointed day five armies, including all the German mechanized divisions, crossed the Polish frontiers.

Even at this last moment Chamberlain had difficulty in accepting that war was inevitable. There were contacts with Hitler and Goering through a Swedish intermediary, the industrialist Birger Dahlerus, to which he attached considerable weight; and in addition the Italian government showed clear signs of being anxious to prevent war, and proposed a conference of the same character as Munich.[28] The French, whose air defences were weaker than those of Britain, wanted extra time to mobilize their forces and to evacuate Paris; and in any case some of their ministers seemed to want to keep out of war altogether. Ever since 1936, when the opportunity of dealing with the

28. Feiling, *op. cit.*, pp. 416f., quoting a letter of Chamberlain of 10 Sept., 1939.

nascent German threat had been let slip, French morale
in the face of aggression had been crumbling.

It was significant that there had been no attempt at co-
ordinating mobilization policy between the two countries
in the event of need. As the crisis developed, there was
frantic telephoning between London and Paris which led
to no agreement about the timing of an ultimatum. Meanwhile, Poland was suffering all the horrors of an invasion
by vastly superior forces. In Britain, suspicion grew that
Chamberlain was himself supporting the idea of a new
surrender. A Cabinet meeting in the afternoon of September 2nd declared unanimously for war, an ultimatum to
be timed to expire at midnight. But the French government
was still dragging its feet. When Parliament met, ministers
outside Chamberlain's immediate circle were 'aghast' to
hear no announcement of the decision.[29] They met separately after the Parliamentary statement and demanded
immediate action. Later that night the Cabinet as a whole
again went into session and the decision for an ultimatum
was confirmed, though this time it was to expire at 11
a.m. next day. This was the decision which, after immediate action at the Foreign Office, allowed Halifax to
relax and gave Dalton his 'good news'.

Even so, co-ordination with the French continued to
be poor. The French Cabinet's ultimatum, although sent
on the same day, was timed for six hours after the British.
A French military attaché flying back to Britain shortly
after the expiry of the British ultimatum, arrived without
the proper recognition signal and so set off the London
air raid sirens by mistake.[30] And the British Cabinet still
had to decide who should be the Commander-in-Chief
for the tiny expeditionary force of four divisions (without
armour) which were to go to France in the next few days;
and it still had to consult with the French government
about the role of the force and the sector of the front
which it should occupy.

29. Minney, *Hore-Belisha*, p. 226.
30. Slessor, *Central Blue*, p. 234.

## 2.  Attitudes to War, 1939

'It is evil things that we shall be fighting against,' said
Chamberlain in his broadcast on the outbreak of war:
'brute force, bad faith, injustice, oppression and persecution.'[1] It need be no reflection on the Prime Minister's sincerity to point out that so far as he was concerned, it was
only 'brute force' and 'bad faith' that had actually precipi-
tated Britain into war. Hitler's oppression and persecution
of German citizens, especially Jews and political liberals,
would not of themselves have led to a direct conflict with
Britain, at any rate while Chamberlain was in power. It
was, indeed, a principle of the National Government's
foreign policy that relations between states should not be
based upon ideological considerations, but that good feelings should be cultivated with all foreign countries which
were prepared to reciprocate them. To be sure, Conservatives had a special dislike of Soviet Russia; but this was
due to specific reasons—the expropriation of British
property interests by the Bolsheviks, and the support still
given by the Russian dictator Joseph Stalin to the Communist parties in Britain and the British Empire. By the
mid-1930s these reasons were counting for less than they
had done previously. 'We ourselves,' said Eden as Foreign
Secretary in 1937, 'have no greater desire than to co-
operate fully with others, and herein we make no excep-
tions. We shall respond fully to the same desire, wherever
it manifests itself.'[2]

The government's empirical attitude to foreign policy
was well exemplified by the special case of the Spanish
Civil War. In 1936 a group of army leaders, including

1. Feiling, *Chamberlain*, p. 416.
2. Hansard 319, 108 (19 Jan., 1937).

General Franco, supported by nearly all right-wing and propertied elements and by the hierarchy of the Catholic Church, had risen in revolt against a left-wing government. Spain was strategically important for Britain, but British policy was at once directed towards an attempt to 'hold the ring' for the contestants and to prevent intervention by other powers. It was assumed that it would be perfectly possible to establish good relations with the victors in the Spanish war, whatever their political complexion, provided that they had not become too dependent upon some foreign power or powers. As it turned out, British policy could not prevent continuous German and Italian intervention on Franco's side, and Russian intervention against him; but in the end the presumption that a new Spanish government of any complexion would consult its own interests before it responded to those of its civil war allies was vindicated by Spanish neutrality in the World War.

The minds of Liberal and Labour politicians worked in a very different way on questions of foreign policy. They started off with the belief that not only the democratic nations, but also—at any rate since its admission to the League of Nations in 1935—the Soviet Union could be regarded as 'peace-loving'; while on the other hand countries with right-wing authoritarian regimes, and in particular Germany, Italy and Japan, were inherently militaristic and expansionist and hence sooner or later likely to attack Britain. This interpretation of the international scene was partly based on the fact that Germany, Italy and Japan had all breached the law of the League of Nations; and the British Left, which had always held much higher hopes of the League than the Right had done, was naturally the more aggrieved. But Socialists also accepted the thesis, first advanced by J. A. Hobson at the time of the South African War and later elaborated by Lenin, that countries in an advanced stage of capitalism had a strong impulse to seek markets by political expansion and hence by war.

The Socialists, of course, were well aware that Britain

B.A.S.W.W.

was a capitalist state; and hence they were reluctant to
trust the motives of the existing government in its foreign
policy any more than in its domestic policy. It followed
that many of them were unwilling to respond to the
National Government's call for a bi-partisan attitude to
the question of re-armament. This question was hotly
debated at the 1937 conference of the Labour Party. On
the one hand were the less doctrinaire elements, led by
the influential secretary of the Transport and General
Workers Union, Ernest Bevin, who maintained that British
plans of re-armament had already encouraged 'the liberty-
loving nations of the world';[3] on the other hand was the
Socialist Left with spokesmen such as the fiery Welsh
MP Aneurin Bevan, who held that for Labour to support
re-armament while in opposition was 'to put a sword in
the hands of our enemies that may be used to cut off our
own heads'.[4] Bearing in mind that there was a sizeable
proportion of out-and-out pacifists in the Labour ranks,
and also that it was common ground within the party that
increased expenditure on arms would mean decreased
expenditure on social reform, it becomes easier to understand how it was that Labour dragged its feet in the
acceptance of such a commitment. The trade-union leaders,
with their common-sense attitude to the realities of
power, and their appreciation of the fact that trade unionism had been almost the first thing to be destroyed by the
new regimes in Italy and Germany, led the way in bringing
about a change of view.

These ambiguities on the Left were probably of considerable importance in preventing the Opposition from
emerging, in the Chamberlain years, as a vigorous and
convincing alternative government, or even as a nucleus
for such an alternative government, to which Conservative
dissenters such as Churchill and the Eden group could
gravitate. It is significant that according to the monthly
Gallup poll started in October 1938 Chamberlain regularly
had the support of the majority of the electorate. Nor can

3. Labour Party *Report*, 1937, p. 207.    4. *Ibid*., p. 209.

this be interpreted as a vote against war, for after war broke out his support grew still further.[5]

Yet bitter hostility both to Chamberlain and to his colleagues was general among the Opposition; it was not just something to be found among the left-wing leaders such as Sir Stafford Cripps and Aneurin Bevan, both of whom were expelled from the Labour Party in 1939 for establishing a working political alliance with the Communists. The hostility is to be explained in part by the narrow and unaccommodating personality of Chamberlain himself, who lacked the good humour and indeed the breadth of political understanding shown by his predecessor, Baldwin. But it had its roots in the harsh realities of British social and political life between the wars. In a period when the proportion of the unemployed in the total work-force was hardly ever less than 10%, the Labour and Liberal parties divided the vote of the Left, with the result that Conservative or Conservative-dominated governments held office for eighteen of the twenty-one years between the two wars. For most of this period Chamberlain was in a key position to shape home policy, and as Chancellor of the Exchequer in 1931-7 he had been the champion of orthodoxy at the Treasury.

The inter-war depression was not the fault of the Conservatives any more than of the other political parties. The essential problem was that the staple export industries of the country—coal, textiles and shipbuilding—were suffering from a shrinkage of their international markets. As a result, there was heavy unemployment in the North of England, in Scotland and South Wales, where these industries were concentrated; and nobody at the time had much idea of how the unemployed in these areas could be put to work again. It is true that the economist J. M. Keynes began to work out ways and means of stimulating internal demand by government action in times of depression; and these ideas were taken up by Lloyd George and Sir Oswald Mosley in the 1930's, without achieving

5. *News Chronicle*, 29 Dec., 1939.

much popular impact. But Keynes's proposals would not have done much for the export staples; and in any case there was a considerable expansion of the internal market in the 1930's under Chamberlain's 'cheap money' policy, which resulted in a housing boom, especially in the south, and in the rapid growth of new industries such as motor manufacture and electrical engineering in the London area and in the Midlands. All this augured well for the future: and there was a considerable migration, especially of younger people, from Wales, Scotland and the North to London and the Midlands. In the mining valleys of Wales, however, and in the ship-building towns of Scotland and Northern England, and in the mill towns of Lancashire and Yorkshire, there remained large numbers of unemployed, especially the older unemployed, who had not moved. In the 1935 election many of them had voted Labour once again, even if they had not done so in 1931, the year of the split in the party; and their MPs reflected in their own attitude to the government the bitterness that they found among their constituents.

The bitterness might have been modified if the Labour Party had had more opportunity to form the government in the inter-war period. Unfortunately, although it took office for brief periods first in 1924 and then in 1929-31, it never held a majority of seats in Parliament and was dependent upon support from the other, now declining party of the Left, the Liberals. The conflict on the Left between the Liberals and the Labour Party was damaging to the parliamentary system: it meant that the experienced men of the Liberal Party were unable to display their talents in government, and the inexperienced men of Labour failed to make the best use of their limited opportunities. Above all, it meant that in the first period of virtually full democratic franchise (introduced in 1918) the Conservatives were normally in office and the Left— whether Liberals or Labour—in opposition. Further, the crisis of 1931, when the Labour Party lost its outstanding parliamentary leaders to the National Government and suffered a crushing defeat at the polls, was a traumatic experience for those who stayed in the party. It seemed to many of them that their party's failure at that time was due much more to sinister anti-democratic forces than it was to their own incompetence. Their scapegoats were the international bankers, the City of London, the 'aristocratic embrace' which had corrupted Labour's own leaders, and perhaps also the partisan bias of the King himself.[6]

The remarkable degree of unanimity in the country when war broke out can, therefore, be attributed more to the extent to which the members of all parties had come to dislike Hitler and Nazism, than to any warmth of feeling on the part of the Opposition for the existing Prime Minister and government. In fact, at the moment when Arthur Greenwood, Attlee's deputy in the leadership, was voicing the 'resentment, apprehension, anger'[7] felt by many in Parliament on both sides of the House that the country was not immediately at war after the invasion of Poland, he and his colleagues were also refusing to join a Coalition government under Chamberlain's leadership—a refusal in which the Liberals concurred. And at Bridlington, where the TUC was meeting when war was declared, a motion of support for the war, which spoke of ' a united and resolute nation' entering the struggle 'with a clear conscience and steadfast purpose' was carried by an overwhelming majority;[8] but this motion was carried by men who had been 'glum and angry' when they met Chamberlain at the time of the introduction of conscription, and it was of this encounter that Sir Samuel Hoare, one of Chamberlain's closest colleagues, wrote: 'I had never realized the extent of the personal bitterness felt by the Labour leaders against the Prime Minister.'[9]

When it came to the days of decision, therefore, there

6. For left-wing criticism of the King's role, see R. Bassett, *1931: Political Crisis* (1958), pp. 358ff.

7. Hansard 351, 292 (3 Sept., 1939).

8. TUC *Report*, 1939, pp. 306, 338.

9. Templewood, *Nine Troubled Years*, p. 338.

was a virtual unanimity of the opposition parties as there was of the government supporters in favour of the declaration of war. On the extreme Right there was the tiny Fascist fringe, its leader, Sir Oswald Mosley, a former Labour minister; there were the out-and-out pacifists, many of them with religious objections to taking part in war; and there were the members of the small Communist Party—in some disarray owing to Russia's switch of policy after the Russo-German Pact of August 1939. All these opponents of the war did not amount to much, and it can safely be said that Britain entered the war with a greater degree of unanimity than in 1914; and this was so in spite of the fact that the perils to be encountered were, if anything, exaggerated on this occasion, rather than, as in 1914, hardly appreciated at all. As for the mass of the population, the support for the Prime Minister shown by the Gallup poll is perhaps the best indicator. In April 1939 only 14% of the sample were opposed to the British military guarantees to Poland and Rumania, and there is no reason to suppose that all of these were still hostile to the government when war actually broke out.[10]

A British declaration of war was a declaration on behalf of the United Kingdom of Great Britain and Northern Ireland, and also on behalf of India, Burma and the colonies. Thus the Foreign Office spoke for almost 48 million people in the home country, about 63 millions in the colonial empire, about 370 million Indians (including the inhabitants of what is now Pakistan) and 15 million Burmese. The governments and Parliaments of the self-governing Dominions of the Crown—Canada, Australia, New Zealand, South Africa and Eire—were free to make up their own minds, whether to fight or stay neutral.

The Dominions were the lands of substantial white settlement, but individually they were not heavily populated, Canada, the largest, having only 11 million inhabi-

10. British Institute of Public Opinion, *What Britain Thinks* (1939), p. 20.

tants. Nor did they show much interest in preparations for war, relying for their protection upon their remoteness from potential enemies and upon the strength of the British Navy. Thus none of them, save Eire, had a standing army; and the Irish army was not one to be considered very seriously, as it only numbered 16,000 men. It is perhaps not surprising that Dominion sentiment should be hostile to commitments by Britain on the continent of Europe, as was clearly demonstrated at the time of the Imperial Conference of 1937. Malcolm MacDonald, then the Dominions Secretary, told the British Cabinet after the conference that the Dominion leaders found even the policies of Baldwin and Chamberlain too 'interventionist' for their liking:

> The Canadian Prime Minister had spoken in a slightly isolationist spirit. The Prime Minister of New Zealand had followed with a polite but rather comprehensive attack on the United Kingdom foreign policy. General Hertzog [South Africa] had intimated the view that our attitude to the French was too warm, and towards the Germans too cold. Even the Australian delegate had criticized our opposition to the Anschluss [proposed union of Germany and Austria].[11]

Lack of information was part of the trouble. The Dominion governments had few representatives of their own in foreign capitals, and did not know what was going on in Europe. The Canadian High Commissioner in London was actually forbidden by his government to take part in foreign policy briefings at the Dominions Office.[12] As MacDonald reported, after the discussions 'the attitude of the Dominions had gradually swung round towards our own'.[13] The common heritage of free parliamentary insti-

11. Cabinet Minutes, 16 June, 1937.
12. Massey, *Memoirs*, pp. 236f.
13. Cabinet Minutes, 16 June, 1937.

tutions, and the ties of language and kinship, all helped to make the British case acceptable to the majority.

We have already seen that the Dominions all approved the Munich agreement in 1938. A year later they were much more attuned to the idea of involvement in war on Britain's side. The main difficulty was with Eire, whose very existence stemmed from a revolt against Britain in the middle of the previous German war. Although Eire could not escape close economic ties with Britain, her sense of political alienation was strong. De Valera, the Prime Minister, was on cordial personal terms with Chamberlain, especially after having persuaded the British Cabinet, early in 1938, to hand over the so-called 'treaty ports' which the British government had been entitled to garrison and use as naval bases under the 1921 treaty between the two countries. His success was due, in fact, to the view of the Chiefs of Staff that they could not afford the troops to garrison the ports against a hostile population.[14] But de Valera's satisfaction at the 1938 agreement did not alter his determination to keep Eire out of the war. What happened in the upshot was that, while Eire was technically neutral, large numbers of Irishmen continued to cross to Britain to work in the factories, and many also served in the British armed forces. A dump of civilian clothing was kept at Holyhead for the convenience of Irish servicemen travelling home on leave. But de Valera was unable to have more than a *chargé d'affaires* at Berlin, because the appointment of an ambassador would have required the signature of the King.

All the other Dominions declared war in September 1939, but those with a high proportion of inhabitants of non-British stock had their doubts at first. The greatest problems arose in South Africa, not because of the Africans, who were not of any political significance, but because of the Boers, who were of roughly equal strength with the population of British origin. Some prominent

14. *The Times*, 4 Feb., 1942 (letter from Chatfield).

Boer leaders, in particular General Smuts, sided with the British, and this proved decisive. General Hertzog, the Prime Minister, was against a declaration of war, but the Cabinet split seven to five against him, and the House of Assembly was for war by a vote of 80 to 67. Hertzog resigned and Smuts succeeded him as Premier, and war was declared on September 6th.

In Canada the issue was less in doubt, but the government, mindful of the susceptibilities of the French-speaking population—who had no great feeling of sympathy for the French Republic—felt it necessary to allow Parliament to debate the question thoroughly before any declaration of war was made. After it had been announced that conscription would not be introduced, an overwhelming majority voted for war, which was declared on September 10th. The governments of Australia and New Zealand, which were more homogeneously of British origin, did not deem it necessary even to assert their own right to declare war; for them, a state of war was deemed to have existed from the moment of the British declaration.

The colonies accepted their commitment to the British cause with attitudes varying from enthusiasm to resignation. The inhabitants of most of them, if they thought about it at all, could hardly conceive of any other course. In any case, as there were no German forces outside Europe, the war with Germany did not seem likely to affect them very directly. Nationalist feeling as yet had no real strength except in the Middle East and India, and this meant, so far as the colonial Empire was concerned, that only Palestine was affected. But unfortunately Palestine was very seriously affected, as the Arabs strongly resented the Jewish immigration, which built up a strong minority now numbering about half a million. In 1937 a British Royal Commission had recommended the partition of Palestine, but this had been followed by an Arab revolt, which engaged considerable British forces. On the eve of the war the government, knowing that it had Jewish support in its quarrel with Germany, sought to mollify the Arabs by declaring against partition and by cutting down further Jewish immigration. This policy was designed not merely to win back the Palestine Arabs but also to keep in line the Arab client states Egypt and Iraq, both of which were committed by treaty to provide bases for British troops in war as in peace. No fighting was to be expected in the Middle East until such time as Italy should enter the war: meanwhile an uneasy lull descended on the area, in the expectation that events in Europe would determine the future course of action.

Elsewhere in the colonial empire the outbreak of war changed the normal routine of government but little. The typical colony was ruled by a British governor and a small body of British civil officers of the Colonial Service, backed by exiguous local forces of police and a few predominantly native troops. Each colony enjoyed a great deal of local autonomy, which meant, not that there was much participation in government by the native-born, but that Whitehall did not attempt to interfere. Some governors were in a position to behave like despots; others, however, where there were local assemblies, were more like constitutional monarchs. In any case the junior colonial servants, the District Officers, had wide powers at their discretion. Bound by a code of conduct which derived from British public school education, they sought only to pass on their charges in a slightly better state than they found them. Larger objects were not practicable, for the colonies were poor countries, and the home government had only just begun to provide a trickle of funds for colonial development by an Act of 1929. As the purpose of the Act was not so much to help the colonies as to 'promote commerce with, or industry in, the United Kingdom', and as only £5 million was spent in a decade, it made little real difference. As the Colonial Secretary said in 1940,

> The existence of the Fund has not involved any departure from the old principle that a Colony

should have only those services which it can maintain out of its own resources.[15]

At the outbreak of war there was very little interest in Britain for any discussion of colonial affairs. As Herbert Samuel, the Liberal leader, put it, 'Parliamentary supervision of colonial administration is somewhat perfunctory, and the Secretary of State for the Colonies has a fairly unnoticed and uninterrupted career.'[16] This was partly because there was little serious nationalist feeling in the colonial empire. Even the labour riots in the West Indies in the later 1930s, though they provoked a Royal Commission, did not arouse concern about the loyalty of the islanders to the British connexion. 'In the latest troubles' wrote a close observer, 'strike meetings normally closed with *God Save the King*.'[17]

Things were different in India. This vast sub-continent was still largely a land of peasants, but there were many large cities, a growing industry, and an educated class of some size. A vigorous nationalist movement had for many years demanded constitutional advance, and the principle had long been conceded by the British government. The great difficulty was the mutual hostility of the different communities in India, and in particular the rivalry between the Hindus and the Muslims. But under the Government of India Act, 1935, arrangements were made for elected governments both in the provinces and at the centre. By an Act of 1937 Burma was separated from India and enabled to set up its own elected government. Unfortunately the central government of India had still not been set up when war broke out in 1939, because the princes who ruled a large part of the country, under treaty arrangements with Britain, had for the most part

15. W. K. Hancock, *Survey of British Commonwealth Affairs*, ii (1942), p. 344.

16. Lord Samuel, 'The Colonies at Westminster' (c. 1944), Samuel Papers A/121/129.

17. W. M. Macmillan, *Warning from the West Indies* (1938), p. 60.

not signified their adhesion to the constitution, and this was regarded as an essential preliminary. Thus although India had been admitted to the League of Nations as a founder-member, her central government was still under the control of a British Viceroy, theoretically the representative of the King-Emperor, but in practice appointed by and responsible to the British government. Both the central administration and that of the provinces were run, at the higher levels, by an élite force, the Indian Civil Service, which was originally all-British, but which between the wars recruited members equally from Britain and India. Stalin observed to Ribbentrop at the ceremony for signing the Russo-German Pact in August 1939 that it was 'ridiculous' that India should be run by 'a few hundred Englishmen'.[18] In fact, at the outbreak of war the total membership of the Indian Civil Service (which also looked after the administration of Burma) was 1300, of whom 760 were British. But the British dominated the more senior posts.[19]

The interwar years had seen a considerable breakdown of the old aloofness of the British governing class from contact with the Indian intellectuals. And many of the latter, especially those who had been educated in Britain, had close ties with their British counterparts. But if anything this made them more eager for self-government, and they would have agreed with Stalin and Ribbentrop about the absurdity of British rule in India. The Viceroy's declaration of war on behalf of India, without any consultation with its inhabitants, struck them as a supreme expression of this absurdity. The leaders of the predominantly Hindu nationalist organization, the Congress Party, expressed their resentment at once. The Congress Working Committee declared that while their sympathy was 'entirely on the side of democracy and freedom', yet

18. *Documents on German Foreign Policy, 1918-45*, ser. D, vii (1956), 227.

19. Woodruff, *Men Who Ruled India*, p. 300.

> India cannot associate herself in a war said to be
> for democratic freedom, when that very freedom is
> denied her, and such limited freedom as she possesses
> is taken away from her.[20]

For the future, they demanded 'the elimination of Imperialism and the treatment of India as a free nation' as conditions for their support of the war.[21] The Congress Ministers in the provinces thereupon resigned their offices, and direct rule by the British governors was re-instituted. The Muslim League, however, took a less strongly anti-British line, and Muslim-dominated provincial governments stayed in office, as did the government of Burma. The Indian princes, in accordance with their long-standing alliances with the British crown, as usual offered their services to the Viceroy. Above all, the Indian Army appeared to be as loyal as ever. As even the German consul-general at Calcutta had perceived on the eve of the war, the Indian soldiers 'belong to quite different races from the opponents of the war' and 'are not affected by such talk. They are soldiers by profession and not because of any political ideals.'[22]

This was fortunate for Britain. The Indian Army was an essential element in the strategic thinking of the British Chiefs of Staff. It consisted of some 47,000 British and 140,000 Indian regular soldiers, and there were also auxiliaries and territorials.[23] In peacetime this army, including the British element, was almost entirely paid out of Indian revenues, but it was the regular practice that whenever Indian troops were employed abroad at the behest of the British government, they were paid for by the British government. The army was short of mechanized equipment, and the Indian navy and air force were of quite negligible strength; but the Indian Army was a

20. Mansergh, *Documents and Speeches,* i, 514.

21. *Ibid.*, p. 516.

22. *Documents on German Foreign Policy,* D, vii, 263.

23. Figures from RIIA, *Political and Strategic Interests of the U.K.,* p. 285.

valuable reserve of infantry suitable for use at critical points in the Imperial perimeter, such as in the Middle East, where Italian forces might attack the British position on the Suez Canal, or in the Far East, where the threat came from Japan. The regular British army in 1939 consisted of only 185,000 men (excluding those in India), and of these two-thirds were normally stationed in Britain: so the reserve of trained British soldiers for service overseas was very small.[24]

The tiny dimensions of the land forces available to the British government, to defend an Empire of well over 500 million people (a quarter of the world's population) against all threats, both external and internal, reminds us of the extent to which British strategy relied upon the Navy to prevent any militarily powerful enemy from getting into a position to invade British territory. But as we have seen, although the Navy had a satisfactory preponderance over the German and Italian Navies, it could hardly spare enough ships to cope with the Japanese fleet as well. Furthermore, there was a good deal of doubt as to how far naval power was dependent upon air support: and in 1939 there were very few aircraft to be spared for use in any overseas theatre. The British naval staff stoutly maintained that properly armoured battleships could defy air attack, but the air staff held a contrary view. Obviously this was a matter that could only be settled by war itself. But apart from this question, it was clear that the most vulnerable points of the overseas empire were, first, the Suez Canal, which might be attacked from Libya, and secondly, the naval base of Singapore, on which hinged the defence of Malaya, Australia and New Zealand against Japanese attack. Fortunately as it seemed, in September 1939 these threats were still potential rather than actual. But they had to be taken into account in the disposition of British forces from the beginning of the war.

As Britons went to war, it was not enough for all of them

24. *Ibid.*, p. 284.

to know that they were fighting against Hitler and Nazism. Right from the start there was talk of a positive definition of war aims. H. G. Wells, in a letter to *The Times*, demanded a revival of the vigorous discussion of the post-war order which had taken place in 1917-18, and which he had participated in then.[25] Harold Nicolson wrote a cogent tract entitled *Why Britain is at War*, in which he urged the need for a 'United States of Europe'—a federal authority requiring from existing states a 'sacrifice of national sovereignty': this would, he thought, be a more effective guarantee of peace than the loosely-knit League of Nations had been.[26] At this stage most people were still thinking primarily in terms of Europe and European problems. Attlee, who had recovered sufficiently from ill-health to resume the leadership of the Labour Party, spoke in October of the need for 'a more closely co-ordinated Europe'—a phrase which seemed to imply that he was looking in the same direction as Nicolson without being able formally to commit his colleagues.[27] Sir Archibald Sinclair, for the Liberals, was more definite: there was a need, he said, for 'a substantial limitation upon national sovereignty'.[28]

The Cabinet, however, seemed chary of committing itself to anything specific while the war was only just beginning. It was after all making its plans on the view that the war would last for three years. If there were to be any negotiations, it was desirable that the government should have its hands free of definite commitments. Chamberlain therefore continued to speak in vague and negative terms, as he had done on September 3rd. On September 20th he declared that the British aim was

> to redeem Europe from the perpetual and recurring
> fear of German aggression and enable the peoples

25. *The Times*, 26 Sept., 1939.
26. H. Nicolson, *Why Britain is at War* (1939), pp. 155, 159.
27. Hansard 352, 570 (12 Oct., 1939).    28. *Ibid.*, 574.

of Europe to preserve their independence and their
liberties.[29]

In October he even retreated somewhat from the forth-
right demand that he had made for the overthrow of
Nazism. This was partly a tactical move at a time when
Hitler was attempting to appear as reasonable as possible.
The German government, said Chamberlain,

> must give convincing proof of the sincerity of their
> demand for peace by definite acts and by the
> provision of effective guarantees of their intention to
> fulfil their engagements.[30]

This statement was upsetting to some, like Eden, who
were still suspicious of the revival of the spirit of 'appeasement';[31] but it may also be seen as a return to the logic
of peacetime British foreign policy, which judged foreign
countries by their deeds and not by their ideology. It was
not necessary to be a Conservative to accept this logic,
though to be sure it was not a common view on the Left.
But the Whiggish Sir Archibald Sinclair expressed it very
clearly at the time:

> It is not for us to chastise another people for its own
> mis-government or to go to war on behalf of Pastor
> Niemoeller or German Jews.[32]

This was a view which could still be taken in the lull
before the real conflict. But later the war was to develop
a logic of its own, and Sir Archibald was to find himself
committed to very much sterner policies than those which
he advocated at the outset.

29. Hansard 351, 978 (20 Sept., 1939).
30. Hansard 352, 568 (12 Oct., 1939).
31. Avon, *Facing the Dictators*, p. 72.
32. Hansard 352, 572 (12 Oct., 1939). Dr Niemoeller was a
German Protestant Pastor who suffered imprisonment for his
anti-Nazi views.

Part Two

# The Experience of War

# 3.    The Phoney War

As Lloyd George had discovered in the course of the First World War, the sudden emergencies occasioned by war and the need for quick decisions could only be met by a radical change in the system of government at the top. In place of the large, cumbersome peacetime Cabinet of about twenty members, it was desirable to have a small body, meeting daily, and consisting perhaps of only five or six members. Chamberlain realized that he must try to conform to this pattern, but he did not see any case for immediately depriving himself of the advice of his closest colleagues, or for removing them from jobs which he thought they were competently performing. At the same time, he had to find room for that 'strengthening' of his administration which public opinion would demand. He failed to persuade the leaders of the Labour and Liberal Parties to join the government, though both were willing to agree to an 'electoral truce' for the duration of the war. It was consequently only the dissident members of his own party, and also those of no party at all, who could be used to broaden the base of the government's support. Among the former, it was obviously Churchill, the man of great military experience, who had to be found a leading place in the government; and there was also a strong case for the return of Anthony Eden.

The trouble was that Chamberlain did not want to put Churchill into the position of controlling the entire strategy of the war, which would inevitably be the case if he took a superintending post, or became Minister for the Co-ordination of Defence, in succession to Admiral Lord Chatfield. Chamberlain's solution was to put Churchill at the Admiralty (where he had served in 1911-15) and to bring all three ministers of the defence departments

into the War Cabinet—the others were Leslie Hore-Belisha
at the War Office and Sir Kingsley Wood as Air Minister
—and also to retain Lord Chatfield as Minister for the
Co-ordination of Defence, senior to the departmental
ministers but without their executive powers. For the rest,
Chamberlain was keen to keep in the highest counsels his
immediate colleagues of the appeasement years—Sir John
Simon, Lord Halifax and Sir Samuel Hoare. Simon was
Chancellor of the Exchequer; Halifax was Foreign Secretary; and Hoare, who had been Home Secretary, was
given the non-departmental post of Lord Privy Seal so
that he could supervise policy generally on the home
front. Lord Hankey, the former civil servant who as
Secretary of the Cabinet had prepared the War Book
(which listed the administrative measures to be taken at
the onset of war) was also brought in as Minister without
Portfolio. Like Chatfield he was a man from government
service, not from party politics. This meant a total of nine
members for the Cabinet already; and so Eden was told
that as Dominions Secretary he could attend the Cabinet,
but would have no vote. Sir John Anderson, another non-
party man who had been brought in immediately after
the Munich crisis to prepare a scheme of civil defence,
was in a somewhat similar position: he took over Hoare's
former responsibilities at the Home Office, and also remained in charge of air raid precautions: though technically
outside the Cabinet, he attended its meetings regularly.

The War Cabinet was thus much larger than Lloyd
George's, and it consisted much less of ministers who were
free from departmental responsibilities. This was not
necessarily a bad thing: there was a danger, which had
appeared in the First World War, of too great a divorce
between the decision of policy and its execution. But as
the Cabinet met daily, there was a heavy burden on
ministers, some of whom had already been exhausted by
the crisis at the outbreak of war. The worst thing was that
nearly all the disagreements between the services which
could previously be ironed out at the Committee of Im-

perial Defence were now transferred to the War Cabinet. Furthermore, the new First Lord of the Admiralty at once began to outstrip his colleagues in his activities and attention to affairs, including the affairs of other departments. Churchill came in full of fresh energy and enthusiasm and at once started to bombard the Prime Minister with letters on various topics not necessarily connected with the Navy. He also installed at the Admiralty a 'statistical office' under the supervision of his old friend, Professor F. A. Lindemann, the Oxford scientist, which was to prepare minutes and charts on all sorts of topics, also not necessarily connected with the Navy. Hore-Belisha and Kingsley Wood, who had had no military experience in their lives, could not cope with this; and Chatfield, an experienced sailor but a man of no great administrative or political skill, found himself, as he put it, 'a fifth wheel to the coach.'[1]

Meanwhile Hitler was employing the great bulk of his army, including all the main striking forces, to overwhelm Poland. After little more than two weeks' fighting, Warsaw was surrounded and the Polish armies were broken up. On September 17th, in accordance with the secret agreement made in the Russo-German Pact, Russian troops invaded Poland from the East and occupied a broad band of territory. By the end of the month Polish resistance was entirely at an end. All this had taken place without any hindrance from the Western Allies, although the French Army might have taken advantage of the absence of the bulk of the German troops from the Western Front, and the British Bomber Command, which was designed to attack deep in enemy territory, could have benefited from the concentration of the German Air Force in the East. But the French Commander-in-Chief, General Gamelin, was a strong believer in the superior power of defensive operations; and in any case he had no mobile forces at his command, as there were no French armoured divisions and the infantry mostly lacked motor transport. A body called the Supreme War Council, consisting of the two

1. Lord Chatfield, *The Navy and Defence*, ii (1947), p. 182.

Prime Ministers and their leading colleagues, was set up to
co-ordinate British and French strategy; but it was obvious
that the French would have the real say in what was done
on the Western Front. So far as bombing was concerned,
the British and French leaders including Churchill believed that more was to be lost than gained by initiating
mass air raids. Since the war could probably only be won
by economic blockade, they thought that time was on the
Allied side; and in any case, the neutral countries, including America, would tend to sympathize with whichever
country suffered the first heavy air raid casualties. The
sufferings of Poland, if not ignored, were taken to be the
by-product of an ordinary land campaign and so somehow
less reprehensible.[2]

Thus the British contribution to the war in its first
month seemed to be on a very small scale. The four
British infantry divisions were sent off to France and
placed close to the Belgian frontier in the neighbourhood
of Lille. General Lord Gort, VC, was put in command,
but he was subordinated to the authority of the French
army and was normally to take his orders from General
Georges, Gamelin's North East Front commander. The
Royal Air Force attacked a few selected targets on the
German coast, with little success, and for the rest confined
itself to dropping propaganda pamphlets over the German
mainland. The Navy was more actively involved, as it had
to enforce the blockade and also to face an immediate
attack by German submarines. The passenger liner
*Athenia* was torpedoed off the coast of Scotland on the
very day of the outbreak of war, with heavy loss of life;
and two weeks later the aircraft carrier *Courageous* was
sunk in the Channel.

For the great bulk of the British population, all this
was an anti-climax. They had been led to expect devastating air raids at the very outset of the war. In anticipation
of this, children had been hastily evacuated from the
expected target areas such as London and other large

2. Butler, *Grand Strategy*, ii, 20.

cities. Some of them went with their mothers, some without; in either case, families were broken up. A strict black-out was imposed, the immediate effect of which was to double the number of deaths and injuries in road accidents. At the same time, nearly all forms of popular entertainment—football, racing, and in the target areas, theatres and cinemas—had been abruptly halted. The BBC abandoned all its programmes save one, which was largely devoted to news programmes and light music. When no great onslaught from the air occurred, relief was soon followed by a slackening of precautions. Evacuees who disliked the country, or who failed to get on with their hosts, or who were simply home-sick, returned to the cities in large numbers. The carrying of gas-masks, which had been almost universal at first, began to lapse. People even criticized the full-time civil defence workers, for living idly on public money. There was also some concern about the Allies' failure to go to the aid of the Poles, or at least to take advantage of the German pre-occupation with the Eastern Front in the first month of the war. But it was left to an American, and one who was hostile to the Allied cause—the isolationist Senator William E. Borah of Idaho—to pick the phrase which was adopted in America and Britain alike to describe the unexpected nature of the war at this stage. 'There is something phony about this war', said Borah:

> You would think that they would do what they are going to do now, while Germany and Russia are still busy in the East, instead of waiting until they have cleaned up there.[3]

Borah was evidently holding the balance so carefully between the rival contestants that he had not fully realized how weak the offensive spirit was on the Allied side. But Hitler was ready to take advantage of the lull to see whether in fact it implied an unwillingness to carry on

3. *New York Times*, 19 Sept., 1939.

the war. On October 6th he proposed a peace conference, and spoke to both Britain and France in conciliatory terms. Daladier, the French Prime Minister, replied on October 10th, and Chamberlain on the 12th. They both by implication rejected the proposal, though it was clear, as we have seen, that Chamberlain at least had retreated somewhat from his earlier demand for the extirpation of Nazism. There were, to be sure, a few in Britain who were even now in favour of going to the conference table with Hitler. Conspicuous among them was Lloyd George, who was gloomy about the military prospects, having been coached by the brilliant *Times* defence correspondent, Capt. B. H. Liddell Hart. Lloyd George wrote to Churchill in mid-September to say that the country had been 'man-oeuvred into a terrible conflict under the most hopeless conditions';[4] and now he was writing articles in Beaver-brook's *Sunday Express* and speaking in the Commons in favour of the acceptance of any offer of a conference with Hitler. But although he received a good deal of favourable correspondence from individuals, there was little support for his views and much hostility in political quarters.

As the autumn drew on, the shape of the vast state machine which had been devised to control almost every corner of British life grew ever clearer: though there were some contradictory tendencies, and here and there the controls already imposed were relaxed somewhat. In the summer of 1939 a Minister of Supply had been constituted, and at the outbreak of war four new ministries were established —Home Security, Economic Warfare, Information, and Food. In October a Ministry of Shipping came into exist-ence. The Ministry of Labour took on the title of 'Ministry of Labour and National Service', and on September 29th the Registrar-General supervised the registration of the entire population, as a basis for national service and food rationing. A scheme for petrol rationing had already come

4. Lloyd George to Churchill, 13 Sept., 1939, Lloyd George Papers.

into existence before the end of September; but food rationing was held up for a time because some ministers— in particular Churchill—thought it was unnecessary and would only damage morale. Churchill thought that 'It was open to doubt whether the governmental machine could operate the rationing arrangements without creating resentment and unrest.'[5] He did not appear to realize that local shortage of butter and sugar, partly due to hoarding, had already begun to appear, and that the mass of the population were in favour of the introduction of rationing.[6] In the end rationing of butter, bacon and sugar began on January 8th, 1940.

Meanwhile all the ministries had been assembling staffs and trying out their powers in one way or another. For straight-forward administrative jobs at the higher level, the Civil Service favoured the recruitment of university dons, whom they regarded as more or less their professional equals; but when it came to industrial controls it was necessary to bring in the businessmen, as Lloyd George had done in 1916 and 1917. Naturally there were teething troubles, and they were increased as a result of the dispersal of ministries from London as an air-raid precaution. But the most vulnerable of the new ministries was one largely concentrated in London—the Ministry of Information. It sprang into existence with no period of gestation: within a few weeks of the beginning of the war it had 999 employees, of whom only 47 were journalists.[7] There were 'too few ordinary civil servants in it, and too many brilliant amateurs'.[8] The latter were a remarkable collection:

Ex-ambassadors and retired Indian Civil Servants abounded, the brightest ornaments of the Bar were employed on minor duties, distinguished men of letters held their pens at the monster's service . . .[9]

5. Cabinet Minutes, 28 Oct., 1939.
6. Harrisson and Madge, *War Begins at Home*, pp. 381, 395.
7. Hansard 351, 1209 (26 Sept., 1939).
8. Duff Cooper, *Old Men Forget*, p. 285.

and the minister himself was a distinguished Scottish lawyer of advancing years, Lord Macmillan, who had, it is true, served in the ministry in its earlier existence in the First World War.

It would have required a very skilful minister to make a success of the Ministry of Information. Newspaper editors disliked it, because it rationed the news that they were allowed to disseminate, and thereby took some of the bread out of their mouths. Furthermore it was, to begin with, inefficient—and this the press ascribed to the fact that there were so few journalists on its staff. One serious mix-up took place only a few days after the outbreak of war, when the newspapers had been told that they could announce the safe arrival of the British Expeditionary Force in France. The papers were already in print when the War Office asked the Ministry to withhold the news; and the police were instructed to go round to confiscate copies which were already being distributed. To cap it all, the announcement had already been made the previous evening in the French press.[10] The result of this was that in future the Service ministries were made responsible for their own news—a change that had disastrous results for the government in the following spring. The Ministry of Information also showed great lack of expertise in its efforts to improve public morale. For instance, it distributed a poster which announced that '*Your* Courage *Your* Cheerfulness *Your* Resolution Will Bring Us Victory.' This might almost have been specially designed to emphasize the gulf between the government and the governed, and it was undoubtedly widely resented.[11]

Much of the trouble with the Ministry of Information, as with the Ministry of Food, was that far too little was known about popular feelings and likely reactions to policy. In a war which was regarded by many as being fought on

9. *Ibid.*
10. Templewood, *Nine Troubled Years*, pp. 422f.
11. Harrisson and Madge, *op. cit.*, pp. 8off.

behalf of 'democracy' and against 'dictatorship', it was a paradox that ministers had no means of knowing what people thought, and that large numbers of people found the German propaganda broadcasts by William Joyce ('Lord Haw-Haw') more interesting than their own press and radio. Yet the means of judging popular feeling were at hand. For years the larger commercial companies had been testing the reactions of consumers by Market Research; social patterns were being investigated, admittedly in somewhat amateur fashion (owing to lack of money) by a body called Mass-Observation; and, as we have seen, the Gallup poll had been introduced from America to Britain. Yet the government had the utmost difficulty in starting such a service, because they could not get over the hurdle of their own prejudice that it would be highly unpopular. There was, we are told, 'considerable doubt in official minds as to the reaction of the public to such a service under governmental control'.[12]

In the meantime, the press, having little else to do, concentrated its criticisms on ministers on the home front. The latter suffered because they did not know whether the criticisms were based on genuine popular feeling or not. The ministers also had other grievances. According to Hoare, his colleagues on the Home Policy Committee were 'irritable' because they were 'not in the Cabinet' and felt 'resentment against the Service ministers for getting the credit e.g. Winston on the freedom of the seas and they getting the kicks for restrictions and regulations.'[13] In fact, in spite of everything the government was not at all unpopular with the mass of the people. Towards Christmas there was a distinct slackening of the new wartime austerity: popular sport and entertainment got under way again, and the pools were allowed to start up once more. But on the other hand, in November Sir John Simon

12. Select Committee on National Expenditure 1941-2, Second Report, *P.P.* 1941-2, iii, 74.

13. War Diary Oct.-Nov., 1939, Templewood Papers.

introduced a war budget which put up the income tax from 5/- to 7/6 and increased the taxes on cigarettes, tobacco, beer, spirits and sugar. Yet in mid-December the *News Chronicle* published the results of a Gallup poll which showed that in reply to the question 'Are you satisfied or dissatisfied with the Government's conduct of the war?' 61% were satisfied, 18% were dissatisfied, 10% did not know, and another 11% were against the war altogether.[14] The Prime Minister's personal popularity, which had risen at the outbreak of war, reached a high peak in November when almost 70% of the Gallup sample indicated their approval of him.[15]

Early in January a fresh opportunity for the press to attack the government arose when Chamberlain removed Hore-Belisha from the War Office. Hore-Belisha had been a popular minister, having initiated a number of overdue reforms in the army and being in addition keenly aware of the need for good public relations. But when visiting France he had shown concern about the state of defences on Gort's front; and this and the manner in which he comported himself had annoyed both Gort and his staff. The Chief of the Imperial General Staff, General Sir Edmund Ironside, also disliked Hore-Belisha. Chamberlain began to hear from a number of quarters (including the Palace, for the King had a brother, the Duke of Gloucester, serving on Gort's staff) that his War Minister had lost the confidence of the Army.[16] Since it was clear that the Minister of Information, Lord Macmillan, was not up to his job, Chamberlain's first plan was to put Hore-Belisha in Macmillan's place. But when he consulted Halifax he encountered disapproval: that grave Anglican thought that Hore-Belisha as a Jew was unsuitable for such a ministry, and his methods would prove vulgar.[17] Anxious not to

14. *News Chronicle*, 13 Dec., 1939.
15. *News Chronicle*, 29 Dec., 1939.
16. Wheeler-Bennett, *George VI*, pp. 432f.; Rhodes James, *Chips*, p. 229.
17. Macleod, *Chamberlain*, p. 286.

lose one of his more popular ministers, Chamberlain therefore offered Hore-Belisha the Board of Trade, whose
incumbent, Oliver Stanley, he was proposing to transfer
to the War Office. Hore-Belisha asked for time to think
the matter over; but he could not convince himself that he
should accept the rebuff, even though Churchill urged him
to do so.[18] He therefore resigned from the Cabinet altogether. Stanley went to the War Office; Sir John Reith,
the former director-general of the BBC, was appointed to
the Ministry of Information; and Sir Andrew Duncan, a
leading businessman, went to the Board of Trade.

Although Chamberlain took care to see Lord Camrose,
the owner of the *Daily Telegraph*, he could not prevent
the bulk of the popular press making a great outcry about
'the Generals' and their victory over Hore-Belisha. Hoare
was anxious that Chamberlain should improve his relations
with the press, and should at least see Beaverbrook, who
had wanted to be Minister of Information at the beginning
of the war, and who was now as Hoare put it in his diary
'uncertain between hatred of N[eville] C[hamberlain] and
fear of Churchill being P.M.'[19] No such meeting took
place; but Hore-Belisha made no public attack on Chamberlain; and although the Prime Minister's standing in
the opinion poll fell somewhat, in the third week of
January there were still 56% of people who approved of
his leadership.[20] There remained, in fact, a majority in
favour of Chamberlain until the spring.

Meanwhile Churchill, although accepting the principle that
Britain should not initiate mass air raids, was not prepared to believe that this should mean complete inaction
on the part of British arms. To be sure, the enforcement of
the naval blockade involved clashes with the enemy. In
October the battleship *Royal Oak* was sunk by a daring
and skilful U-boat attack while at anchor in the supposedly

18. Minney, *Hore-Belisha*, p. 273.
19. War Diary Jan., 1940, Templewood Papers.
20. *News Chronicle*, 8 Feb., 1940.

safe and protected harbour at Scapa Flow. In December
the Navy felt that it had got its revenge by the Battle of
the River Plate, when a group of three light cruisers,
though heavily outgunned, managed to ensure the destruction of the German pocket battleship *Admiral Graf Spee*.
Convoy work was on the whole effective, and the new
system of sonic location of submarines ('Asdic') enabled
two destroyers to give as much protection as ten in 1918.[21]
Severe shipping losses were at first caused by the enemy's
magnetic mines, but within a few weeks a method of
counteracting them ('de-gaussing') had been devised.
Meanwhile, Churchill's fertile mind was turning to various
plans for harassing the enemy, many of them very unlikely
to have had much success. One idea was to drop floating
mines in the Rhine, in order to destroy the bridges and
any shipping they encountered. Another was to send a
squadron of old battleships, specially armoured against
air and torpedo attack, to range up and down the Baltic,
perhaps for months at a time. Events were soon to show
that this would have been disastrous.

More serious, because more practical, was a proposal
to mine the Norwegian 'leads' or coastal waters, in order
to prevent the shipment of Swedish iron-ore—a vital
component of the German arms industry. Churchill first
suggested this at a War Cabinet meeting on 19th September, but the Foreign Office raised objections to such an
intrusion into neutral waters, and for the time being nothing
was done. Then in November Stalin, seeking to improve
his northern frontiers in the same way as he had done in
Poland and the Baltic States, demanded territory and bases
from Finland, and on meeting a rebuff, invaded the
country. The Finnish army resisted bravely and, for some
time, with remarkable success. The moribund League of
Nations suddenly came to life, to expel Russia from its
membership. And Churchill produced a plan to kill two
birds with one stone by sending troops to the assistance of
Finland through the Norwegian port of Narvik, which

21. Churchill, *Second World War*, i, 449.

had a railway connexion to the Baltic by way of the Swedish iron-ore district.

This plan was one of the most extraordinary pieces of folly produced in the entire course of the war. In the first place it threatened to involve Britain and France in hostilities with Russia as well as with Germany, thus adding to the tally of the Allies' enemies at a time when it was impossible to see how Germany alone could be overcome. Secondly, as it was very doubtful that Norway and Sweden would allow the Allied forces through without opposition, it would demonstrate to the world, and particularly to America, that the Allies had no more respect for neutral rights than Hitler himself. Thirdly, the plan made no allowance for the counter-measures which Germany could take—and they were likely to have been prompt and effective, as the whole of the southern part of Scandinavia lay under the control of German air power. Any move against Narvik would thus be readily answered by a German occupation of the airfields in the lower part of the peninsula.

In spite of this Churchill succeeded in overcoming the scruples of the other members of the War Cabinet, and in persuading the French of the merits of the scheme. The French, in fact, needed little persuading. They were desperately anxious that the war should be fought anywhere rather than in France. Their object was *la Marne blanche*—a defensive victory without the shedding of blood, at any rate on the Western Front.[22] Churchill's hand was also strengthened by the success of a slighter infringement of neutrality in February, when he ordered a British destroyer to enter Norwegian waters and release some 300 captured British seamen who were below decks on a German merchantman, the *Altmark*. The plans for an expeditionary force therefore went ahead rapidly, and were all but complete when on March 13th the Finns capitulated, and the whole justification for the expedition disappeared. One early consequence was that the French

22. P. Reynaud, *Mémoires* (Paris, 1964), p. 296.

government fell on March 21st, Daladier being replaced as Prime Minister by the more vigorous Paul Reynaud, a critic of Munich.

After this, Allied hopes of intervention in Scandinavia were considerably reduced. Two British divisions which had been standing by for service there were now despatched to France, leaving only a few battalions for possible service at Narvik. The proposal to mine the Norwegian leads still seemed to merit active consideration, and Reynaud's government was as keen as Daladier's on action of some sort in Scandinavia. At a meeting of the Supreme War Council on March 28th, however, Reynaud made a concession: he was willing to accept Churchill's plan for dropping mines in the Rhine, it being understood that this was to take place at the same time as the mining of the leads. Both operations were to take place on April 4th and 5th. The British battalions available for Scandinavian operations were to stand by on the decks of warships so as to proceed to occupy Narvik, in the event of a German invasion of Norway in response to the Allied move. However, Reynaud was faced with a refusal by the French War Committee to endorse his commitment to the Rhine operation. A short delay took place and then the British War Cabinet decided to go ahead with the single operation to mine the Norwegian leads on April 8th.

Meanwhile Hitler had made up his mind that Allied intervention in Norway was inevitable, and that he had better anticipate it. A careful plan was drawn up for the rapid invasion of Denmark and Norway, and late in March Hitler decided to fix the beginning of the operation for April 7th. On April 2nd the operation was delayed two days, and so April 9th, the day after the mining of the leads, was the day when German troops overran Denmark and began the invasion of Norway. The troops were conveyed to Norway in warships, in transports disguised as merchantmen, and also by air, for this was the first military operation in which substantial numbers of troops were flown to the battlefield. A clever deception plan was employed to give the British Admiralty the idea that the German battleships were making for the open Atlantic. As a result, the British Home Fleet was ordered to disembark its expeditionary force and to go out to challenge the German ships, which however quickly headed back to port. Meanwhile Denmark was occupied almost without resistance and German troops seized Oslo, the Norwegian capital, and many of the principal ports including even Narvik in the far North. Resistance was patchy, but government and King escaped from Oslo to fight on further north, and two German cruisers were sunk by shore batteries.

In Britain the first reaction was one of disbelief that the enemy should have ventured to throw his forces so far around the Norwegian coast, where they could be harried from the sea. When the truth became clear, this was succeeded by an atmosphere of optimism: as Churchill put it, Hitler had committed 'a strategic error comparable to that of Napoleon's invasion of Spain.'[23] Nor was this remark simply made to revive public morale at a moment of danger; for he had just written to the First Sea Lord:

> There is no reason to suppose that prolonged and serious fighting in this area will not impose a greater drain on the enemy than on ourselves.[24]

Increasing German naval losses, partly as a result of Norwegian action, partly from Allied surface and submarine attacks, tended to confirm this view. Two battles in Narvik fjord resulted in the sinking of ten German destroyers for the loss of two British. And on April 12th a British force of brigade strength was despatched to seize Narvik, more or less in accordance with plans made before the German invasion, but now with the knowledge that they had the more formidable task of ousting a newly arrived German garrison. The troops were told to land

23. *The Times*, 12 Apr., 1940.
24. Churchill, *op. cit.*, i, 541 (letter of 10 Apr., 1940).
B.A.S.W.W.                                                           C

near the port and to prepare an assault: further reinforcements would follow.

At this stage the British counteraction began to show
signs of confusion. The operations were being directed by
a sub-committee of the War Cabinet concerned with
questions of defence, known as the Military Co-ordination
Committee, acting on the advice of the Chiefs of Staff.
This committee was no longer presided over by Chatfield,
who had resigned at the beginning of April, finding that his
duties as Minister for the Co-ordination of Defence had
virtually disappeared. His vacant post was not filled, but
the chairmanship of the committee passed to Churchill,
who continued as First Lord of the Admiralty. Samuel
Hoare had just replaced Kingsley Wood as Air Minister
in a reshuffle of the Cabinet, Wood assuming Hoare's

Scandinavia

The Narvik-Lulea
railway is
marked thus: ▪▪▪▪▪▪▪▪▪▪▪▪▪▪▪▪▪▪▪▪▪

duties on the home front; and besides Churchill and Hoare, Oliver Stanley as War Minister and Leslie Burgin as Minister of Supply were on the committee. Although Churchill was in the chair, nobody was fully in control, and decisions had to be reached by compromise. Furthermore, orders to naval and military commanders on the spot were not properly co-ordinated, as became apparent very soon at Narvik.

What was still more unfortunate, however, was that after the destruction of the German naval forces at Narvik it was assumed that the port could be captured by only a small force; and as the Norwegians were demanding aid for their army in central Norway, on the night of the 13th the rear half of the Narvik expedition while still at sea was diverted to Namsos, with the intention that it should move overland from there to occupy the major port of Trondheim. The War Office was particularly upset by this change of plan which Churchill insisted on in his capacity as chairman of the Military Co-ordination Committee. As General Ironside, the Chief of the Imperial General Staff, put it:

> We cannot have a man trying to supervise all military arrangements as if he were a company commander running a small operation to cross a bridge.[25]

The result was that the forces at Narvik were still not adequate for their task, and those at Namsos, which were entirely without artillery, faced the problem of moving a hundred miles through heavy snow to their objective. A further landing also directed at Trondheim took place at Aandalsnes, but this was as far south of Trondheim as Namsos was north of it. Finally, a plan was made to send a force of battleships into Trondheim Fjord in order to make a direct attack on the German forces in the city; but the Chiefs of Staff decided on April 19th that this

25. Macleod and Kelly, *Ironside Diaries*, p. 260.

was too hazardous an operation for the battleships to undertake, as they would be very exposed to air attack in the narrow waters of the fjord. This view was accepted by Churchill, and also by Chamberlain, who at Churchill's insistence was now presiding at the meetings of the Military Co-ordination Committee, in order to ensure that definite decisions were taken.

In the next few days the campaign in central Norway, although it was the first priority, went very badly for the Allied forces. The Germans were attacking fiercely with the aid of tanks and bombers. Fighter aircraft from Britain did not have the range to cover troops and ships in the area, and an attempt to establish an airfield on the spot proved unsuccessful. It soon became clear that the only thing to do was to abandon Trondheim, evacuate the troops, and concentrate on Narvik. A decision to this effect was taken on April 26th, and on the nights of May 1st and 2nd the evacuation was carried out. This meant that all hope of prolonging the main Norwegian resistance had to be abandoned; but the operation had at least encouraged the Norwegian government not to capitulate. The battle for Narvik went on, and the town was eventually captured on May 28th, only to be evacuated shortly afterwards owing to the changed strategical situation on the Western Front.

The Norwegian campaign had shown that combined operations need good intelligence, careful planning and firm control. All these requirements were lacking on the British side. About half the German fleet had been destroyed or seriously damaged, and this was to have an important effect on future operations. But on the other hand, the Germans had secured many more bases for their submarines and their aircraft. The importance of air power, and the dangers run by the most heavily armoured warships when exposed to air attack without fighter support, had become apparent for the first time. The tiny Allied expeditionary force had learnt its lesson at the cost of less than 2,400 casualties on land. But Hitler did not propose to allow the Allies to draw the right lessons from the campaign and to reorganize their forces accordingly. Only one major change was possible in Britain before the German forces struck again. Churchill demanded, and Chamberlain agreed, that he should have the right to preside over the meetings of the Chiefs of Staff and in emergency act without consulting his colleagues of the Military Co-ordination Committee, provided that Chamberlain himself should be informed and should have no objection to the measures proposed. This would have made Churchill a virtual Minister of Defence: it was a prospect that his colleagues on the Military Co-ordination Committee, after their experience of his activities over the preceding month, viewed with mixed feelings. But the new arrangements, which were announced on May 1st, were to last only a week.

We have seen that even at the end of March Chamberlain still stood high in popular esteem. His plans for staying on the defensive and building up the armament and training of the forces seemed to be sensible and successful. In November 1939 the American Congress had been persuaded to amend its neutrality legislation to enable Britain and France to purchase armaments in the United States on a 'cash and carry' basis—that is to say, the goods were to be paid for at once and conveyed in Allied shipping. This meant that American industry could help to fortify the Allied cause, though its adaptation to military purposes was bound to be slow. Meanwhile inside Britain the production of aircraft, which had been at the rate of 650 a month in 1939, reached over 1,000 a month in April 1940. The total British aircraft production in the months from September 1939 to May 1940 was already slightly greater than the German output, though this was not known at the time.[26] The naval war had moved in Britain's favour; shipping losses were declining and in March 1940 they amounted to less than 40,000 tons. The expeditionary

26. Postan, *British War Production*, p. 109.

force in France had expanded from four divisions to ten, and more would soon be available. On many counts, therefore, there was reason for optimism, and several ministers displayed it. Towards the end of January Churchill had said in a speech at Manchester:

> These additional months of preparation have been a godsend to us . . . Herr Hitler has already lost his best chance.[27]

Over two months later, Chamberlain saw no reason to disagree with this view. Speaking to a Conservative meeting, he said on April 4th that he was 'ten times as confident of victory' as at the beginning of the war, and that Hitler had 'missed the bus'.[28]

When in late April the course of events went so much against British arms, public opinion was ill-prepared for the reverse. Things might well have been easier to take if the service ministries had not been in charge of supplying news of operations during this period: the optimism that they generated worried the Cabinet in the later stages of the campaign.[29] But the high hopes expressed by leading ministers only a few days earlier had also played their part. It was, in particular, the remarks of Chamberlain that were remembered: Churchill was to a large extent absolved from blame as not having been in any way responsible for the slow re-armament of the country before September 1939. So far, opposition to the government in Parliament had been muted, and the reconstruction of the ministry at the outbreak of war had done something to heal the rifts within the Conservative Party. But a group of anti-Munich Conservatives still met weekly under the chairmanship of Leopold Amery.[30] An All-Party Action Group under the chairmanship of Clement Davies, an independently-minded Liberal National member, was at

27. *The Times*, 29 Jan., 1940.     28. *Ibid.*, 5 Apr., 1940.
29. Reith, *Into the Wind*, p. 377.
30. Amery, *My Political Life*, iii, 339.

first a more likely focus of opposition: its object was to discuss, with the aid of experts, questions of policy which could not readily be debated in public.[31] Then in April, just before the invasion of Denmark and Norway, an influential 'Watching Committee' of leading Conservatives in both Houses was formed by the veteran Lord Salisbury, who had been advocating a coalition government before the war.[32] The anti-Munich Conservative leaders including Amery were members of this body and were able to see the crystallization of opinion against Chamberlain in the last days of April, after the Trondheim operation was abandoned. Although there was agreement that the Chamberlainites were primarily to blame for this, there were some who were sufficiently in the know to realize that Churchill had been responsible for much of the policy uncertainty over Norway. Harold Nicolson, one of Churchill's best friends on the back benches, thought even in early May that Lloyd George would be a more likely Prime Minister.[33] On May 6th the *Daily Mail* demanded a change of government, and on its front page an anonymous politician (in fact, Sir Stafford Cripps) suggested names for a new Cabinet with Halifax as Prime Minister.

On May 7th the Commons met to debate the Norwegian campaign. This was on a motion by the Labour Opposition, but at first it was not clear that it would be pressed to a division. Clement Davies, however, after discussing the situation with Amery and others, urged Attlee to demand a vote.[34] Attlee at first hesitated but later agreed, and with the help of his colleague Herbert Morrison won over the Labour front bench. Morrison also sent a message to Lloyd George asking him to attend the debate, which he did.[35] Chamberlain for his part took counter-measures: he sent his Parliamentary Private Secretary, Lord Dun-

31. Boothby, *I Fight to Live*, p. 195.
32. Amery, *op. cit.*, p. 355.
33. Nicolson, *Diaries*, ii, 75 (4 May, 1940).
34. Amery, *op. cit.*, p. 365.
35. Morrison, *Autobiography*, p. 174.

glass, to the different Conservative groups to offer them a reconstruction of the government in return for their support in the lobby. When Dunglass approached the secretary of the Watching Committee, P. V. Emrys-Evans, however, he found him unwilling to discuss such terms.[36] Meanwhile the debate went badly for the government: Admiral of the Fleet Sir Roger Keyes, the hero of the Zeebrugge exploit in the First World War, appeared in full uniform to denounce the failure to send the Navy in at Trondheim, and Lloyd George, misunderstanding Churchill's responsibility, implored him not to 'allow himself to be converted into an air raid shelter to keep the splinters from hitting his colleagues.'[37] The greatest impact, however, came from Amery's speech which ended with the words of Cromwell, 'In the name of God, go!'[38] When the vote was taken on the evening of May 8th, according to Dalton the Opposition lobby 'seemed to be full of young Conservatives in uniform, khaki, Navy blue and Air Force blue all intermingled.'[39] 'Full' is an exaggeration: there cannot have been more than a dozen Conservative rebels under the age of forty, let alone in uniform. But though the government won its vote of confidence, it had suffered a severe blow. Its majority had dropped from the customary figure of over two hundred to no more than 81. About forty of the ministerialists had changed sides, and many more had abstained.

Chamberlain at once began to think that he ought to resign. But he realized that he had one last chance if he could persuade the Labour Party to serve under his leadership. He summoned Attlee and Greenwood to Downing Street on May 9th to ask them under what circumstances they would join the government. Meanwhile Churchill had been lunching with Kingsley Wood, hitherto one of the most loyal of the Chamberlainites, formerly an insurance

36. Amery, *op. cit.*, p. 367.
37. Hansard 360, 1283 (8 May, 1940).
38. *Ibid.*, 1150 (7 May, 1940).
39. Dalton, *Fateful Years*, p. 306.

solicitor and hardly a warlike figure, but now a convert
to Churchill's cause. Kingsley Wood said that Chamberlain
would try to survive as Prime Minister, or, failing that,
would prefer Halifax as his successor. If Churchill was
asked to support Halifax, said Kingsley Wood, he should
not do so, but remain silent.[40] That afternoon, the opportunity came. Chamberlain sent for Churchill, Halifax and
David Margesson, the Chief Whip, and told them that he
was almost certainly going to resign. He hinted that
Churchill might find it more difficult than Halifax to win
the support of the Opposition. Churchill deliberately did
not speak, and for some moments there was silence. Then
Halifax declared that he, at any rate, could not be Prime
Minister as he was in the Lords.[41]

Halifax's excuse was no more than a technical one,
for the constitutional difficulty could easily have been
overcome if all the parties had been willing to support his
government. And indeed, it seems that Chamberlain was
right in supposing that Labour preferred Halifax as
Premier, if it came to a choice with Churchill.[42] He was
naturally also the choice of Chamberlain himself and
of Chamberlain's personal following—still much the larger
element in the Conservative Party, and hence of great
importance in the House of Commons. The King, too,
preferred Halifax to Churchill, who had been a partisan of
the former King Edward VIII at the time of the Abdica-
tion.[43] So the outcome was by no means decided. In any
case, there was the possibility that Chamberlain might yet
be saved by the Labour Party. At Chamberlain's invitation,
Churchill and Halifax waited with him to see Attlee and
Greenwood, who had come in answer to Chamberlain's
summons. When Chamberlain asked the Labour leaders
under what circumstances they would join the government,

40. Avon, *Reckoning*, pp. 96f.
41. Churchill gets the date wrong in *Second World War*, i, 597.
42. Amery, *op. cit.*, p. 371; Birkenhead, *Halifax*, p. 453.
43. Wheeler-Bennett, *George VI*, pp. 443f.

they refused to give a definite answer, but said they must consult their party's national executive. This cautious response was due to the strict rules of conduct for the party leadership which had been laid down after the 'betrayal' by Ramsay MacDonald in 1931. But they took care to leave Chamberlain with the impression that their executive was very likely indeed to demand a change 'at the top'. Churchill left the meeting with the feeling that he would be Prime Minister in a few hours.[44]

But Chamberlain had not yet resigned; and next day, when the long-awaited attack on the Western Front began, he thought for a time that he should carry on to cope with the immediate crisis. Thereupon Kingsley Wood again played an important role, urging him to resign as soon as possible.[45] Chamberlain decided to wait for the formal reply from the Labour Party: and in the meantime he made one more bid to persuade Halifax to accept the Premiership. He told Lord Dunglass to ring up the Under-Secretary at the Foreign Office, R. A. Butler, and ask him to see Halifax and press him to change his mind. Butler had to confess that he could do nothing: the Foreign Secretary had gone to the dentist.[46] Then at 5 p.m. Attlee telephoned from Bournemouth, where the Labour Party conference was meeting, to say that the party's National Executive had resolved that it would be prepared to serve in a new government, but only 'under a new Prime Minister'.[47] So Chamberlain went to Buckingham Palace, formally submitted his resignation, and advised the King to send for Churchill. At 6.30 p.m. Churchill visited the Palace in his turn and was invited to form a new government.[48]

44. Churchill, *op. cit.*, i, 598.

45. War Diary 10 May, 1940, Templewood Papers; Churchill, *op. cit.*, i, 597.

46. Rhodes James, *Chips*, p. 249.

47. Dalton, *op. cit.*, pp. 311f.

48. A diary of Churchill's engagements in this period, drawn from official sources, was sent to him by the Prime Minister's secretary on 18 Sept., 1946. Copy in Attlee Papers. (U).

Thus Churchill, the pre-eminent man of war within the administration—yet the opponent of rationing and controls—received the summons to preside over the nation's affairs. But to the last moment it was touch and go whether he would have the chance of 'walking with destiny', as he put it.[49] In the end, the decisive factors were Halifax's unwillingness to serve, and his own readiness for the task. When Halifax first heard Chamberlain's suggestion that he should be Prime Minister, he felt 'a bad stomach-ache'.[50] Indeed it is very doubtful whether a man of such languid airs and sober temperament could have inspired the nation as Churchill was able to do. But even in early 1940 the need for such a leader was not yet clear. Churchill's friend Harold Nicolson thought his broadcasts were 'a little too rhetorical' and 'too belligerent for this pacifist age.'[51] Early in May, those who were in the know thought it strange that he should gain the main advantage from the failure of the Norwegian campaign. As his colleague on the Military Co-ordination Committee, Oliver Stanley, put it in conversation later, 'This man climbed to power on Norway who, on his record, least deserved it.'[52] Samuel Hoare agreed: 'Norway failed because of his meddling.'[53] And Liddell Hart, the great military writer, was later to put it even more strongly:

It was the irony, or fatality, of history that Churchill should have gained his opportunity of supreme power as the result of a fiasco to which he had been the main contributor.[54]

49. Churchill, *op. cit.*, i, 601.
50. Diary, 9 May, 1940, quoted Birkenhead, *Halifax*, p. 454.
51. Nicolson, *Diaries*, ii, 59.
52. Diary, 28 Apr., 1941, Dalton Papers.
53. War Diary 12 May, 1940, Templewood Papers.
54. Liddell Hart, 'Churchill as a Military Leader', *Encounter*, Apr., 1966, p. 17.

# 4. Dunkirk and the Battle of Britain

As Churchill formed his government the onslaught on the Western Front was just beginning. Although the immediate military reaction was planned in advance and needed no new consultations, he felt it necessary to form his government as quickly as possible, so as to ensure a rapid transfer of offices. Churchill chose to form a really small War Cabinet, as critics had been demanding: but it had to be a Cabinet of the parties, rather than a Cabinet of expert administrators as Lloyd George's had been towards the end of the 1914-18 War. In the first place, Chamberlain, who was still leader of the Conservative Party, had to be included; and secondly the Labour Party had to be given generous representation at every level. Churchill at first proposed to make Chamberlain Leader of the Commons: but Attlee and Greenwood protested vigorously, demanding that this post go to somebody acceptable to all parties.[1] In the end Churchill himself assumed the Leadership of the Commons, and gave Chamberlain the less conspicuous office of Lord President of the Council. Halifax was asked to continue as Foreign Secretary, and Attlee and Greenwood joined the War Cabinet as ministers without portfolio. Churchill himself also took the title of Minister of Defence, which had not previously existed, and decreed that the three departmental heads of the armed services should be outside the War Cabinet. For these subordinate but responsible offices Churchill chose men whom he regarded as personally congenial to himself: A. V. Alexander, of the Labour Party, as First Lord of the Admiralty, where he had already served in the previous Labour government of 1929-31; Anthony Eden as Secretary of

1. Williams, *Prime Minister Remembers*, p. 35.

State for War; and as Air Minister, the Liberal leader Archibald Sinclair, who had been Churchill's second-in-command in the First World War when he had for a time commanded a battalion in France. The Liberals had wanted a place in the War Cabinet, but Churchill was not prepared to give them this, as their numbers in the Commons were not great, and he wanted to keep the War Cabinet really small.[2] Also, he was hoping that he might be able to persuade Lloyd George to join the government, and this could only be done by offering him, sooner or later, a place at the top level.

With these main offices determined, Churchill could proceed to allot the remaining offices with a judicious mixture of the political parties, retaining also the able non-party men whom Chamberlain had brought in. Of the leading Chamberlainites, Simon, the former Chancellor of the Exchequer, who was a lawyer, could readily be moved 'upstairs' to the post of Lord Chancellor; and Kingsley Wood, who had given such signal help to Churchill by changing sides at the right moment, was rewarded with the Exchequer. Of the most prominent Chamberlainites, only Hoare, whom Churchill most disliked, was left out of the new administration altogether.[3] Leading anti-Chamberlainites in the Conservative Party now attained high office once more—Lord Lloyd as Colonial Secretary, Leopold Amery as Secretary for India, Duff Cooper as Minister of Information. Of the non-party men, Anderson was to remain as Home Secretary and Minister of Home Security, Andrew Duncan stayed at the Board of Trade, and Lord Woolton at the Ministry of Food. Hankey ceased to be in the War Cabinet but retained the rank of Minister. Ernest Bevin, the ablest and most powerful of the trade-union leaders, but not yet a Member of Parliament, was brought in as Minister of Labour, and other members of the Labour Party to get senior posts were Herbert Morrison as Minister of Supply and Hugh

2. Churchill, *Second World War*, ii, 11.
3. Avon, *Reckoning*, p. 96.

Dalton as Minister for Economic Warfare. Churchill also after some effort persuaded Beaverbrook to abandon his attitude of aloofness from the war and to join the government: his task was to be the urgent one of creating a Ministry of Aircraft Production.

The system of government that Churchill operated was, in its main elements, simpler than Chamberlain's. The Prime Minister himself now became the controlling authority in all detailed matters of defence operations, dealing directly with the Chiefs of Staff and referring only specially important questions to a Defence Committee consisting of three members of the War Cabinet—himself, Chamberlain and Attlee—and the three armed service ministers. For a time, there were daily meetings of the War Cabinet to supervise the main lines of strategy in both the military and the civil sphere. On the civil side the committee system operated more fully, although there was first a considerable pruning of the total number of committees which had operated previously.[4] Since the senior minister on the civil side was the Lord President, the most important committee was the Lord President's Committee, over which Chamberlain presided with the same efficiency that had marked his Cabinet chairmanship in the past. The Labour ministers were impressed to find how swiftly decisions could be achieved under Chamberlain's aegis. 'Always very business-like. You could work with him,' said Attlee later.[5] But of course the urgency of these critical days muted past antagonisms and encouraged rapid action.

Meanwhile on the continent a grim struggle was now in progress between the armies and air forces of five countries. The Belgian and Dutch forces were resisting invasion as well as they could, and French and British troops had entered Belgium to go to their support. The British Expeditionary Force numbered about 400,000 men, but the number of divisions available for the front was only

4. Williams, *op. cit.*, p. 40.    5. *Ibid.*, p. 37.

ten, although another three were employed in the rear on works and training. The ten BEF divisions were at least motorized, which was more than could be said of most of the French divisions. But they were only about one-tenth of the fighting strength available to the French command in the area north of the Swiss border. The German Army had substantially more troops at its disposal for its offensive—136 divisions, including ten armoured. But the forces on the two sides were not markedly unequal if the Belgian and Dutch divisions are added to those of the French and British. The Allied strategic situation, however, was poor. Although the Belgians and the Dutch had feared a German invasion very much more than a French one, they had been afraid to co-ordinate their plans for resistance with the French. As for the French, they had only recently begun to form armoured divisions, and the great majority of their tanks, which were quite numerous, were allocated in small numbers to the infantry units.[6] The French Air Force had few modern machines and was pitifully weak compared with the German. Finally, the long-meditated defensive plans of General Gamelin were quite erroneous. Discounting the possibility of an attack just north of the Maginot Line, in the Ardennes, where the country was hilly and wooded, he put his best and most mobile troops on the extreme left wing, where on the invasion of Belgium they were to move rapidly along the coast and try to assist the Dutch north of Antwerp. On their immediate right flank the BEF under Gort was to advance to the River Dyle. The Allied front would then run north and south through the middle of Belgium along the line Antwerp-Louvain-Meuse. But in the Ardennes, the line was thinly held by troops from French reserve formations.

When the German offensive began, it was at first difficult to tell where the main enemy thrust was to be expected, as heavy fighting developed on the entire front north of the Maginot Line. But the strongest and most dangerous

6. A. Goutard, *The Battle of France* (1958), p. 30.

attack came in the Ardennes, where seven of the ten German armoured divisions were available to exploit the first infantry advances. In the early days of the campaign the British forces were not heavily engaged, as their task was to move forward to the River Dyle behind the retreating Belgian Army. But British bombers of the Advanced Air Striking Force stationed in France were employed in daylight raids on the bridges over the river Meuse, suffering heavy losses as a result. After four days' fighting the Dutch army capitulated, and—what was more serious for the whole campaign—a German breakthrough took place in the Sedan area, where armoured divisions began a rapid scythe-like thrust around the northern armies. Soon the roads in Belgium and northern France began to fill with streams of refugees, seeking to evade the advancing enemy tanks and Stukas or dive-bombers.

The breakthrough caused the retreat of the Allied forces to the north. Gort's nine divisions (the tenth was on detachment in the Maginot Line area) had been defending the line of the Dyle from the 12th; on the 16th they were instructed to withdraw to the Scheldt. Meanwhile Churchill flew to France to find out what Gamelin's overall strategy was. He was disconcerted to find that the General had no strategic reserve, and that government offices in Paris were already burning their papers. Reynaud urged Churchill to reinforce the front with ten more squadrons of fighters from Britain, and Churchill agreed to recommend this to the War Cabinet. But although the squadrons were duly assigned, Air Chief Marshal Dowding, the Commander-in-Chief of Fighter Command in Britain, successfully argued that the bulk of the squadrons should continue to be based in England, as the French bases were so insecure. This undoubtedly helped to save many aircraft from being lost in France, but it meant that liaison with the ground forces became very poor. At about the same time the Air Ministry in Whitehall gave orders for the beginning of a Strategic Air Offensive by night attack from Britain against oil refineries and other targets

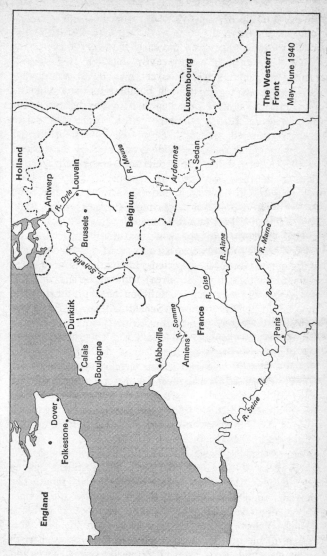

on the far side of the Rhine—a curiously irrelevant campaign at such a moment, and one that was very ineffective owing to the difficulty of locating the targets.

On May 19th it became clear that the BEF was in danger of being cut off, as the German thrust was making rapid progress towards the Channel coast at Abbeville. Preparation therefore began in Britain for the evacuation by sea of the British and other Allied forces that might become trapped. Meanwhile scratch forces of British troops, including the training divisions, held up the advance of the German tanks for a few hours here and there as they made their way through the Allied lines of communication. On May 20th General Gamelin, whose plans had proved so disastrous, was replaced by General Weygand, a man of 74, but still vigorous. But Weygand took several days to find out what was happening, and his orders, when they were issued, were out-of-date and inadequate. Gort was supposed to send two divisions for a counter-attack to the south on May 26th, and this was to link up with a French attack from the south northwards, thus cutting off the head of the German thrust. But a gap suddenly appeared on the British left, where the front joined that of the Belgian Army, and so Gort cancelled his offensive to the south. The French armies to the south were also unable to mount any attack. It was on the 26th that Gort decided that he must begin to retreat towards the coast and prepare an evacuation. His decision was approved by the British Cabinet. The port for evacuation had to be Dunkirk, for on that day German armoured forces had taken both Boulogne and Calais in spite of gallant resistance by hastily-assembled British troops.

On May 27th Gort's decision was justified by the capitulation of the Belgian Army on his left flank. The Belgians, under the command of their King, were no longer able to fight as a coherent force in conjunction with the British. Two days later Weygand accepted the inevitable and also authorized the withdrawal of as many French troops as could reach Dunkirk. Now the British Navy and

Air Force put out a supreme effort to save the troops from
the port and beaches of Dunkirk. Fortunately, this was a
point within the reach of fighters based in England; though
there were times when the harbour and the whole embark-
ation area suffered severely from enemy bombing. All sorts
of craft—pleasure steamers and little ships from the
Channel ports and the Thames—were used to supplement
destroyers and minesweepers in carrying troops from the
harbour mole and the beaches. At first it had seemed that
only a small proportion of the BEF could be saved from
such a perilous situation. But the German command was
husbanding its armoured divisions for the next advance
deeper into France, and seems to have expected that air
attack would prevent the escape of any substantial body
of troops. Furthermore, Gort, that 'simple, straightforward,
but not very clever man',[7] showed the traditional skill of
British commanders in organizing retreat. When the
evacuation of British troops was completed on the night of
June 2nd/3rd, some 198,315 British soldiers had been
saved. This was nearly all of the front-line BEF which
had been caught in the Dunkirk pocket. French troops
acted as a rearguard and a considerable number of them
were forced to capitulate when evacuation finally ended on
June 4th. But by this time a total of 338,226 Allied troops
had escaped, though the great bulk of their equipment had
been lost.[8] Nine British destroyers were lost and twenty-
three damaged, but otherwise the Navy did not suffer
seriously.

When evacuation began Churchill warned the British
public to prepare for 'hard and heavy tidings'.[9] But when
so many men escaped there was a tendency to regard the
Dunkirk operation as a sort of victory, and the King, in a
message to the forces, hailed it as a 'triumph'. Churchill
had to say at once 'We must be very careful not to assign
to this deliverance the attributes of a victory. Wars are not

7. Spears, *Assignment*, i, 34.
8. Ellis, *War in France and Flanders*, p. 247.
9. Hansard 361, 422 (28 May, 1940).

won by evacuations.'[10] And indeed the prospect looked very black for the remaining forces under Weygand's command, heavily outnumbered as they were by the German troops now facing them across the Somme. There were now two British divisions which were hastily brought into the line near the Channel Coast: the 51st Highland Division, which had raced back from its temporary detachment, for training purposes, in the Maginot Line; and the 1st Armoured Division, which had been preparing to cross the Channel from England when the offensive began. Altogether, including troops from the British lines of communication, some 140,000 British soldiers were still in France. But the odds against Weygand's hastily-assembled divisions were heavy.

On June 5th a new German offensive took place across the Somme. On the left flank the 51st division was soon cut off from other forces and pinned against the coast at St Valery, where it was battered into capitulation, this time without sufficient opportunity for escape by sea. The 1st Armoured had already lost many of its tanks in attacks on German positions on the Somme, and its remaining elements retreated towards the west. On June 14th—the day of the fall of Paris—General Alan Brooke, one of Gort's corps commanders who had been sent back to France to take charge of the remaining British forces, reported that the state of the French Army was such that it was impossible to hold any line. He urged the immediate withdrawal of the remaining British troops. Together with Polish troops and others who wished to escape, they were evacuated from Cherbourg and other points on the Channel and Atlantic coasts. The proportion of casualties incurred by the BEF in the Battle of France was of the order of one in six: some 11,000 were killed, 14,000 wounded, and 41,000 missing or prisoners of war.[11] Considering the extent of the German victory, these casualties were sur-

10. Hansard 362, 791 (4 June, 1940).

11. F. A. E. Crew, *Army Medical Services—Campaigns*, i (1956), p. 112. Figures corrected to August, 1945.

prisingly small. It is worth recalling that at the Battle of the Somme in 1916 nearly 60,000 troops were killed or wounded in a single day.[12]

Meanwhile the tragedy of the French collapse was being enacted. Although Reynaud wished to fight on, his colleagues in the French Cabinet began to speak of an armistice. Churchill sought to persuade them to carry on the struggle from French North Africa if necessary, but he had no success. A last British effort to prevent a surrender was made on June 16th, when a plan for an indissoluble union between the two countries (originally based on suggestions by Jean Monnet, the French economist, and by Sir Robert Vansittart of the Foreign Office) was put forward by the British War Cabinet to the French government, now at Bordeaux.[13] But Reynaud was unable to get his colleagues to accept the proposal, and so he resigned, to be succeeded by the aged Marshal Pétain, a military hero of the First World War. Pétain immediately set on foot negotiations for an armistice, and this led to acceptance of the German terms on June 22nd. A large part of France including Paris and the whole of the northern and western coasts were to be occupied by German troops. The new French government established itself at the spa of Vichy, in the unoccupied zone. On June 18th General Charles de Gaulle broadcast from London an appeal to Frenchmen to carry on the fight under his leadership, but he was no more than a junior figure in the French government, and at first there were few who could or would respond to his call.

It did not need the fall of France to persuade people in Britain that there was a danger of the invasion of their own country. They had already taken to heart significant details of the campaign against Norway—in particular, the use of parachute and airborne troops to capture key points,

12. C. R. M. F. Cruttwell, *History of the Great War, 1914-1918* (Oxford, 1934), p. 268.

13. Thomson, *Proposal for Anglo-French Union*, pp. 8-12.

and the rapid emergence of Nazi sympathizers, led by Vidkun Quisling, to form a government of collaborators. The Chiefs of Staff, indeed, had reported to the Chamberlain Cabinet on May 9th that they thought Hitler was more likely to strike against Britain than against France, and that preparations to deal with this eventuality should begin at once.[14] On the following day all male enemy aliens living in coastal areas liable to invasion were ordered to be interned, and six days later the order was extended to the entire country. When Eden took over the War Office he found that plans were already being made for the recruitment of a local part-time militia to help in guarding against parachute troops.[15] On May 14th he broadcast an appeal for volunteers, and the response was immediate—prompted by news and rumours of the effective use of parachutists in the Low Countries and France. Soon hundreds of thousands of men of all ages between 17 and 65 were donning armlets with the initials 'LDV' (Local Defence Volunteers) and were drilling with improvised arms and keeping watch at vantage points throughout the country. On May 22nd the Home Office decided to intern suspected fascist sympathizers: Sir Oswald Mosley and other members of the British Union of Fascists were immediately arrested, together with Captain A. H. M. Ramsay, a Conservative MP known to have similar associations. On the same day Parliament hastily passed an Emergency Powers Bill which conferred on the government a wide-ranging authority over persons and property. The measure had been drafted by Chamberlain and Attlee, working together.[16] The second reading of the bill was introduced by Attlee in a speech in which he also announced that Excess Profits Tax would henceforth be at the rate of 100%.

All these developments indicated the common determination that the war should now be fought more vigor-

14. Butler, *Grand Strategy*, ii, 172.
15. Avon, *Reckoning*, p. 103.
16. Feiling, *Chamberlain*, p. 448.

ously than before. The French request for an armistice might have had the opposite effect, and persuaded people that there was no longer any hope of victory. But there was surprisingly little defeatism. In mid-June it was decided to intern the great majority of enemy aliens, without waiting to establish which of them were really sympathetic to the Allied cause. As additional precautions, the Ministry of Information urged the public to join a 'Silent Column' pledged not to talk about the course of the war; and the Home Office issued a regulation which authorized the prosecution of anyone whose talk was likely to cause 'alarm and despondency'. But these latter measures were clearly more trouble than help and after vigorous protests in Parliament and in the national press they were jettisoned after a few weeks. Criticism of the indiscriminate internment of enemy aliens took rather longer to build up, and for some time was largely confined to the left-wing press and MPs. Distrust of foreigners was widespread; but the general level of morale remained high, for whether through ignorance or through a sense of national continuity the great majority of people were quite confident in the outcome of the war. To fight 'alone' was no doubt unfortunate in many respects; but it did not quite mean what it said, for there were after all the British Dominions, and the United States could be relied upon for assistance with arms and supplies. Not to have to maintain a fighting front on the continent of Europe might well be a positive advantage: it had certainly been terribly expensive in life and wealth in the previous war. The King, as so often, reflected the popular view: 'Personally I feel happier now that we have no allies to be polite to & pamper', he wrote to his mother, Queen Mary.[17]

But the fall of France brought one serious danger which had to be faced at once. The French fleet was much more powerful than the German, and if it were taken over by the enemy, the Royal Navy would be hard put to it to

maintain superiority at sea. This was especially serious
as the Italian government had declared war on Germany's
side on June 10th; and although it was generally recognized that the Italian forces were relatively weak, their
navy was, on paper at least, the strongest of the three
arms. The War Cabinet reluctantly decided on a drastic
remedy for this situation: the Commander of the British
fleet at Gibraltar, Admiral Sir James Somerville, was
ordered to deliver an ultimatum to the French naval commander at the North African base of Oran: he was to
agree to put his ships under British control, or to undertake
to despatch them to a neutral port, or they would at once
be destroyed. The French admiral rejected the ultimatum
and his ships were thereupon bombarded, all being destroyed or seriously damaged, and more than twelve hundred
French sailors being killed. Other French warships were
taken over or immobilized in British ports and at Alexandria, and only light forces remained under the control of
the Vichy government. Somerville hated this task of destroying a fleet with which he had so lately been co-operat-
ing, and later described the action as 'the biggest political
blunder of modern times.'[18] The immediate result was that
the Vichy regime broke off diplomatic relations with
Britain, and General de Gaulle's task of rallying Frenchmen to carry on the war by Britain's side became much
more difficult. But a major element of uncertainty in
Britain's prospects of survival had now been removed;
and many people throughout the world took this as an
indication of the fighting spirit of the new British government.

The prime mover in the Oran affair, and the embodi-
ment of Britain's fighting spirit, was Churchill himself.
For several weeks his popularity had been rising. His
somewhat old-fashioned and elaborate oratory at last struck
the right note with a public which was conscious of the
challenge of the times and anxious to be reminded of the
previous occasions when invasion of Britain had been

18. Macintyre, *Fighting Admiral*, p. 69.

attempted and successfully resisted. As de Gaulle put it, he could now use his eloquence to 'stir up the heavy dough of the English.'[19] He did this by speaking directly to the people through the medium of radio—a way of strengthening his political position which was not open to Lloyd George in the First World War. But also unlike Lloyd George he had a great respect for Parliament, and all his finest speeches at this time were delivered first to his fellow-members of the House of Commons. At the outset, on May 13th, he told them that he had 'nothing to offer save blood, toil, tears and sweat'.[20] On June 4th, before the fall of France, he anticipated the threat of the invasion of Britain:

> We shall fight on the beaches, we shall fight on the landing-grounds, we shall fight in the fields and in the streets, we shall fight in the hills; we shall never surrender.[21]

On June 18th, when it became known that France was seeking an armistice, he declared:

> I expect the Battle of Britain is about to begin . . .
> Let us therefore brace ourselves to our duty, and so bear ourselves that if the British Empire and its Commonwealth last for a thousand years men will still say, 'This was their finest hour'.[22]

When, on July 3rd, his oratory was transformed into ruthless action—unhappily, at the expense of a former ally —the climax came, and after his explanation to the Commons of the reasons for the bombardment of the French fleet he received a tremendous ovation. Now for the first

19. '. . . remuer la lourde pâte anglaise.' C. de Gaulle, *Mémoires de Guerre*, i (Paris, 1954), p. 47.
20. Hansard 360, 1502.
21. Hansard, 361, 796.
22. Hansard 362, 60f.

time even the Chamberlain Tories who had sat silent on
their benches for several weeks joined in the cheering with
enthusiasm.[23] Early in August, the popularity of the new
Prime Minister was confirmed in a striking way by a
Gallup poll. Asked whether they approved or disapproved
of Churchill as leader, 88 per cent of the sample replied
in the affirmative, and only 7% were hostile, with 5%
doubtful.[24] This was far better than the score that Chamberlain ever achieved.

But there was by no means the same degree of approval
for all of Churchill's colleagues. Chamberlain was the
target of much hostile criticism, and as early as May 15th
he received a report from the Conservative party organization to say that his position had much deteriorated even
in his home town of Birmingham.[25] Among the leading
politicians, Lloyd George was one of the most critical of
Chamberlain, and privately told Churchill, when the latter
tentatively offered him a place in the War Cabinet:

> Several of the architects of this catastrophe are still
> leading members of your Government, and two of
> them are in the Cabinet that directs the war.[26]

But Churchill replied that he had been 'touched' by
Chamberlain's 'kindness and courtesy . . . in our new
relations' and said 'I have joined hands with him, and
must act with personal loyalty'.[27] So Lloyd George stayed
outside the government. But the 'feeling against what is
known as the "Old Gang" ', as Harold Nicolson put it,
continued to grow, as the troops who had returned through
Dunkirk told their tales of shortages of equipment.[28] In
mid-June Churchill was obliged to ask for a truce to
recrimination:

23. Churchill, *Second World War*, ii, 211; Rhodes James,
*Chips*, p. 260.
24. *News Chronicle*, 8 Aug., 1940.
25. Reith, *Into the Wind*, p. 389.
26. Owen, *Tempestuous Journey*, p. 749.      27. *Ibid.*
28. Nicolson, *Diaries*, ii, 94 (letter of 6 June).

If we open a quarrel between the past and the present we shall find that we have lost the future.[29]

In early July, however, there was published an anonymous book entitled *Guilty Men*, written by three Beaverbrook journalists, bitterly assailing the record of the leading Chamberlainites, and this fed the demand for their early retirement from the government. A Gallup poll found that more than three-quarters of those who could decide thought that Chamberlain should be dropped from the government, and more than half also thought that Simon, Halifax and Kingsley Wood should go.[30] Chamberlain wrote optimistically to Hoare, now the ambassador at Madrid, on July 15th:

On the home front the campaign for the elimination of the 'Old Gang' & particularly your humble servant though it has not yet come to an end seems nevertheless to be petering out. I have done nothing to counter it except to get on with such work as falls to me and I have some reason to think that my colleagues, Attlee, Greenwood & Alexander have considerably revised their ideas of my value in the government.[31]

But there was no real 'petering out' of the campaign, not even when in late July Chamberlain fell ill and had to undergo a major operation. Halifax, who was the leading available scapegoat after Chamberlain, also received a good deal of unfavourable attention.[32] As Foreign Secretary he had to try to keep Spain out of the war and to prevent the military faction in Japan from finding an excuse to attack British possessions in the Far East. This meant, in effect,

29. Hansard 362, 52 (18 June, 1940).
30. *News Chronicle*, 8 July, 1940.
31. Chamberlain to Hoare, 15 July, 1940, Templewood Papers.
32. Atticus in *Sunday Times*, 21 July, 1940; Birkenhead, *Halifax*, p. 464.

appeasement once more: the Spaniards had to be allowed to get supplies through the blockade—in spite of the reluctance of Hugh Dalton, the Minister of Economic Warfare, to permit this;[33] and the Burma Road, by which the Chinese were being supplied, had to be closed for three months as a result of Japanese pressure. The critics were not to know that Halifax was much braver in the face of the Japanese than Churchill himself. He wrote privately at the time

> My own inclination has been to tell the Japs to go to the devil . . . but Winston is not unnaturally anxious about risking another war.[34]

Similarly, when in mid-July Hitler paused in his invasion plans to make a final offer of peace, it was not the men of Munich who wished to take this seriously, but rather a small band of pacifists and pessimists, mostly from the former opposition parties. Some of them, such as Richard Stokes, a Labour MP, looked to Lloyd George for leadership;[35] and indeed he rather than Chamberlain was fitted for the role of a British Pétain, listening regularly as he did to the German radio and contrasting the present situation unfavourably with that which he had faced in the worst days of the First World War.[36] The Foreign Office permitted certain informal contacts with enemy agents in neutral countries, possibly as a delaying tactic; and Lord Lothian, the ambassador in Washington, thought that Hitler was offering not unfavourable terms.[37] But it was Halifax himself who in a broadcast decisively rejected the German initiative after only three days. And Chamberlain described Hitler's speech in his diary as 'the familiar

33. Halifax to Hoare, 23 Aug., 1940, Templewood Papers.
34. Halifax to Hoare, 8 July, 1940, *ibid*.
35. Stokes to Lloyd George, 25 June, 1940, Lloyd George Papers.
36. F. Lloyd George, *The Years that are Past*, p. 269; T. Jones, *Diary with Letters, 1931–1950* (1954), p. 469.
37. Nicolson, *op. cit.*, p. 104.

round of distorted history, megalomania, self-righteousness and threats.'[38] He at least had learnt his lesson.

But the German dictator was still not ready to begin the invasion, or even to unleash the air offensive which was to be its preliminary. Contrary to the current assumption in Britain, he had had no plans ready for such operations before his attack on France, and time was required to work them out and to set on foot the necessary redeployment of men and material. It was only at the beginning of July that the German armed forces started reorganizing for an invasion. Two weeks later, on July 16th, Hitler issued a directive which declared his intention, 'if necessary', to invade Britain at a date not earlier than mid-August.[39] The operation was given the code-name 'Sealion'. But while the German armed forces made their preparations, so did the British. By mid-August the military strength of the defence had been considerably enhanced. In the air, Fighter Command's total of Spitfires and Hurricanes, which had fallen to 331 after Dunkirk, rose to 620; fighter aircraft in reserve rose from 36 to 289.[40] Beaverbrook as Minister of Aircraft Production was straining every nerve to increase the supply, and although his unorthodox methods won him the enmity of the Air Ministry, it seems clear that he managed considerably to boost the short-run availability of fighters. This was done by cutting down on other types of aircraft, by increasing the hours of work in the factories and by ensuring the immediate repair of damaged planes. Meanwhile, the Navy was busy sowing mines on invasion paths and organized raiding forces to deal with any transports that might set forth on the North Sea or the Channel. This meant the withdrawal of most of the destroyers from convoy duties, on which they were badly needed: but the risk had to be taken.

38. Feiling, *Chamberlain*, p. 450.
39. Wheatley, *Operation Sealion*, p. 37.
40. Richards, *Royal Air Force*, i, 156.

On land, Ironside, who had been made Commander-in-Chief, Home Forces, at the end of May, had ordered the construction of static defences in the form of anti-tank ditches and concrete pillboxes, along lines well inland from the beaches. But in mid-July he was replaced by Alan Brooke, whom Churchill preferred because he was in favour of hitting directly at the invader with all his strength at the point of landing.[41] For this purpose Brooke organized mobile reserves which could at once reinforce the forward troops. Only twenty-five tanks of the seven hundred sent to France had been saved, and less than five hundred remained in Britain, mostly in training units; but another three hundred were delivered from the factories in June and July.[42] Brooke also had his difficulties with Beaverbrook, who acquired supplies of armour plating and fitted it on cars, which he called 'Beaverettes', and proposed to use for the defence of aircraft factories.[43] The artillery and rifle shortage was considerably relieved by shipments of First World War stocks from the United States in July. In that month the Home Guard (as the LDV had now been re-christened) passed the million mark; many of them received American rifles, and others had shotguns. All open fields had obstacles placed on them to prevent the landing of air transports; signposts had been removed from the roads and railway stations; and in general it seemed reasonable to expect that airborne invaders would have a difficult time.

But in any case, before attacking it was necessary for the Germans to win air superiority over England. On August 12th they began an air offensive with the object of destroying the resistance of Fighter Command. Radar stations, which provided vital advance warning of enemy aircraft, were attacked on that day, and one was put out of action. On succeeding days attacks were made on RAF airfields and stations, and also on aircraft factories. A total of 1790 German aircraft flew sorties on August

41. Bryant, *Turn of the Tide*, pp. 197f.
42. *Ibid.*, p. 205.          43. *Ibid.*, pp. 205f.

15th, and almost as many re-appeared next day.[44] But the defending Spitfires and Hurricanes took a heavy toll, roughly at the rate of two German aircraft for every one of their own. Since damaged aircraft mostly fell on British soil, or close to the coast, the loss of pilots was proportionately even greater on the enemy side. This was especially important, because the reserves of trained pilots threatened to run out more quickly than the reserves of new aircraft. The total of RAF pilots engaged in the battle was little more than a thousand: and it was with justice that Churchill said in August 'Never in the field of human conflict was so much owed by so many to so few'.[45]

The critical stage of the German attack came in the last week of August and the first week of September. Throughout this period the resources of Fighter Command, both in pilots and aircraft, drained away more quickly than they were replenished. Furthermore, airfields and command posts were suffering heavy damage and the strain on the control system was becoming acute. German losses in this fortnight were less than two to one, and in view of the Luftwaffe's substantial superiority in numbers it began to look as if it would complete the attrition of the RAF in a few weeks. But a change in tactics by the German high command proved helpful at this juncture. British bombers had been attacking targets in Germany, and after a few bombs had fallen on London it was decided to extend the raids as far as Berlin. Apparently enraged by this, Hitler decided that the main target of German bombers should henceforth be London, rather than the RAF stations which sustained the air defences. In the ensuing fortnight (from September 7th) London suffered a great deal; but Fighter Command began to recover. The relative losses of German and British aircraft returned to the ratio of about two to one, and the British reserves began slowly to recover.[46] Both sides thought they were winning, because returning

44. Richards, *op. cit.*, i, 170, 172.
45. Hansard 364, 1167 (20 Aug., 1940).
46. Richards, *op. cit.*, p. 186.

pilots tended to exaggerate their success. On September 15th it was reported in Britain that 183 German planes had been shot down for the loss of less than forty. Everyone from Churchill downwards was much encouraged by this, and it was only much later that the figure of German losses on that day was discovered to be only 56.

All the same, there can be no doubt that the Battle of Britain had worked out to the advantage of the Royal Air Force. For this, 'the few' above all deserve the credit, and after them, Air Chief Marshal Dowding and his staff, then the skilled designers of the aircraft, the scientists led by Henry Tizard who devised the radar system, and finally the peacetime governments of MacDonald, Baldwin and Chamberlain which had the foresight to give priority to the air defence of the country. Because the Luftwaffe failed to overcome this obstacle, Hitler was unable to launch an invasion of Britain. In early September large numbers of barges had been massed at the Channel Ports, and British bombers went out to attack them: it has been calculated that they destroyed about 12% of them.[47] On the night of September 7th, however, invasion seemed imminent, and an alarm was given, which resulted in the church bells being rung—the pre-arranged warning of an actual attack. But in fact Hitler had been putting off his decision to invade from day to day, and on September 15th he decided to postpone it indefinitely. This information was naturally not immediately available to British intelligence, but a gradual dispersal of the invasion fleet was reported; and as the difficulties of making a crossing increased with the worsening of the weather, it gradually became clear that Hitler had accepted the necessity of postponement at least until the spring of 1941.

Meanwhile the civil population had encountered for the first time the strain, discomfort, damage, risk and injury which were caused by persistent air raids. The civil defence

47. *Ibid.*, p. 187.

organization set up by Anderson before the war was now really tested in the late summer and autumn of 1940. In June only about 100 civilians were killed in air raids; in July the total rose to 300; in August to 1150.[48] But in the two months beginning September 7th no less than 11,700 died, over four-fifths of them in London.[49] This was nowhere near the rate of casualties that was expected before the war, but for Londoners, and particularly for the inhabitants of the crowded East End boroughs in the neighbourhood of the docks, which suffered more than other districts, it was certainly a testing time.

The 'Blitz' as it was called—although it had little to do with the concept of the Blitzkrieg or 'lightning war'—began to all intents and purposes on the night of September 7th, when heavy day raids which had left the East End ablaze were followed by night attacks on a large scale. Day raids became less frequent; but thereafter until November 2nd London was bombed every night, by a nightly average of 200 planes. Few of the planes were brought down, for night fighters were not yet able to locate their targets with success, and anti-aircraft guns were ineffective at high altitudes. To begin with, the guns were not very numerous, as many of the batteries originally stationed in London had been sent to defend other targets. But after a few days many of them were brought back, and if they did nothing else they heartened the civilian population. It was soon clear that morale was a factor of great importance, and the government became worried by the fact that it was the poorer parts of London which were suffering so much more than those inhabited by the wealthy. The Communist Party was agitating for the provision of deep shelters, which Anderson had ruled out as being unduly expensive. Sir Harold Scott, a senior official of the London civil defence, has said that he was 'in a way relieved' when Buckingham Palace was raided

48. Titmuss, *Social Policy*, p. 253.
49. O'Brien, *Civil Defence*, p. 388.

on September 11th, at a time when the King and Queen were in residence.[50] The King and Queen themselves, though shaken by the experience, also came to feel that it was a good thing that they had shared the misfortunes of fellow-Londoners, at least to this extent. Apart from the East End, the old City was badly damaged, and St Paul's Cathedral was for a time threatened by a large unexploded bomb, which was eventually removed intact by a bomb disposal unit of the Royal Engineers.

The main surprise of the raids, from the point of view of the civil authorities, was the 'relatively small loss of life accompanied by . . . relatively high amount of damage to all types of building.'[51] This meant that the casualty services and the hospitals were used less than had been expected, but rescue services were in much greater demand. In addition, there were formidable problems of care, feeding and rehousing of people bombed out of their homes, or forced to leave by unexploded bombs. Emergency arrangements had to be made by the Ministry of Health to expand and co-ordinate existing services provided by the local authorities, which were quickly overborne. Additional problems were created by damage to power supplies and communications, though it was found that in most cases damage of this sort could soon be repaired. The extent of human suffering would have been reduced if more people could have been persuaded to leave the metropolis before the raids started: but although efforts had been made to get all the children away, and most schools in London were now closed, some 279,000 children of school age remained in the London evacuation area throughout the worst of the raids.[52] At West Ham, after much damage on the night of September 11th, the local authorities panicked and demanded the immediate evacuation of Silvertown; the Minister of Health wisely agreed to the demand and offered transport next day for all who wished to leave, but less than 3,000 took advantage

50. Scott, *Your Obedient Servant*, p. 131.
51. O'Brien, *op. cit.*, 392.    52. *The Times*, 18 Nov., 1940.

of the offer.[53] Elsewhere, without any panic, many people took matters into their own hands and settled down for the night on the platforms of underground stations. Since they bought twopenny tickets they could not be stopped at the barriers. On the night of September 27th it was reckoned that there were some 177,000 persons sheltering in the tubes.[54] But this was not a large proportion of the total population of London, and while many more occupied the previously provided communal shelters on the surface, the great majority of people stayed in their own homes, and either used a household shelter of their own or did without any protection better than that provided by an ordinary roof. The standard household shelter was the Anderson, which provided quite reasonable protection against blast or falling masonry if properly installed. But unfortunately it could not be used indoors, and so was only of help to those with gardens.

But nobody had envisaged the continuous nature of the attack, which forced on people the need not only for shelter against bombs, but for beds, proper drainage and ventilation, and washing and toilet facilities within the shelter. The rest centres provided by the local authorities often lacked these amenities, as the accommodation used for this purpose was not always available in advance, and so could not be properly prepared. This was because the local authorities had no powers to requisition in advance of need. There was also an urgent demand for communal feeding centres. As often happens in emergencies, the charitable societies had to step in to try and cope until the government caught up with the problem. Soon the Minister of Health gave the London County Council authority to spend as much as was required for all these purposes. The difficulties had been caused, to no small degree, by Treasury resistance to the idea that the government should pay for services which it was the legal obligation of the local authorities to provide.[55]

53. Titmuss, *op. cit.*, p. 259.    54. O'Brien, *op. cit.*, p. 392.
55. Titmuss, *op. cit.*, p. 252.

Justice, if not generosity, to the victims of air raids thus became an essential of policy. As early as June a scheme had been introduced for the provision of compensation to people of limited means who had lost their household requirements and clothing, so that at least these essentials could be replaced. Later, in October, it was announced that there would be a compulsory scheme for the insurance of all property against war damage; and all householders, and not just the poor, were guaranteed a certain amount of immediate compensation. Another measure to raise morale was the institution of the George Cross, as a recognition of heroism comparable to that shown on the field of battle by recipients of the Victoria Cross. What was important for Londoners, however, was not the exceptional bravery of a few but rather the ordinary, persistent fortitude of the many—the capacity to carry on with their ordinary work under conditions of constant strain and loss of sleep and moderate but continuous danger. The discovery of this fortitude in themselves and in their fellow-citizens was a source of pride to men and women alike. John Strachey, the left-wing author and politician who was serving as a part-time air raid warden, noticed that

> Nearly all women Civil Defence workers . . . derived the utmost reassurance from the discovery that they were quite as capable of facing the Blitz as were men.[56]

Throughout it all, the city, though scarred, continued to fulfil the main functions of a great metropolis. Plans made before the war to evacuate the seat of government to the Midlands were quietly abandoned, after Churchill and others had reported unfavourably on the chaos and confusion caused by the move of the French government from Paris to Tours and then to Bordeaux.[57] The Cabinet and

56. Strachey, *Post D*, p. 23.
57. Churchhill, *Second World War*, ii, 323; O'Brien, *op. cit.*, p. 362.

the House of Commons moved out of their existing homes, but not more than a few hundred yards—the Cabinet to the well-protected Annexe at Storey's Gate, and the Commons to Church House. The knowledge that the government was still in London undoubtedly helped to maintain morale. People liked to feel, as J. B. Priestley put it, that they were 'in the middle of the world's stage with all the spotlights focused on us.' The Londoners were indeed soldiers fighting a battle: 'As a kind of civilian life this is hell; but as battles go, it is not at all bad.'[58]

The Battle of Britain and the London Blitz were watched with close attention and concern throughout the world, not least in the United States, where President Roosevelt and his administration saw the preservation of Britain's capacity to resist Hitler, and above all the survival of the British fleet, as essential for the security of their own still inadequately defended land. Since the first month of the war, as we have seen, American supplies had been made available to the Allies on a 'cash and carry' basis, and both Britain and France had placed large orders for planes and other munitions of war. When France fell, Jean Monnet, who was in charge of the programme for the French government, saw to it that the French orders were transferred to Britain; and during the crisis of the summer the British purchasing mission substantially increased their requirements as a matter of urgency. The half-million First World War rifles and the artillery and machine guns that were hastily shipped over made an important contribution to the defence of Britain in the face of the invasion threat. Then in August a deal was carefully worked out whereby fifty over-age American destroyers were transferred to Britain in return for the cession to the United States of naval and air bases on British islands in the West Indies and elsewhere on the Atlantic seaboard. The War Cabinet also gave the American government solemn assur-

58. J. B. Priestley, *Postscripts (1940)*, pp. 69, 75 (8 and 15 Sept.).

ances about the disposal of the fleet in the event of a successful invasion of Britain. Since only nine of the destroyers were sufficiently serviceable to be used by the
Royal Navy before the turn of the year, it may well be
thought that the Americans got much the better of the
bargain.[59] But it was a presidential election year, and this
prevented the American administration from acting more
generously. Churchill calculated, with reason, that a long-
term result of the deal would be that henceforth Britain
and the United States would be 'somewhat mixed up
together in some of their affairs for mutual and general
advantage.'[60]

For when members of the British government looked
ahead to try to estimate how Britain could possibly win
the war, it seemed as if the generous assistance of the
resources of the United States would be essential. It is
true that very optimistic views prevailed about the poten-
tialities of the economic blockade of Germany and about
the prospect of effective resistance by the populations of
the defeated European countries. Dalton, the new Minister
of Economic Warfare, wrote to Attlee late in May:

> Even if the worst happens across the Channel,
> Germany will begin to feel the oil squeeze by the
> Autumn and will become dangerously short by the
> Spring of 1941. Holding down Europe will need
> strong and mobile garrisons, and mobility needs oil.[61]

Dalton also advocated that guerilla activities in Europe
should be organized from Britain, along the lines of the
Sinn Fein movement in Ireland, the Spanish guerillas of
the Peninsular War, and the Chinese resistance fighters
who were presently defying the Japanese Army in occupied areas. In July Churchill decided to accept this idea,
and placed Dalton himself in charge of a secret organiza-

59. Butler, *Grand Strategy*, ii, 245.
60. Hansard 364, 1171 (20 Aug., 1940).
61. Dalton to Attlee, 27 May, 1940, Dalton Papers.

tion called the Special Operations Executive which was to prepare sabotage and subversion on the Continent.[62] Thus Dalton was responsible for both the negative and positive aspects of undermining the enemy grip in Europe. But whatever the prospects of these activities, it hardly seemed possible that Britain could win without a substantial advantage over Germany in sheer military strength; and to achieve this, it was essential to rely upon American supply. At the beginning of the war, it looked as if Britain had sufficient dollar resources to pay her way, provided she kept up her exports and also did not order too many items of munitions from America. But during the Battle of Britain all moderation in placing defence orders had been abandoned, and exports had also suffered. By July it had become clear to Treasury officials that the dollars that they had been husbanding would run out early in 1941.[63] Britain was winning the Battle of Britain 'alone'; but this 'splendid isolation' would not have much permanent significance unless economic resources, beyond the power of the British Commonwealth to provide, could be thrown into the balance on her side.

62. Dalton, *Fateful Years*, p. 369; Foot, *S.O.E. in France*, p. 8.
63. Hancock and Gowing, *British War Economy*, p. 232.

# 5.   The Ocean and the Desert

As the immediate threat of invasion receded in the autumn of 1940, the prestige of the Churchill government stood at an exceptionally high level. There was no obvious need for reconstruction of the Cabinet at such a time. Nevertheless Churchill was forced into it by the illness of Chamberlain. The ex-Premier, who had incurable cancer, resigned office at the end of September, and died on November 9th. Churchill had come to rely upon Chamberlain for his work in supervising domestic administration, and at first he did not know how he could replace him.[1] He eventually decided to appoint Anderson, the former civil servant who as Home Secretary and Minister of Home Security had been dealing with a whole range of critical problems on the home front, including civil defence. Since civil defence policy had now become a highly-charged political question, it was desirable to place Anderson's former responsibilities in the hands of a skilled politician; and this Churchill now did, by choosing Herbert Morrison, for several years the leader of the Labour majority on the London County Council, as well as a former Labour Cabinet minister.[2] Anderson became a member of the War Cabinet, which had already been enlarged by the admission of Beaverbrook in August; and Bevin and Kingsley Wood, both retaining their existing posts, were also brought in. Thus, allowing for the loss of Chamberlain, the size of the War Cabinet had grown from five members to eight.

Another consequence of Chamberlain's retirement was that the leadership of the Conservative Party fell vacant.

1. Avon, *Reckoning*, p. 138.
2. Churchill, *Second World War*, ii, 326.

Since even Chamberlain's closest supporters had risen to enthusiastic approval of Churchill's conduct as Prime Minister during the summer, there could be no hesitation about the party's wish that he should take the post of leader. The only question was whether, after so many years of disregard by his fellow-Conservatives, he would decide to spurn the offer and assume a position above the parties. But Churchill saw clearly enough that since the Conservatives still had a large majority in Parliament, he had either to accept the post of Conservative leader or place himself at the mercy of whoever should take the leadership instead. The party's second choice would probably have been Halifax; and although Churchill and Halifax had worked together quite well in the preceding months, there was a temperamental barrier between the two men. Churchill was an extrovert, a creature of moods, yet sceptical of organized religion; Halifax was an Anglo-Catholic, by character reticent and even devious, described unkindly by Beaverbrook as 'the holy fox'.[3] Churchill disliked ordinary office hours, got up late, took naps in the late afternoon and then expected his colleagues to debate policy with him in the small hours; Halifax detested these 'midnight follies' as they were sometimes called, believing in regular hours of work and proper rest: even in the first days of the Churchill government he was 'seeking to organize a rebellion on the subject.'[4] With a campaign against the remaining Chamberlainites smouldering in the press, and an alternative Foreign Secretary (Eden) at his elbow, it is not surprising that Churchill contemplated with equanimity the idea of finding Halifax a new job away from Whitehall.

The opportunity came in mid-December with the sudden death of Lord Lothian, the ambassador to the United States. The post was one of vital importance and at first Churchill thought it might be a suitable opening for the talents of Lloyd George. The veteran war leader, now

3. Young, *Churchill and Beaverbrook*, p. 174.
4. Birkenhead, *Halifax*, p. 457 (diary 12 May, 1940).

77 years old, considered it at least to the extent of having
a medical examination, but probably to his own relief
and certainly to the relief of the Americans, he was
advised against acceptance.[5] Then Churchill turned to
Halifax, who after expressing the utmost reluctance eventually consented to go as a matter of duty.[6] He proved
to be a successful ambassador, and stayed at Washington
for over five years. Eden became Foreign Secretary once
more, rejoining the War Cabinet; and as Eden's successor
at the War Office Churchill unexpectedly chose the Conservative Chief Whip, David Margesson, who had at
least shown in his former office that he could display
fidelity to his new leader. Thus the team at the top
became personally more congenial to Churchill than before.

In the late autumn of 1940 the night air raids on London
continued, though less continuously, owing to poorer
weather and because provincial targets were also heavily
attacked. One of the most serious raids in the provinces
was that on Coventry on the night of November 14th.
Aided by a full moon and good weather, some 450 enemy
aircraft easily found their target and dropped both explosive and incendiary bombs, starting innumerable fires in
the old city centre and destroying it almost completely.
A total of 554 people were killed, and of the old fourteenth-
century cathedral only the spire and an empty shell of
walls remained. But the aircraft factories on the outskirts
were not badly damaged, partly because they were less
combustible.[7] The news of this raid, together with photo-
graphs of the damage to the cathedral, was released almost
immediately, and had a powerful influence on American
opinion. But nearly all the main industrial centres of
Britain suffered heavy attacks in the succeeding months
of the winter and early spring. The west coast ports

5. F. Lloyd George, *The Years that are Past*, p. 268; Churchill, *Second World War*, ii, 504.
6. Avon, *op. cit.*, p. 182; Birkenhead, *Halifax*, pp. 468f.
7. Collier, *Defence of the U.K.*, p. 265.

began to receive special attention from the enemy, who hoped to damage docks and shipping and thus starve out the fortress that he could not invade. Of provincial targets, Merseyside was attacked more heavily than any other area, but in proportion to size none suffered more than Coventry and Plymouth.[8]

It became increasingly evident in late 1940 that fire was an especially dangerous hazard of the air raids, and one that was largely unnecessary if proper precautions were taken. Incendiary bombs could easily be dealt with by individual action, if they could be reached quickly; but often they fell on roofs of empty buildings where they were not at first noticed, or where they were inaccessible, perhaps because the buildings were locked. The need for an effective system of fire watching was therefore already evident when on December 29th a heavy raid on London led to widespread fire damage in the largely unoccupied area of the City.[9] The Guildhall was destroyed; eight Wren churches were burnt out; and a large part of the business quarter was lost. Two days later Morrison announced that the War Cabinet had decided to institute a scheme for compulsory fire watching by male civilians. He also appealed for volunteers to form street fire-fighting parties. His mind was already moving towards plans for the merging of the local fire brigades into a national service;[10] but this required legislation and the establishment of a new administrative machine; and although an Act for the purpose was passed in May 1941, it did not take effect until the following August. The provision of emergency water tanks for the use of fire engines was also considerably, if gradually, extended.

Meanwhile there had been more heavy raids in early 1941, mostly directed against the ports, but culminating in an attack on London on the night of May 10th in which the Chamber of the House of Commons was destroyed and all but one of the main line railway stations tem-

8. *Ibid.*, p. 281.　　9. See, e.g., Strachey, *Post D*, p. 64.
10. Morrison, *Autobiography*, p. 184.

porarily put out of action. Though heavy damage was done, the fire watchers with their stirrup pumps and buckets of sand proved their worth on this occasion. For the first time, too, night fighters, using airborne radar, brought down a number of enemy bombers.[11] Other devices which were now in use by the defence included rocket batteries, the lighting of decoy fires, and interference with enemy direction-finding radio.[12]

Although Britain was to suffer heavily from air attack in later stages of the war, there was never again the continuous battering which had taken place in the eight months from September 1940 to May 1941. The surprising thing, in retrospect, is how slight the damage to the war effort had been in this period. Although some supplies— for instance, sugar—were seriously depleted for a time, no grave shortages resulted. Factories were sometimes put out of action, but rarely for long periods. Road and rail communications could be restored with very little delay. To be sure, the tonnage of bombs dropped was small compared with that later devoted to targets in Germany. By the later stages of the war, however, methods of air raid protection had been distinctly improved. At any rate in this phase of the war the enemy did not come near his object of disabling Britain's capacity to resist.

At sea, the danger to the country's capacity to survive and fight was undoubtedly more critical. Britain depended, in war as in peace, upon a constant flow of imports of food and raw material. The collapse of France and the entry of Italy into the war meant that the Mediterranean could no longer be used, and this imposed an extra burden of distance on all shipping to and from the Far and Middle East. Further, although the enemy's submarines were but few in the summer of 1940, they could make their attacks in the shipping lanes almost with impunity, for the destroyers which normally escorted the convoys were concentrated instead to guard against the threat of an invasion.

11. Douglas, *Years of Command*, p. 127.
12. Collier, *op. cit.*, pp. 277-9.

The U-boat captains were later to speak of the summer of 1940 as 'the happy time';[13] and their success was considerable, for British, Allied and neutral shipping losses by submarine attack, which had averaged less than 100,000 tons per month in the first nine months of the war, rose to an average of 250,000 tons in the last seven months of 1940. In 1941 the losses remained at a high level, and a menace of almost equal importance appeared in the form of attacks on the high seas by aircraft from enemy bases all the way along the European coastline from northern Norway to the Spanish border. The intensification of this type of warfare was the result of an order by Hitler on February 8th, 1941 that all German striking power should be directed against the British shipping routes. Hitler's order in its turn led to Churchill's directive of March 6th giving the highest priority to defeating 'the attempt to strangle our food supplies and our connection with the United States'.[14] The action to be taken included bombing raids on enemy submarine and aircraft bases; improved aircraft cover and anti-aircraft defence for shipping and for ports; and efforts to reduce the delays at docks both at home and overseas. Compared with the ravages of submarines and aircraft, enemy surface raiders were comparatively ineffective, but there was always the danger of one or other of the few large German surface craft emerging into the shipping lanes. The Admiralty, and indeed the entire nation, went through a period of particular concern when the newly completed enemy battleship *Bismarck* moved through Norwegian waters into the North Atlantic and then sank the battle-cruiser *Hood*, which had for long been the pride of the Royal Navy. After eluding pursuit for a time the *Bismarck* was brought to bay west of the French coast and destroyed by a combination of air attack, gunfire, and torpedoes from a naval task force.[15]

The Battle of the Atlantic, as Churchill called it, went on

13. Roskill, *War at Sea*, i, 348.
14. *Ibid.*, p. 339; Churchill, *op. cit.*, iii, 107.
15. Roskill, *op. cit.*, pp. 395-418.

through 1941 with varying fortunes. On the one hand, the number of U-boats increased rapidly as German construction programmes got under way. But on the other hand the supply of British escort vessels also improved, and Coastal Command of the RAF, using American-built Hudson and Catalina aircraft, grew more and more effective. Late in the year British convoys were supplied with catapult fighter aircraft or even auxiliary aircraft carriers to ward off enemy attack. By late 1941, with many of the U-boats moving into the Mediterranean, the Atlantic shipping routes became safer. On a tonnage basis losses of shipping in the Atlantic in the whole of the last quarter of the year were less than the loss in any single month of the spring and summer.

It was against this background of difficulty, if not dislocation, of overseas supply and home manufacture that the government sought to expand the production of armaments and thereby prepare the ground for eventual victory. In August 1940 plans were being drawn up not only to strengthen the navy and the air force but also to provide the equipment for an army of fifty-five divisions, as had been agreed in September 1939, at a time when it was thought that the army's heaviest task would be to supplement the French Army on the Western Front.[16] A mere fifty-five divisions would not be sufficient to challenge the entire German Army, but it was now assumed that air attack, blockade and subversion would all have taken their toll of the enemy before any major encounter took place. The fifty-five divisions would not absorb a very large proportion of British manpower, as they were to include only thirty-four divisions of British troops, the remaining divisions being manned by India, the Dominions and the colonies, albeit with British equipment. There were in fact to be nine Indian divisions, four from the African colonies, three each from Canada and Australia and one each from South Africa and New Zealand.[17]

16. Butler, *Grand Strategy*, ii, 32.     17. *Ibid.*, p. 347.

Large orders for munitions of all types had already been placed in the United States and Canada, and still more were planned for the autumn. Even so, the demands for increased production from British industry, combined with the manpower demands of the services, were so gauged as to require the most efficient use of the available resources of the nation's labour force. It was not easy to ensure that the competing demands of industry and the forces were properly catered for—still less that the three separate ministries concerned with supply to the three services worked in proper co-ordination. When the Coalition took office Arthur Greenwood was given the task of presiding over the Production Council, which was supposed to resolve disputes in this sphere: [18] but the friction which arose, for instance, between Bevin, the Minister af Labour, and Beaverbrook, the Minister of Aircraft Production, showed that this task was not being satisfactorily accomplished. Beaverbrook's motto, 'Committees take the punch out of war' did not augur well for his relations with other ministers.[19] His methods, which Dalton summed up as 'constant banditry and intrigues against all colleagues'[20] may have served the nation well in the critical summer of 1940, when aircraft had to take priority over all other needs: they were less suitable for the longer haul of the autumn and winter months, or for the succeeding year. Churchill tried to solve the difficulty in late September 1940 by urging Beaverbrook to take on the Ministry of Supply as well as Aircraft Production, and to unite them into a single Ministry of Production, from which only Admiralty orders would be excluded. But Beaverbrook refused, pleading reasonably enough that his chronic asthma prevented him from undertaking extra work.[21]

A few months later, however, in January 1941 Churchill decided that Greenwood was not a strong enough per-

18. Hancock and Gowing, *op. cit.*, p. 217.
19. Scott, *Your Obedient Servant*, p. 165.
20. Diary, 11 Dec., 1940, Dalton Papers.
21. Young, *op. cit.*, pp. 160ff.

sonality to oversee the work of national production, and moved him to the less urgent task of organizing studies of post-war reconstruction. A smaller Production Executive was constituted under Bevin's chairmanship, with the three ministers in charge of the service supply programmes as its other members; but it was to have a court of appeal in the form of the Lord President's Committee, which thus assumed an importance on the home front roughly comparable to that of the Defence Committee in the sphere of operations.[22] As time went on, it became clear that the allocation of manpower by the Lord President's Committee was the key to the effective co-ordination of industrial production for all purposes. It governed the standard of domestic consumption as well as the supply programmes of the armed forces.

It was Bevin, the leading trade unionist of his day, who had the responsibility for reshaping the work force of the nation, and for drawing into its ranks many who had not previously been in employment. He expanded the scope of the Ministry of Labour, which he correctly described when he first came to it as no more than a 'glorified conciliation board.'[23] It was true that the initial weakness of the Ministry was partly due to the fact that Bevin and his trade-union colleagues had in the past been reluctant to co-operate with the government. Now, however, the situation had been transformed by the formation of the Coalition and by the events of the summer; and the Emergency Powers Act of May 1940 endowed the Ministry with virtually dictatorial powers to conscript labour. But while Bevin recognized his responsibility to supply skilled and unskilled labour where it was needed, he was mindful of the workers' dislike of compulsion. He acted quickly on taking office to establish a National Arbitration Tribunal as a final resort for disputes between employers and workmen, and issued an Order (No. 1305) to prohibit all strikes and lockouts. But he refused actually to direct

22. Hancock and Gowing, *op. cit.*, pp. 219-221.
23. Williams, *Prime Minister Remembers*, p. 36.

labour until it was absolutely necessary; and when it was necessary, he sought to cushion its effects by making the direction as agreeable as possible for the workers concerned. To begin with, there was no great problem of unskilled labour, as there were still about 700,000 unemployed in the summer of 1940.[24] The need was to persuade the skilled workers to accept the 'dilution' of labour, that is, the up-grading of the less skilled. Following the pattern of Lloyd George's Treasury Agreement of 1915, he induced the skilled unions to give up some of their restrictive practices for the duration of the war on the understanding that they would be restored afterwards. In order to end the 'poaching' of workers by rival employers, he made it compulsory for employers to engage their labour only through the employment exchanges or the trade unions. And he appointed inspectors to supervise the use of skilled men, and expanded the government training centres where skills were taught.[25]

As time went on, the remaining pools of unemployed workers were absorbed, and there developed a general shortage of labour. After an examination of future manpower needs had been made by a committee under Sir William Beveridge, Bevin introduced in March 1941 an order requiring skilled workers to register and to be directed if necessary to undertake what was described as 'essential work'. But as compensation for this degree of direction, he insisted that all undertakings classified as 'essential' should satisfy certain standards of wages, conditions and welfare. At the same time the Schedule of Reserved Occupations, which exempted skilled men from call-up into the services, was adjusted to make sure they were suitably employed. Finally, a start was made on the registration of successive age groups of women, with a view to encouraging them, and if necessary directing them, into essential occupations. Cases of actual direction of women were to begin with rare, as Bevin was reluctant to cause hardship

24. The figure includes 67,000 in N. Ireland.
25. Bullock, *Bevin*, ii, 22-28.

in individual cases; but it was clear from opinion polls that on the whole the public was on the side of compulsion if necessary.[26] This was partly, perhaps, because so many people had already responded to the national call in one way or another: it was calculated that by July 1941 about 49% of the total occupied population was engaged in some type of employment for the government.[27]

The Board of Trade also had an important contribution to make to the mobility of labour, by its measures for the reduction of civil production. In the course of 1940 controls were instituted on the supply of raw material and on factory space and new building. At the same time, the supply of consumer goods to the home market was held back by a system of quotas. Then in March 1941 a scheme was introduced for concentrating the production of individual industries in a limited number of factories. At first, however, there was too little distinction between goods which were genuinely essential, such as saucepans, and those for which the demand was less immediate, such as pianos. In June 1941 clothes rationing was introduced, despite opposition from Churchill;[28] but it was already a matter for complaint that clothes were unduly expensive, and later in the year it was decided to introduce standard lines of 'utility' clothing, which would be restricted in price.[29]

The rationing of food, which had begun early in the war, was considerably extended in this period, owing to the shortage of shipping space. Lord Woolton, who had become Minister of Food in Chamberlain's last reshuffle, and who was a former retail business magnate, was very successful in securing the confidence of the housewife at a time when shortages were constantly becoming more severe. Part of his difficulties was the absence, until the end of 1940, of

26. *News Chronicle*, 22 May, 1941; *Mass-Observation Bulletin*, July, 1941
27. Hancock and Gowing, *op. cit.*, p. 297.
28. Chandos, *Memoirs*, p. 205.
29. Hargreaves and Gowing, *Civil Industry and Trade*, pp. 431-3.

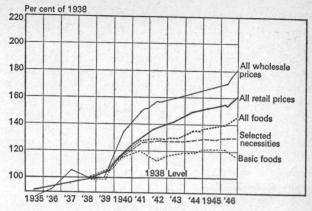

Effect of Subsidies and Controls on Wartime Inflation 1939-1946
Redrawn from a diagram in the *Report of the Economic Co-operation
Administration Mission to the United Kingdom* (London 1948)

any satisfactory system of allocating priorities in the use
of shipping.[30] Consequently there were some unusual fluc-
tuations in the rations, which in general became more
stringent in the period. The rations of sugar and bacon
were cut in the spring of 1940, and the meat ration which
was fixed on its introduction in March 1940 at the rate of
two shillingsworth per person per week was cut by half in
1941. Tea, cooking fats and margarine were rationed from
July 1940, and cheese from mid-1941. Heavy workers were
given supplements to the basic ration; cheap milk was
supplied to expectant and nursing mothers and to children
under five; the provision of school meals was encouraged;
and restaurants and canteens were allowed their own supplies. A flexible system of 'points' rationing covering a
wide range of less essential foods was introduced in 1941.
But Woolton kept bread and potatoes—'the fillers'—off
the ration altogether. Some foods which were expensive to
import, such as bananas, grapes and tinned fruit, disappeared altogether.

30. Hammond, *Food*, i, 162.

The shortages that existed before particular items came to be rationed, and also the increased costs of import and distribution, led to price rises which threatened a severe inflation. To keep this at bay, food subsidies had been introduced as a temporary measure in December 1939. They were extended in 1940, and maximum prices were fixed for a wide range of foodstuffs in general use. Kingsley Wood's budget of April 1941 extended what was now openly called a policy of 'stabilisation' to all essential goods, so as to keep the cost-of-living index at not more than about 25-30% above the pre-war level. The 'utility' scheme for cheaper clothing, already mentioned, had a place in this policy, though little of it became available before the end of 1941. But in general these methods, combined with the moderation of trade-union wage demands, helped to restrict the inflationary spiral in the second year of the war. In July 1941 earnings were 43% above the level of October 1938, but this was largely because longer hours were being worked, wage rates having risen by only about 18%.[31]

In the task of achieving the necessary flow of armaments the War Cabinet was increasingly looking to the United States for help. The careful husbanding of American dollars, on the assumption of a three-year war, had been abandoned during the Battle of Britain; and in the late summer of 1940 it became apparent that further orders for American goods could only be paid for on credit. Since a presidential election was pending, it was difficult for Roosevelt to make any immediate arrangements for this; but in the autumn he allowed further substantial orders to be placed, only stipulating that a fair proportion of the munitions should be of American pattern, so that the factories which fulfilled the orders could at once switch to supplying the United States forces if required.[32] It was fortunate for Britain that not only the President but

31. Hancock and Gowing, *op. cit.*, p. 339.
32. Langer and Gleason, *Undeclared War*, pp. 186, 188.

also the Chiefs of Staff, General George C. Marshall and Admiral Harold R. Stark, took the view that it was to America's advantage to sustain Britain. Meanwhile the Canadian government extended generous financial aid to enable British orders in Canada to be expanded.

The United States, unlike Canada, was not at war; and, as opinion polls showed, its citizens did not wish to become involved in war. Before the elections Roosevelt had to exercise great caution in what he said about aid for Britain. But his Republican opponent, Wendell Willkie, shared his view that it was desirable to help Britain as far as possible. So in a speech at Boston on October 30th, just before polling day, Roosevelt could safely take pride in the enormous contribution American industry was making or going to make. He announced that Britain would shortly have placed orders for 26,000 aircraft in the United States. But he pointed out that this meant the creation of a substantial munitions industry, which would be for the benefit of American defence. And as for actually joining in the shooting war, he gave this pledge to his audience: 'Your boys are not going to be sent into any foreign wars'.[33] The result of the election was a substantial if not overwhelming victory for Roosevelt, who could now enter his third term in the White House.

After the election it became possible for the administration to deal with the question of how the British orders should in future be paid for. Already in October Henry Morgenthau, the Secretary of the Treasury, had urged that financial aid to Britain should take the form of a gift rather than a loan.[34] This was because of the unhappy history of war debts in the inter-war years. In November, just after the election, the issue was brought to a head by an apparently calculated indiscretion on the part of Lord Lothian, the British ambassador, on his return from London. 'Well, boys,' Lothian said to the reporters, 'Britain's broke; it's your money we want.'[35] Roosevelt pon-

33. *Ibid.*, p. 207.   34. *Ibid.*, p. 188.
35. Butler, *Lothian*, p. 307.

dered the reaction to this statement and also the detailed statistics that the British Treasury supplied about the country's remaining dollar assets. The latter were still very considerable, but that portion of them that could readily be realized was almost exhausted. Roosevelt indicated his intentions at a press conference on December 17th. In the relations between Britain and America it was necessary, he said, to get rid of the 'silly, foolish old dollar sign.' With great skill, he used the analogy of the garden hose, which a man would readily lend to his neighbour if his neighbour's house was burning down. In such a situation there would be no cash transaction, but the hose would be returned. This was the origin of the Lend-Lease Bill, which was drafted and sent to both Houses of Congress in January and passed after vigorous debate but by substantial majorities on March 11th, 1941. Two weeks later an appropriation of seven billion dollars was made, and the operation of Lend-Lease began.

The impact of the new financial arrangements upon the military situation in 1941 must not be exaggerated. Although by the time the United States entered the war in December 1941 the appropriations for aid to Britain had risen to fourteen billion dollars, only a little over one billion's worth of Lend-Lease goods had been delivered by that date. Throughout 1941 the great bulk of deliveries were of material for which Britain had contracted to pay, and the Treasury was in considerable difficulties to find the means of payment. Emergency shipments of gold from South Africa and borrowing from Canada and Belgium helped.[36] So did the sale of a Courtauld subsidiary, the American Viscose Company, though it had to be offered at much less than its real value.[37] Nor were the total military supplies to Britain and British forces overseas as considerable as might have been expected: only 2,400 aircraft were sent in the last nine months of 1941 (the equivalent of about six weeks' production in Britain) and of these a

36. H. D. Hall, *North American Supply* (1955), p. 272.
37. *Ibid.*, p. 275.

mere hundred went under Lend-Lease. Of a total of 951 tanks (also about the same as six weeks' production in Britain) some 786 went under Lend-Lease.[38] The largest single category of aid in this period consisted of food— dried eggs, evaporated milk, and the varieties of tinned meat such as Spam which became familiar to the British public for the first time.

What was of the greatest immediate help to the British war effort was the growing participation of the American Navy in the Battle of the Atlantic. Staff talks in Washington between British and American officers in early 1941 paved the way for this. A general agreement was reached that in the event of the United States joining the war it would be desirable to take the offensive against Germany first, while maintaining a defensive position in the Pacific, whatever the Japanese might do. In the spring the US Atlantic Fleet was strengthened and in April the President ordered a number of measures to assist in the naval war: ten coastguard cutters were transferred to Britain, British warships were allowed to refit in American dockyards, and American merchantmen were allowed to go to Red Sea ports. In July a British garrison which had been sent to Iceland, a Danish dependency, was reinforced by American troops, and the American Navy was ordered to escort ships of any nationality to and from Iceland. In August Churchill and Roosevelt met at sea off the Newfoundland coast and drew up a statement of the common purpose of the two countries which became known as the 'Atlantic Charter'. This seems to have been Roosevelt's moment of decision: henceforward the United States was involved in an 'undeclared war'. In September the American Navy was instructed to escort convoys comprising ships of any nations in the western Atlantic, and to shoot at submerged or surface raiders. In October one American destroyer was damaged and another was sunk while on escort duties. But Roosevelt did not want the onus of actually declaring war. Hitler was also anxious to keep America neutral as

38. Hancock and Gowing, *op. cit.*, p. 239.

long as possible; and so the final commitment came by the action of another power—Japan.

Meanwhile the one theatre where British troops were in regular contact with the enemy was the Middle East. The news from this quarter had done much to encourage those who were enduring the Blitz at home. It had always been the intention of the British and French commands in the early months of the war to take advantage of Italy's weakness and to make her the target of early offensive action.[39] But Mussolini thought he had avoided the danger by not entering the war until nearly all the fighting appeared to be over. After the French armistice, the British forces in the Mediterranean and in North Africa were heavily outnumbered by the Italian; and in many respects, particularly in the air, they were in no way ready to assume an offensive role. But there were enough indications of poor morale, equipment and planning on the part of the Italians to justify preparations for early offensive action against them. The first measures taken, however, were defensive: the Mediterranean Fleet was concentrated at Alexandria, the frontier posts in the Western Desert of Egypt were pulled back, and troops were withdrawn from British Somaliland, which was occupied by superior Italian forces.

In August General Sir Archibald Wavell, the British Commander-in-Chief, Middle East, visited London, and it was bravely decided, in spite of the threat of an invasion of Britain, to send out some 150 tanks and a hundred guns immediately.[40] But before Wavell could get his reinforcements, which had to go round the Cape of Good Hope, an expedition had been sent out to the west coast of Africa in order to try and rally the French territories to General de Gaulle's Free French cause. General de Gaulle himself accompanied the force, which tried to take over the port of Dakar by a mixture of persuasion, bluff and bombardment Unfortunately some Vichy French warships appeared on

39. Butler, *Grand Strategy,* ii, 299.　　40. *Ibid.,* p. 308.

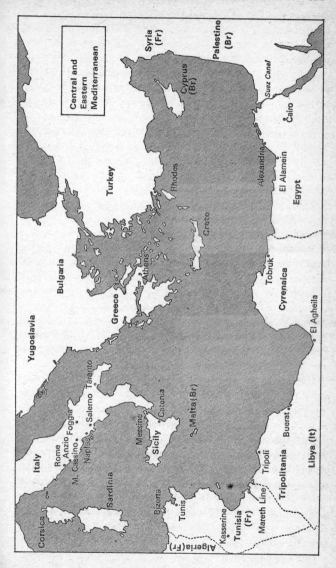

the scene to stiffen the resistance, having escaped from the Mediterranean without being intercepted. The result was that after an inconclusive exchange of salvoes at the port the attempt was abandoned. General de Gaulle had to be content with winning over French Equatorial Africa, which at least provided a route whereby aircraft could be flown to the Middle East. The whole of Western and Northern French Africa remained loyal to Vichy.

On October 28th, before Wavell could take the offensive against the Italian forces in Africa, Mussolini launched an attack on Greece from his bases in occupied Albania. Greece had been given a guarantee by the Chamberlain government in April 1939, shortly after the guarantees to Poland and Rumania; and in response to a Greek request for aid, the War Cabinet decided that troops and aircraft should be sent to defend the island of Crete, which was vulnerable to enemy naval attack. But the Italian fighting capacity was soon shown to be very poor. Carrier aircraft of the Navy scored a remarkable victory over the Italian fleet in November by disabling three Italian battleships in Taranto harbour. And on the Albanian border, Greek resistance was unexpectedly successful and the Italian advance was thrown back with heavy loss. Then in December Wavell with little more than two divisions of troops in the Western Desert attacked and severely defeated an Italian army of seven divisions. The British force rapidly advanced into Italian Libya and in January occupied the port of Tobruk. By February 8th the whole of Cyrenaica was in British hands, but Wavell's troops halted short of Tripolitania. This was in part because the Italians now had the aid of German bombers based in Sicily; in part because of other demands on Wavell's limited forces. Mussolini was unable to reinforce the Italian garrisons in Abyssinia and Somaliland, and Wavell sent small expeditions to eliminate them. But major elements of the Middle East field force had to be prepared for service in Greece, where German intervention became likely.

Hitler was worried about the threat to the Rumanian

oilfields, one of his most important areas of supply, if British air bases should become established in Greece. He was also anxious that Mussolini should not suffer a serious setback in Albania as a result of his ill-judged offensive. On December 13th, therefore, he issued orders for preparations to be made to attack Greece from bases in southern Rumania. In the face of the new threat the Greek government appealed for ground support, and the British War Cabinet, having sent Eden and General Sir John Dill, the Chief of the Imperial General Staff, to consult with Wavell and the Greek leaders, decided to send an expeditionary corps to the Greek mainland.[41] This was a strategic error: the Allied forces were bound to be outnumbered and outgunned, and although the generals thought it possible to hold a line in the Greek mountains, they had made no reconnaissance of the area. The British troops would have been better employed in advancing into Tripolitania, where there was a chance of destroying the last Italian foothold. This now proved to be impossible: and as the Germans moved into Bulgaria in March, a British force with as its main components one Australian and one New Zealand division, together with a British armoured brigade, was ferried to Athens from Egypt. The Italian navy was unable to intervene to prevent this move, its morale having been further reduced by a fleet action at night off Cape Matapan in which British warships sank three heavy cruisers without loss to themselves. Lack of training in night warfare and absence of radar were the Italians' undoing.[42]

The attitude of Yugoslavia, which lay on the flank of the German advance into Greece, now became crucial. Late in March the Yugoslav government declared its willingness to collaborate with Germany, but a *coup d'état* took place and the Germans were obliged to invade both Greece and Yugoslavia simultaneously. There was, however, no possibility of effectively co-ordinating the defence of the two countries; and even the Greeks failed to adhere to their

41. Avon, *op. cit.*, pp. 197f.
42. Cunningham, *Sailor's Odyssey*, pp. 336f.

joint defence plan with the British, whereby their line was to be shortened by a withdrawal from Albania. The result was that the British force found itself constantly being outflanked; and late in April it had to be evacuated to Crete and Egypt. Out of a total of 62,000 who were sent, over 50,000 were re-embarked; but as was usual in these evacuations by sea, the bulk of their equipment was lost. Meanwhile a division of German troops which had landed at Tripoli in February under the command of General Rommel took the offensive against the weakened British garrison in Cyrenaica and drove it back to the Egyptian border, except for elements which were invested in Tobruk. In the general setback to British arms, fresh troubles appeared. A hostile regime emerged in Iraq, which was in treaty relations with Britain, and to forestall enemy occupation small forces had to be sent in from both the Palestinian and Indian sides. Then on May 20th the Germans invaded Crete with parachute and airborne troops. The garrison, consisting of two New Zealand brigades and a few British battalions, put up a bitter resistance, but as the Germans had air superiority and the garrison was not large enough, it proved impossible to hold the island. After a week of fighting, the troops were ordered to withdraw by sea. The Mediterranean Fleet suffered severe losses in carrying out the evacuation, and some 12,000 troops had to be left behind to become prisoners of war. Although there had also been severe losses among the German paratroop élite, the action was really a remarkable success for the enemy.

It looked as if the next German advance would be into Syria, where the Vichy French were in control. To prevent this, Wavell was instructed to invade the country and occupy its key positions. The Vichy French put up a stiff resistance which ended only in mid-July. Meanwhile in May the main force of the Italian troops in East Africa was forced to surrender, and in June the Red Sea coast was cleared. Prodded by Churchill, Wavell also undertook a new offensive in the Western Desert, hoping to relieve

Tobruk. But the attack, which started on June 15th, was an immediate failure, many of the British tanks being destroyed. The trouble was that British tanks lacked the mobility and firepower of those of the enemy, and their commanders and crews were not properly trained.[43] As Dill later pointed out, 'The fault was not Wavell's, except in so far as he did not resist pressure from Whitehall with sufficient vigour.'[44] But Dill himself might have helped by putting up a firmer opposition to Churchill's insistence on premature offensives.

It was however clear by June that Churchill had lost all confidence in Wavell, whose abilities he had always reckoned as not more than those of 'a good average colonel'.[45] This was an underestimate of a skilful commander whose reticence in discussion gave a false impression of his knowledge and quality. It was true that Wavell was overloaded with responsibilities and had had to be goaded into at least one vital operation—the attack on Iraq, which was strictly not within the Middle Eastern theatre. But Churchill intervened too much in the details of Wavell's command, and in particular would have been wiser to allow him more discretion in the timing of attack in the Western Desert. In June the War Cabinet decided that Wavell should exchange posts with Auchinleck, who was now the Commander-in-Chief in India; and a minister of Cabinet rank, Oliver Lyttelton, was sent out to the Middle East as Minister of State to advise the Commanders-in-Chief on political questions and to supervise the arrangements for supply.

To Hitler, the operations in the Balkans and in the Desert were minor matters—a clearing of his flank preparatory to the great offensive against Russia that he had planned for the main campaigning season of 1941. Although he had

43. Connell, *Wavell*, i, 495-500.
44. Dill to Auchinleck, 26 June, 1941, quoted Connell, *Auchinleck*, p. 247.
45. Avon, *op. cit.*, p. 133.

ordered preparations for this offensive as early as December 1940, it did not begin until the following June, apparently because the Russian plains were slow to dry out after a late spring.[46]

Ever since the fall of France it had been hoped in London that the Russians would realize the dangers to themselves that would arise from the defeat of Britain. Sir Stafford Cripps, who had been an enthusiastic advocate of close collaboration between Britain and Russia, was sent to Moscow in June 1940 as ambassador, in the hope of improving relations and negotiating a trade settlement. Unfortunately Stalin, the Russian dictator, felt that his position after the fall of France—which he had not expected—was so weak that he was obliged to go on appeasing Hitler. Consequently no Anglo-Soviet trade treaty could be negotiated, and Russian economic aid to Germany went far to make the British blockade ineffective. Evidence of German preparations for an attack on Russia began to mount in the spring of 1941, and in April Churchill sent Stalin a personal message about the impending threat. But Stalin took few precautions, evidently being afraid that they might provoke attack, or at least expecting that demands for further concessions would be the prelude to invasion. The result was that when the attack actually began on June 22nd the Russian army and air force were not ready. The troops had no clear orders to fire back at once, and many aircraft were destroyed on the ground. The German armies made rapid advances in the first days of their assault.

The British War Cabinet was better prepared and had already decided on its attitude to the new struggle. Churchill, on behalf of his colleagues, at once hailed the Russians as allies and offered them such aid as Britain could provide. In public there was enthusiasm and relief at this turn of events. In official circles, however, there was little expectation that Britain would derive advantage from it. At the

46. Fergusson, *Business of War*, p. 87; H. Baldwin, *Battles Lost and Won* (1967), pp. 112f.

War Office nearly all the experts believed that Russia would be 'knocked out in ten days'.[47] A Joint Intelligence Committee report concluded that the occupation of the Ukraine and the capture of Moscow could be accomplished in three to six weeks.[48] Then the entire German army would be free to attack Britain, either across the Channel or in the Mediterranean or Middle East. Even Cripps believed that Russian resistance would collapse in a few weeks.[49] Churchill therefore gave instructions that measures to counter the threat of an invasion should be strengthened, the lessons of Crete being taken into account: preparations were to be 'at concert pitch' by September 1st.[50] For the rest, reinforcements had to be sent urgently to the Middle East, which might be the objective of a German offensive directed either through Asia Minor or through the Russian Caucasus, as well as by the use of the existing Sicilian supply line. Another possibility to be guarded against was a German advance through Spain: to meet this, all available British landing craft, together with a small expeditionary force, were earmarked for the occupation of the Canary Islands, Madeira and the Azores, so as to protect the Atlantic shipping routes.[51]

Contrary to expectation, however, the Russians kept on fighting, although they continued to suffer heavy losses. Enormous territorial gains were made by the advancing enemy armies: by mid-August they were at the Leningrad perimeter in the north, only 150 miles from Moscow in the centre, and deep into the Ukraine in the south. It was only the extent of their trained or half-trained reserves that enabled the Russians to survive: the Germans expected to face two hundred divisions but after a few weeks reckoned that they had identified 360.[52] But the German

47. Nicolson, *Diaries*, ii, 175.
48. Butler, *Grand Strategy*, ii, 543.
49. Dalton, *Fateful Years*, p. 365; Gwyer, *Grand Strategy*, iii, 90.
50. Hansard 373, 1300 (29 July, 1941).
51. Gwyer, *op. cit.*, pp. 94f.
52. Halder, quoted A. Clark, *Barbarossa* (1965), p. 96n.

advance went on. By October the danger to Moscow was acute, and the government departments were being evacuated to Kuibyshev.

In July Britain had made an agreement with Russia whereby the two countries undertook to aid each other and promised not to make a separate peace with Germany. A beginning was made in sending supplies from Britain to Russia, and by late August some 440 planes had been promised, including the Hurricanes of two RAF squadrons which operated from Murmansk for several weeks in the autumn in order to protect shipping in the port. British and Russian troops also moved into Iran to round up German agents there and to organize supply routes. An Anglo-American Supply Conference was held in London in mid-September, and this resulted in decisions to allocate to Russia a proportion of American munitions output—almost entirely at the expense of what had been designated for Britain. But it was impossible to provide what Stalin most urgently demanded, namely, the opening of a new battle-front in Europe which would draw off a considerable part of the enemy armies. Churchill ordered his staff to consider various possibilities, such as a landing on the tip of the Normandy peninsula or an invasion of Norway; but after exhaustive discussions he had to agree with the Chiefs of Staff that the projects were impracticable, owing to shortage of landing craft and lack of bases sufficiently close to ensure air superiority.

It only remained to carry on the campaign in the Western Desert, hoping that this would to some extent relieve the pressure on the Eastern Front. Auchinleck, the new Commander-in-Chief in the Middle East, was left in no doubt about public opinion at home: Dill wrote to him in October to tell him about the 'clamour, which grows, that we should do something for Russia' and about the 'more dangerous' fact that the press campaign was being backed within the Cabinet by Beaverbrook, who, he thought, might 'stage a resignation on the grounds that he cannot continue to be a member of a government which has so signally failed to help Russia'.[53] Once again a Middle East commander was being pushed into making an early attack. It was true that he had a small preponderance in aircraft and tanks; but his tanks were still outgunned by the enemy. The prospects of success were therefore doubtful. Nevertheless, when he announced to Churchill his plans to advance in November with the hope of relieving Tobruk, the Prime Minister responded with a message to the troops telling them that they might well 'add a page to history which will rank with Blenheim and with Waterloo.'[54] What followed was a period of severe fighting in which neither side secured any great advantage. The whole of Cyrenaica was retaken and Tobruk relieved, but there was no question of Rommel's forces having been destroyed. At the end of the year his position was considerably strengthened by an increase in German airpower in the Mediterranean, and by the movement of a number of U-boats from the Atlantic. The British squadron at Gibraltar lost a battleship and an aircraft carrier; Malta was heavily blockaded; and a daring raid by Italian 'human torpedoes' on Alexandria harbour resulted in serious damage to two battleships of the main fleet. If British action had succeeded in diverting some elements of German strength from the Russian front, at least temporarily, it had been done only at exceptionally heavy cost.

Although the high degree of national unity which marked the Battle of Britain was largely preserved in the succeeding year, it was natural that political differences should emerge rather more clearly as the immediate threat of invasion receded. On the whole the period was one of disappointment for the Left, which had hoped that the establishment of the Coalition would result in a major shift in the direction of radical policies. But the fact was

53. Dill to Auchinleck, 25 Oct., 1941, quoted Connell, *Auchinleck*, p. 326.

54. Connell, *op. cit.*, p. 336.

that the Conservative Party still dominated the House of Commons, and Churchill, who had now assumed the leadership of the party, was on many issues far on its right wing. The government's failure to take any steps to reconcile Indian political opinion was largely due to him, for he discovered that the enthusiasm of Amery, the Secretary of State, for a fresh approach to Congress leaders was not shared by the Viceroy, Lord Linlithgow, and he promptly put a stop to it.[55] Nor did Churchill favour any real attempt to fight an ideological war with the Nazis, as had been widely advocated in the summer of 1940. In spite of his own ability as an orator he had little sense of the importance of propaganda. He rarely sided with his Minister of Information, Duff Cooper, against the Foreign Office and the Service Departments. And the Foreign Office in this period was very anxious to keep on good terms with Spain and with Vichy France. It was the old policy of judging countries by their deeds and not by their internal politics. Consequently, no declaration of war aims was published, apart from the vague Atlantic Charter agreed with Roosevelt in August 1941; and the control of what became known as 'political warfare' was gradually taken out of the hands of Dalton, who had the responsibility for continental subversion, and placed under the Foreign Office.[56] In the absence of clear policy directives British propaganda competed somewhat ineffectively with that of Joseph Goebbels. All this, as well as other political discontents, made Dalton begin to feel, as he wrote to Attlee, that the Labour Party was 'in this government as poor relations of the Tories.'[57]

Hitler himself described Britain as a 'plutodemocracy' and as a country governed by 'a thin upper class, which class always sends its sons to its own educational institutions.'[58] Left-wing publicists in Britain, such as J. B.

55. Halifax to Hoare, 30 July, 1940, Templewood Papers.
56. Bruce Lockhart, *Comes the Reckoning*, p. 126.
57. Dalton to Attlee, 25 Sept., 1941, Dalton Papers.
58. *The Times*, 11 Dec., 1940.

Priestley, felt that these charges could only be effectively answered by a national commitment to a more equalitarian post-war society. Priestley's Sunday evening broadcasts, which had proved so popular during the Battle of Britain, were continued for a time in early 1941, but were then terminated as being too controversial. But Priestley and others of similar views organized a body called the '1941 Committee', which sought to keep alive the demand for radical change at a time when party politics were muted by the electoral truce and by the existence of the Coalition government.[59] Priestley sensed a movement of public opinion to the Left which deserved but could not obtain proper recognition. 'It is absurd', he wrote, 'to pretend that this House of Commons, brought together by Baldwin in the Stone Age, elected on issues as remote as the Repeal of the Corn Laws, really represents the country.'[60]

This was an underestimate of the House of Commons in wartime. It is true that the very existence of the Coalition took much of the usual cut and thrust of partisanship out of the debates. It is also true that the mild and elderly H. B. Lees Smith—a man not recommended by Attlee to Churchill for office in the Coalition owing to his being 'too slow'[61]—was not a very vigorous acting leader of the Opposition, which was indeed why the ministerial group of Labour leaders had insisted on his appointment to this post.[62] This was irritating to another obvious claimant, Emanuel Shinwell, who had refused office under Churchill because the post offered was not sufficiently senior. He and Earl Winterton, a front-bench Conservative critic of the government, formed an informal alliance which Kingsley Martin, the editor of the *New Statesman*, described as 'arsenic and old lace' (after the title of a current play).[63]

59. Kingsley Martin, *Editor*, p. 304; 1941 Committee, *Planning and Freedom* (1941).
60. *News Chronicle*, 11 Nov., 1940.
61. Diary, 18 May, 1941, Dalton Papers.
62. Dalton, *Fateful Years*, p. 332.
63. Lord Winterton, *Orders of the Day* (1953), p. 261.

Their attacks on the government helped to keep alive the traditions of debate and criticism.

In this period, the high peak of parliamentary review of the government's performance came in May 1941, when the Whips arranged for a motion of confidence to be debated after the unsuccessful Greek campaign. This brought out Lloyd George, who attacked Churchill for surrounding himself with 'yes-men' rather than with 'absolutely independent men, men of experience' on the pattern of his own First World War Cabinet.[64] Churchill made a powerful debating reply, comparing Lloyd George to Pétain—perhaps not an unjustifiable thrust in view of the veteran leader's pessimism about the prospects of winning the war. In the upshot the government received an overwhelming vote of support—447 to 3, the minority with two tellers consisting of one Communist, one fellow-traveller and three pacifists. Lloyd George and Shinwell did not vote. All the same, as Hankey, himself still a member of the government, wrote privately at the time:

> Ll. G.'s warnings . . . have set people talking . . . Although the façade is almost as strong as ever, I fear that the structure behind is not quite as sound as it was.[65]

At least the debate had shown that the Commons was not as incapable of effective criticism as Priestley implied. It could well voice the widespread public dissatisfaction with aspects of the government's policies, though this was by no means incompatible with an even more widespread conviction that Churchill was still the essential Prime Minister. Such attitudes were confirmed by the Gallup poll in June, which showed that while 87% of people approved of Churchill as Prime Minister, only 58% were satisfied with the government's conduct of the war. While Churchill's high rating remained almost undiminished,

64. Hansard 371, 880 (7 May, 1941).
65. Hankey to Hoare, 18 May, 1941, Templewood Papers.

the number satisfied with the government's conduct of the war dropped to only 44% in October, when the agitation for a 'Second Front' to aid Russia had developed.[66]

But although strategy became a matter of increasing concern to the public in late 1941, Churchill seems to have had no doubt that his methods of determining it were satisfactory. He showed less confidence in the sphere of the administration of war production, which was constantly a target of press and parliamentary criticism. Frequent changes were made in the chain of command in the hope of finding a satisfactory arrangement. In May Beaverbrook was transferred from the Ministry of Aircraft Production to a supervisory role over all production as Deputy Chairman of the Defence Committee (Supply). This did not work, as Beaverbrook hated committees and could not control the departments.[67] In June Churchill placed him at the Ministry of Supply itself, and here he proceeded to obtain as much publicity for tank production as he had obtained for aircraft in 1940. It helped a good deal that Russia had been drawn into the war, and that Britain had promised to supply her with tanks: for many of the engineering shop stewards were Communists, and they set to work to break all records for production. Beaverbrook organized a 'Tanks for Russia' week, promising that all the tanks made that week would be sent to the Eastern Front. This resulted in an output considerably beyond the target. But the tanks were not as good as those being manufactured in Germany, or for that matter in Russia. And in the meantime the new Minister of Aircraft Production, J. T. C. Moore-Brabazon, was finding it quite impossible to fulfil his targets, which had been laid down in 1940 by his predecessor. In 1941 the rate of output of aircraft was only about two-thirds of what had been planned. The supply of heavy bombers was particularly behindhand, being only at the rate of about sixty a month in late 1941

66. *News Chronicle*, 23 Oct. and 3 Nov., 1941.
67. Beaverbrook to Churchill, 3 June, 1941, quoted Young, *Churchill and Beaverbrook*, pp. 192f.

in place of the projected 150-200. The trouble arose partly
from the increasing size and technical complexity of the
aircraft; partly from Beaverbrook's belief in the psychological effects of optimism.[68] But the outcome did not
augur well for the bomber offensive against Germany, on
which the War Cabinet's hopes of ultimate victory largely
rested.

Suddenly, however, on December 7th, 1941, another
avenue towards victory suddenly opened, though hardly in
a way calculated to suggest that victory would be won very
soon or very easily. Japanese planes without warning
bombed the American Pacific Fleet at Pearl Harbour,
destroying four battleships and crippling two others. At the
same time, troop landings were made on the coast of
Malaya. Thus Japan chose to make war on both Britain
and America; and on December 11th Germany and Italy
also declared war on the United States.

68. Postan, *British War Production*, pp. 170, 173.

# 6. The Crisis of the Empire

Churchill's reaction to Pearl Harbour was one of relief: 'So we had won after all!' The Japanese, he saw, had sealed their own doom and Hitler's, by bringing the United States with themselves into the war.[1] But Pearl Harbour itself was a crippling blow to American seapower in the Pacific; and it set the stage for the Japanese invasion of the Philippines, Hong Kong and Malaya and the eventual conquest of the Dutch East Indies, many of the Pacific Islands, and Burma. For a long time, the new turn of events made things much more difficult for the British, in spite of their new certainty of ultimate victory.

The weakness of the British position in Malaya and Singapore was due primarily to the nation's limited resources and to the heavy demands of other already active theatres of war. It had been a principle accepted by the Chiefs of Staff and by the Committee of Imperial Defence before the war that the maintenance of the British position in the Far East was second only in importance to the defence of the British Isles, and if necessary should take precedence over the defence of the Middle East.[2] This principle had been accepted largely in order to secure Australian and New Zealand participation in imperial defence strategy; for in reality Singapore was less important for military than for psychological reasons. It could easily be bypassed by a Japanese fleet on its way to attack Australia or even to break into the Indian Ocean. These facts were admitted in the course of the Anglo-American staff talks in Washington in February-March 1941, when

1. Churchill, *Second World War*, iii, 539.
2. Kirby, *War Against Japan*, i, 17.

the Americans firmly refused to send any of their own
forces to help defend the island.[3]

Even so, Churchill was unwise not to pay more attention
to the advice of Dill in the spring of 1941, to the effect
that Malaya and Singapore ought now to be given a
higher priority for reinforcements.[4] Churchill was influenced in part by the belief that the Japanese army and air
force were not very efficient—a belief which stemmed from
their relative failure against the Chinese.[5] He also shared
the Foreign Office view that Japan was unlikely to enter the
war until Russia had been defeated.[6] To make matters
worse, he had the quite mistaken idea that Singapore was
a fortress capable of all-round defence, and that it could
effectively resist an enemy assault even after the loss of
Malaya.[7] The upshot of this was that the aircraft available
for the defence of Malaya and Singapore at the outbreak
of hostilities with Japan amounted to only one-third of
what the Chiefs of Staff thought necessary; and that the
fighters, which were of the American-built Buffalo type,
were inferior in quality to the Japanese Zero, which was
at least the equal of the Hurricane. The principal field
forces available for the defence of Malaya consisted of
two Indian divisions, so far poorly trained, and one
Australian division. There were no tanks; the troops were
not trained in jungle warfare; and proposals to raise labour
battalions from the indigenous population foundered on
the parsimony of the War Office, which would not offer
sufficient pay.[8] Co-ordination of defence with the Dutch
and the Americans was rudimentary. Even the British
command was lacking in unity: central control of both
Army and RAF had only been achieved in late 1940, and
the Navy operated as an independent force. Civil and
political authority was quite separate from the military

3. Matloff and Snell, *Strategic Planning*, p. 36.
4. Dill to Churchill, 15 May, 1941, quoted Butler, *Grand
Strategy*, ii, 581.
5. Kirby, *op. cit.*, i, 166f.   6. Gwyer, *Grand Strategy*, iii, 280.
7. Churchill, *op. cit.*, iv, 43.      8. Kirby, *op. cit.*, i, 161.

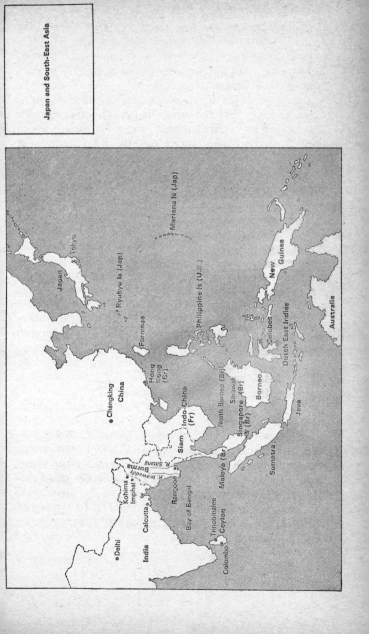

Japan and South-East Asia

until after the invasion began; and then Duff Cooper, the former Minister of Information who was sent out on a mission of enquiry, and who was appointed Resident Minister for Far Eastern Affairs, tried hard to achieve some sort of belated co-ordination.[9]

The Japanese invaders were numerically inferior, but in every other way they had the advantage. They had a supply of tanks and an overwhelming superiority in the air, which resulted in the destruction of half the RAF strength in the first day's fighting. The lack of air power also proved disastrous for the British battleships *Prince of Wales* and *Repulse*, which had been sent out to Singapore in the autumn of 1941, and which on the news of the Japanese invasion of the Malayan coast sought to intercept the transports and harass the landings. It had originally been intended that the battleships should have the protection of an aircraft carrier, but the vessel chosen, the *Indomitable*, went aground on the Jamaican coast and had to be repaired; and no other carrier could be spared.[10] The result was that on December 10th the *Prince of Wales* and *Repulse* were caught by strong forces of Japanese aircraft and were both sunk by bombs and torpedoes, with the loss of a thousand men.

After this, the Japanese landings were free to continue without interference, and throughout December and January the British troops were steadily pressed down the peninsula towards Singapore. The defence, under General A. E. Percival, was to say the least unimaginative. New positions taken by his forces were constantly being outflanked, sometimes even by the use of small craft on the west coast of the peninsula where the Japanese Navy had so far no control. Meanwhile Hong Kong, which was fighting its own lonely battle with a garrison of 12,000 men, mostly Canadians, was forced to capitulate on Christmas Day 1941 after eighteen days' resistance.

9. Duff Cooper, *Old Men Forget*, 292f.
10. Kirby, *op. cit.*, i, 85.

By the end of January the Japanese had captured the whole of Malaya, and the last British troops who had not been cut off made their way across the causeway on to Singapore Island. Now the weakness of the island defences on their own became apparent. The big naval guns could only fire out to sea, and General Percival had refused to take any steps to fortify the landward side of the island, on the grounds that this would be bad for morale while the battle in Malaya was as yet undecided.[11] Churchill now contemplated organizing a Dunkirk operation, but the Australian government would not agree, and insisted on an attempt to hold the island. A fresh British division, the 18th, was therefore brought in as a sacrifice to imperial unity. But there were still no tanks, and the frontage of about forty miles in the Johore Strait could not easily be manned. The arrival of a few Hurricane fighters temporarily encouraged the garrison, but they were soon destroyed in battle with a vastly superior enemy. The naval base and the airfields were now under enemy artillery fire and had to be abandoned. Finally, General Percival's defence plans were faulty: he assumed the main attack would come on the east side, whereas in fact it came on the west; and he kept very few troops in reserve, to counter unexpected action on the part of the enemy.[12] When the Japanese assault began on the night of February 8th it rapidly gained a foothold. By the 15th it had become impossible to carry on the struggle: the water supply had been cut, artillery ammunition was almost exhausted and there was no reserve of petrol. With authority from London General Percival agreed to an unconditional surrender. Taking the Malayan campaign as a whole 140,000 troops were lost, and of these only 8,000 or so were battle casualties. Of the total, 38,496 were British, 18,490 Australian and 67,340 Indian. Japanese battle casualties amounted to less than 10,000; and to add to the humiliation the total enemy strength on Singapore Island at the time

11. Barber, *Sinister Twilight*, pp. 67-72.
12. Kirby, *op. cit.*, i, 404-5.

of the capitulation was probably only about a third that of the defeated forces.

This was a staggering defeat—in Churchill's words 'the worst disaster and largest capitulation in British history.'[13] It was not merely that a large British army had been overwhelmed by a much smaller Japanese force. The Malayan peninsula, with its rich resources of rubber and tin, had been lost; and the Australian and New Zealand governments had been severely shaken by the failure of the imperial defence strategy. An enemy invasion of Burma became much more practicable as a result of the weakness of British naval power in the Indian Ocean; and beyond Burma lay the Indian Empire, by far the most populous of Britain's dependent territories and the recruiting ground for many of her infantry divisions. Probably Malaya and Singapore could have been held if five hundred up-to-date aircraft had been available, instead of less than one-third that number of obsolescent machines. But the stringency of Britain's resources in the face of so many enemies was made startlingly clear by the disasters that befell her arms in the Far East.

Churchill's first thought after Pearl Harbour had been to make a visit to see President Roosevelt, so that the joint war strategy could be planned to the best advantage. He was afraid that the Americans would abandon their earlier commitment, undertaken in the milder atmosphere of friendly neutrality, to devote their major efforts in the event of war to the defeat of Hitler and to settle with Japan afterwards. Furthermore, there was a danger that the armament programmes of the two countries might get out of proportion to the real needs of the war. 'What will harm us', wrote Churchill, 'is for a vast United States Army of ten millions to be created which for at least two years while it was training would absorb all the available supplies and stand idle defending the American continent.'[14]

13. Churchill, *Second World War*, iv, 81.
14. *Ibid.*, iii, 581.

He hoped that some American troops would at once be sent to Northern Ireland, to free British troops for operations elsewhere, and as an earnest for future campaigns in Europe; and, assuming the success of Auchinleck against Rommel, he looked to early Anglo-American co-operation in a move to free French North Africa from Vichy control, so as to give the Allies command of the Mediterranean. In addition, American air squadrons, he thought, should be stationed in England to join in the bombing of Germany. In the longer term—perhaps in 1943—British and American armies might land at various points in Europe 'to enable the conquered populations to revolt.' He still assumed that 'the uprising of the local population' in the continental countries would 'supply the corpus of the liberating offensive.'[15] Since these were the objects of policy, it was necessary to persuade the American leaders to agree that—as the British Chiefs of Staff put it—'only the minimum of force necessary for the safeguarding of vital interests in other theatres should be diverted from operations against Germany.'[16]

Churchill reached Washington on December 22nd, and the two war leaders and their staffs at once started their discussions. The American administration had not had time to draw up fresh strategical plans; and the main lines of the British proposals were soon accepted, although there were reservations on the American side as to how the assault on Europe was eventually to take place. General Marshall, the American Chief of Army Staff, favoured a single thrust onto the continent of Europe, rather than a series of assaults at different points.[17] These differences remained for subsequent resolution. It was also decided that a united command should be established for the south-west Pacific area, to co-ordinate all American, British, Dutch and Australian forces there. General Wavell was appointed to this command. It was a hopeless task, for the forces in the area were already fast disintegrating

15. *Ibid.*, iii, 582-4.  16. Gwyer, *Grand Strategy*, iii, 345.
17. *Ibid.*, p. 358.

under the Japanese attack; and in the end the command only lasted a few weeks. But this turned out to be the pattern for future co-operation between the new allies— to appoint a Supreme Commander for a distinct theatre of the war, with a staff drawn from all the national forces involved.

Finally, it was agreed that the joint Anglo-American strategy of the war should be determined with the advice of a new body called the Combined Chiefs of Staff, sitting in Washington. This body was to consist of the British and American Chiefs of Staff in joint session; but as the British Chiefs were normally located in London, they had to be represented at over half of its meetings by deputies who were permanently posted in Washington. Fortunately Dill, who had just been replaced by General Sir Alan Brooke as Chief of the Imperial General Staff, was available to become the head of the British military mission in Washington. Committees to determine the allocation of war supplies were also to be established in both London and Washington, and were to be under the control of the Combined Chiefs: but control of strategy at the highest level remained in the hands of the President and, on behalf of the British War Cabinet, the Prime Minister.

These arrangements marked the beginning of an even more intimate collaboration between Britain and the United States—a collaboration that was unique, for it had no parallel in the relations between either America or Britain on the one hand and Russia on the other. The Soviet leadership, while willing to receive all the assistance it could get, was reluctant to agree to any close collaboration of military forces—except momentarily in the desperate crisis of the autumn of 1941, when Stalin asked for the dispatch of British divisions to the Caucasus. But Rommel's success in Libya and the emergency in the Far East put paid to this possibility.[18] The few RAF planes which operated from bases in North Russia for a few weeks in the early autumn of 1941, and again in 1942, did so only

18. *Ibid.*, pp. 320f.

in order to protect the convoys; and in each case when the snows began the crews returned to Britain. It seemed that the best service that the western powers could provide for Russia would be to ensure that the promised supplies of aircraft, tanks and other munitions were delivered according to programme. Under the circumstances they could hardly complain about Stalin's unwillingness to declare war against Japan at this stage of the war.

To begin with, the collaboration of Britain and the United States was on more or less equal terms. The United States had much greater potential, but its actual military production was not yet on a par with Britain's. The only trouble with the new arrangements was that the small powers which had been Britain's partners in the war since 1940 or earlier—particularly those now faced by the Japanese advance, such as Holland (on behalf of the Dutch East Indies), Australia and New Zealand—felt that strategical decisions arrived at in Washington might very well ignore their own interests. The Australian government was already very indignant about what had happened in the Far East, for Australian troops had been despatched to the Middle East on the assumption that Britain had made proper arrangements to defend Singapore. Even before Singapore fell John Curtin, the new Australian Prime Minister, had published a signed article in the *Melbourne Herald* in which he said that 'Australia looks to America, free of any pangs as to our traditional links with the United Kingdom'.[19] As a result of pressure from him and from the New Zealand and Dutch governments, it was agreed that a Pacific War Council should be set up in London. Later a similar body was established in Washington. But although these bodies went some way towards providing opportunities for consultation, they could not direct policy.

Unhappily nothing could now save the Dutch East Indies from conquest by the Japanese. As for the Austra-

19. *Melbourne Herald*, 28 Dec., 1941, quoted Mansergh, *Problems of Wartime*, p. 133.

lians, they were anxious to bring back to their homeland at least two of the three divisions of their troops which were now in the Middle East; and in February Curtin refused an urgent request from Churchill that one of these divisions, which was en route south of Colombo, should be diverted to Rangoon in order to defend Burma. Curtin's decision may well have been justified on military grounds, for the division's arrival would probably have failed to turn the tide. When Rangoon fell in March, its remaining defenders under the skilful command of General Sir Harold Alexander made a long and difficult march through jungle and mountain to reach the Indian border at Imphal. Meanwhile it was indeed the Americans, as Curtin had forecast, who had to come to the aid of Australia and New Zealand. American troops were sent to Australia, and General Douglas MacArthur, the resolute defender of Bataan in the Philippines, arrived in Australia in March to take over the new South-West Pacific Command. New Zealand came under the command of the American Admiral Nimitz. Thus Britain had to acknowledge that American armed strength was necessary to defend the remotest but hitherto most loyal of her Commonwealth partners.

The flow of disasters in the Far East not unnaturally released fresh criticisms of the Churchill government. At the end of January—when Malaya had been lost, and Singapore was awaiting assault—a three-day debate took place in the Commons on a Vote of Confidence. As in May 1941 Churchill had no difficulty in securing overwhelming endorsement for his own leadership, for there was no possible alternative Prime Minister. Richard Stokes, the Labour MP who was one of the government's leading back-bench critics, besought Lloyd George to act as the 'Queen Bee to which the Drones can swarm',[20] but Lloyd George probably realized that his day was now past: although he attended the debate he did not speak. Church-

20. Stokes to Lloyd George, 22 Jan., 1942, Lloyd George Papers.

ill promised that he would appoint a Minister of Production—a reform that critics of the government had been demanding as a means of securing effective co-ordination between the competing demands of the existing supply ministries.[21] After this the Vote of Confidence was carried by 464 votes to 1—the little anti-war group of three ILP members constituting the entire opposition (two of them having to act as tellers).

Churchill's decision to appoint a Minister of Production stemmed, he said, from the fact that Roosevelt had appointed a War Production Board, with whose Chairman there was need for direct liaison at the appropriate level. It was indeed true that external factors dictated the appointment—as Beaverbrook put it, the Ministry was 'born in Moscow' where he had made decisions about the whole field of supply to Russia in collaboration with the American representative, Averell Harriman.[22] Beaverbrook himself, who was now Minister of Supply and who had been Minister of Aircraft Production, was the natural appointment for the new post. But as usual he was at odds with several of his Cabinet colleagues, and in particular with Ernest Bevin, who as Minister of Labour had responsibilities which overlapped considerably with those of the new office. The drafting of a White Paper to define the powers of the Ministry of Production caused great difficulty, and Beaverbrook found the ministry was to be an 'ugly duckling' and not a 'swan' as he had hoped.[23] Churchill was now also anxious to bring Sir Stafford Cripps into the ministry, for Sir Stafford, who had returned to England from his post at Moscow, obviously had strong qualifications for office and was widely regarded as a potential member of the War Cabinet.[24] People seemed to think that he, and not Hitler, had brought Russia into the war.

21. Hansard 377, 1008 (29 Jan., 1942).
22. Hansard (Lords) 121, 799 (12 Feb., 1942).
23. Beaverbrook to Hoare, 17 Feb., 1942, quoted Young, *Churchill and Beaverbrook*, p. 228.
24. See, e.g., Gallup poll in *News Chronicle*, 22 Jan., 1942.

Churchill offered Cripps the Ministry of Supply, but Cripps refused to serve under Beaverbrook and, to the Prime Minister's chagrin, demanded a place in the Cabinet as a condition of taking office.

Meanwhile Singapore had fallen and—what seemed to many people even more humiliating—three major German warships, the battlecruisers *Scharnhorst* and *Gneisenau* and the cruiser *Prinz Eugen*, had managed to make their way up the English Channel from Brest to German home waters. They had been heavily attacked by torpedo boats, torpedo bombers and bombers, but had escaped apparently undamaged.[25] The move of the three ships was a defensive move by Hitler, as he feared a British attack on Norway; but it seemed to provide a demonstration of Britain's failure to command the seas so close to her home bases, even after two and a half years of war. Beaverbrook chose this moment to lay down his portfolio of office after only two weeks. The official reason given was ill-health; and it is true that he was suffering severely from asthma. It may be that he expected the government to fall shortly and it is possible that he was hoping to become Prime Minister himself. There were rumours about 'the formation of a so-called Centre Party composed of Liberals, disgruntled Conservatives, etc., with Beaverbrook at its head.'[26] Beaverbrook had long been known to favour a policy of closer collaboration with Russia than his colleagues would accept. He wished, for instance, to recognize the Soviet frontiers of 1941, which would have meant acknowledging the legality of her absorption of half of pre-war Poland.[27]

Churchill's reaction was prompt: he now knew that he had to accept Cripps's terms for entry into the government. He decided to make him Leader of the House of Commons and, in place of Greenwood, who was not a success as a

25. Roskill, *War at Sea*, ii, 149-161.

26. Rhodes James, *Chips*, p. 321.

27. Beaverbrook to Churchill, 17 Mar., 1942, quoted Young, *op. cit.*, p. 237.

minister, a member of the War Cabinet. Attlee agreed to
this only reluctantly, for Greenwood was very popular in
the Labour Party, while Cripps was not even a member,
having been expelled for left-wing deviation in 1939.[28]
There was also a Puritan streak and intellectual arrogance
in Cripps which made others uncomfortable. 'There, but
for the grace of God, goes God' was the comment of
Churchill himself. The Conservative Chief Whip, however,
thought that Cripps would be 'welcome to our people
because unwelcome to Labour.'[29] Beaverbrook was replaced
as Minister of Production by Oliver Lyttelton, the shrewd
Conservative businessman who had been a successful
Minister of State at Cairo. Other changes appeared to be
dictated by the need to placate the Labour leadership:
Margesson, who was a reminder of the Chamberlain era,
was replaced at the War Office by his Permanent Secretary,
Sir James Grigg; and Dalton was promoted to the Board
of Trade. Dalton's move suited Eden as he was now able
to secure the Ministry of Economic Warfare (with which
the Foreign Office had close contact) for a comparatively
pliant Conservative, Lord Wolmer. Col. J. Llewellin after
only eighteen days at the Board of Trade took over the
Ministry of Aircraft Production from Moore-Brabazon,
who had been foolish enough to imply in a speech, albeit
in private, that he thought Russia and Germany ought to
be left to fight it out among themselves.[30] Kingsley Wood,
although still retained at the Exchequer, was asked to relin-
quish membership of the War Cabinet so that its regular
party members could be kept in balance after the departure
of Greenwood. The shock to ministers who were relieved
of office was even greater because Churchill, to save himself embarrassment, notified them all, including even
Greenwood, by letter rather than by telephone or interview.[31] But the critics were satisfied, and even before the
reconstruction was complete there was, as *The Times*

28. Beaverbrook to Hoare, 17 Feb., 1942, Templewood Papers.
29. Avon, *Reckoning*, p. 321. 30. *The Times*, 4 Sept., 1941.
31. R. A. Butler to Hoare, 6 Mar., 1942, Templewood Papers.

Parliamentary Correspondent reported, 'a marked change in the mood of the House of Commons, as was made evident both by the cordiality of the Prime Minister's reception yesterday and by the tone of the debate.'[32]

Unfortunately a reconstruction of the government could not halt the consequences of defeat in the Far East. Wavell's South-East Asia Command was dissolved on February 25th, as the forces he had controlled had been destroyed or thrust aside. He reverted to his former duties as Commander-in-Chief in India. The British troops retreating through Burma under Alexander reached the Indian frontier by late May, when the monsoon fortunately put an end to the danger of an immediate land attack on India. The Japanese had already achieved one of their main objects, which was to cut the supply route through Burma to China. But they had also acquired the flexibility which comes from command of the sea. Already in April they had struck at Ceylon across the Bay of Bengal, damaging the harbours at Colombo and Trincomalee and sinking two British cruisers and a light aircraft carrier which were at sea. Merchant shipping losses rose as Japanese aircraft and submarines began to move into hitherto safe waters. And Wavell had to face the enormous task of preparing the Indian frontier with Burma and the long eastern coast against a Japanese invasion.

The problem of winning the support of the Indian parties for the defence of their country against the Japanese now assumed great urgency. For two years Churchill had maintained almost unaided a firm resistance to attempts to break the constitutional deadlock; and in September 1941 he had infuriated nationalist opinion by saying that the Atlantic Charter with its promise of self-determination of peoples was 'primarily' intended to apply to Europe.[33] But as the war approached Indian soil President Roosevelt pressed Churchill to take action; General Chiang Kai-shek

32. *The Times*, 25 Feb., 1942.
33. Hansard 374, 69 (9 Sept., 1941).

visited India from China and made no secret of his concern that a solution should be found; and inside the War
Cabinet the newcomer Cripps, who was especially interested in India, urged a fresh initiative. Late in February
Churchill gave way and agreed to accept the recommendations of a Cabinet Committee which under Attlee's chairmanship was to draw up new proposals.[34] As Amery, the
Secretary of State for India, put it in a private letter:

> After all the difficulties I have had with Winston
> during the last two years . . . he has suddenly seen
> the red light—especially as far as America and the
> Labour Party here are concerned.[35]

Cripps who was a member of the Committee put up a
proposal for summoning an Indian constituent assembly
to shape a new constitution. This would provide for self-
government along the lines of that achieved by the British
Dominions. It was agreed to put this proposal to the
Indian political parties, with the proviso, however, that
while the war lasted the control of Indian defence must
remain in British hands.

The difficulty was to persuade the Indian leaders that
this was a genuine offer of self-government, not subject
to withdrawal as soon as the military situation improved.
Cripps undertook to go out to India and to explain it to
the parties on the spot. But not even Cripps's obvious
sincerity and enthusiasm for the Indian national cause
could convince the leaders of the Indian Congress Party.
Gandhi himself was reported as speaking of the offer as
'a post-dated cheque on a crashing bank.'[36] The Muslim
League, which was concerned about the position of the
Muslim community in an independent India, also rejected
the offer. Cripps had to return to London without securing
any agreement.

It was fortunate indeed for India, and also for the British

34. Mansergh, *op. cit.*, p. 145.
35. Amery to Hoare, 11 Mar., 1942, Templewood Papers.
36. I. Stephens, *Monsoon Morning* (1966), p. 31.

in India, that the Japanese axis of advance now changed
to a southerly rather than a westerly direction. Landings
were made in the Solomon Islands and a threat to New
Guinea and Australia began to develop. But two remarkable American fleet actions, one in the Coral Sea and the
other across the Pacific near Midway Island, blunted
Japanese offensive power. In both these battles carrier-
based aircraft played a decisive role. The threat to India
loomed less large in the summer than it had done in the
spring of 1942; and gradually the defences of India and
Ceylon were improved with the aid of new forces and
equipment from Britain.

All this was providential for the British control in India,
for in August there developed a serious threat to internal
order. The Congress Party adopted a policy of civil dis-
obedience in order to enforce their demand to the British
to 'Quit India'. The principal leaders of the party were
promptly put in prison, where some of them spent the
greater part of the war; but in their absence the movement
became violent: there were serious riots in many places,
and communications broke down, especially in the United
Provinces and Bihar. For a time, British troops which had
come to India to fight the Japanese found themselves employed on internal security duties. But order was gradually
restored, and although the British civilians in India never
quite overcame their shock at what had happened, there
were very few casualties among them or in the forces. The
Muslim League supported the government throughout,
and the Indian Army showed little sign of disaffection.
It was only among the Indian prisoners of war taken in
Malaya or at Singapore that the Japanese secured recruits
for an 'Indian National Army', led by Subhas Chandra
Bose, the Indian politician who had been in Berlin early
in the war.

Meanwhile the reinforcement of India and Ceylon, and
the return home of two of the Australian divisions, had
weakened the Middle East Command. The German and
Italian forces in Libya, on the other hand, could now easily

be reinforced, for German aircraft and submarines had moved to the Mediterranean in strength, and the British battleships based on Alexandria were immobilized for repairs. Malta was under heavy siege and could be supplied only at great cost in sinkings. General Auchinleck, the Commander-in-Chief, Middle East, had to guard against the possibility of a German break-through in the Caucasus or through Turkey or an attack on Cyprus, as well as to deal with General Rommel in the Western Desert. But Churchill was anxious for an early attack on Rommel, so as to open the way for the relief of Malta, to prepare the way for American intervention in French North Africa, and to show the Russians that the British Army was making some direct contribution to the destruction of German power. He therefore coaxed Auchinleck to prepare an offensive, at any rate by mid-June.[37] But in fact it was Rommel who took the initiative by launching an attack on May 26th.

Rommel had no superiority in numbers of tanks, but he relied for success on his own tactical skill and on the fact that the British tanks were less mobile and armed only with 2-pounder guns. For several days the battle swayed to and fro without decision, but in mid-June the British armoured units suffered a heavy defeat in an attack on a strongly-held German position. General Ritchie, the British army commander, then gave the signal for retreat, leaving a South African division with supporting troops to hold the port of Tobruk. Rommel at once assaulted Tobruk, whose defences were not in a good state of repair, and partly for this reason and partly because the South African general and his staff were inexperienced in tactical control, the port was captured and with it a total of 33,000 prisoners and a rich supply of stores.[38] Rommel then pushed on in pursuit of the remainder of the British army, now under the personal control of Auchinleck who had taken over from Ritchie. Rommel was not seriously held up

37. Connell, *Auchinleck*, ch. 17.
38. Playfair, *Mediterranean and Middle East*, iii, pp. 261-275.

until he came to the strong defensive position at El Alamein, well inside the Egyptian frontier. Something like panic prevailed in Cairo, where July 1st became known as 'Ash Wednesday', because of the burning of documents which took place on that day.[39] But this was the limit of Rommel's success: he could not summon sufficient strength to break through, and by mid-July the initiative had passed to the defending forces.

These Middle East reverses—and particularly the loss of Tobruk—were very discouraging to the British public, and led to a further political crisis in late June and early July. But before examining this it may be useful to consider whether, in the existing state of British resources, such setbacks could have been avoided. In retrospect, it is apparent that the effort devoted to the strategic air offensive against Germany at this time was largely wasted, and that the aircraft and aircrews devoted to the task could have been better employed elsewhere—either in providing greater assistance to Coastal Command in the struggle to protect the seaways, or in reinforcing the air strength of the Middle East or India.

The trouble was that Churchill and the Defence Committee had accepted the view that Germany could be very seriously weakened, if not completely destroyed, by bombing alone. This was partly due to pre-war doctrine which had placed too much weight on the military importance of the bombing of cities; partly to poor intelligence which, until late 1941 at least, grossly exaggerated the success of the small RAF night raids on German industrial targets. It was only by accident that Professor Lindemann, or Lord Cherwell as he had now become, discovered that the success of the raids was exaggerated. After a careful enquiry, he reported in August 1941 that only one-third of the bombers despatched on raids got within five miles of their targets; over the Ruhr, the main target inside Germany, the proportion fell as low as one-tenth. Never-

39. Casey, *Personal Experience*, p. 112.

theless, Bomber Command was allowed to go on building up its strength on the argument that, although precision bombing was difficult, it would be possible to achieve success by widespread disruption of the life of the civil population. In February 1942 a new directive was issued by Sir Archibald Sinclair, the Air Minister, which said that the 'primary object . . . should now be . . . the morale of the enemy civil population and in particular of the industrial workers.'[40]

This policy received support from further calculations by Lord Cherwell. In March he submitted a paper in which he argued that by mid-1943, if bomber production targets were achieved, it should be possible to have 'turned out of house and home' one-third of the German population. Cherwell thought this would 'break the spirit of the people'.[41] In order to show what could already be done with his existing forces, Air Chief Marshal Sir Arthur Harris of Bomber Command arranged exceptionally heavy attacks on several German towns in succession, culminating in a thousand-bomber raid on Cologne in May. Apparently no senior minister or officer condemned the policy on moral grounds. But there were sceptics, such as another scientific adviser, Sir Henry Tizard, who distrusted the statistics that Cherwell produced; and there were other critics including the First Lord of the Admiralty and his staff, and also the Commanders-in-Chief of various overseas commands, who thought that the air power so dramatically employed over Germany—incidentally, with heavy losses—could be better used in the difficult but essential defensive operations which they themselves were undertaking. As Wavell wrote in the spring of 1942, before the first 'thousand-bomber' raid:

> It certainly gives us furiously to think when after trying with less than twenty light bombers to meet an attack that has cost us three important warships

40. Webster and Frankland, *Strategic Air Offensive*, i, 323.
41. *Ibid.*, p. 332.

and nearly 100,000 tons of merchant shipping, we see that over two hundred heavy bombers attacked one town in Germany.[42]

But 'Bomber' Harris had direct access to Churchill—for High Wycombe, where he had his headquarters, was very close to Chequers—and so he largely got his way.

Although the overseas commands were obvious claimants for more air support, the degree to which they could be supplied also depended directly upon the amount of shipping available, and here too air power could play an important part in preventing the ravages of enemy U-boats. It is true that a high proportion of the sinkings in the early months of 1942 took place near the Atlantic coast of the United States, owing to the culpable failure of the American Navy to establish a convoy system and other elementary precautions as soon as hostilities began.[43] Sinkings of Allied or neutral merchant shipping at the hands of U-boats alone ran at an average of over half-a-million tons a month in the first seven months of 1942; and the toll would have been even heavier if Hitler had not held many of his U-boats back in Norwegian waters, fearing a British attempt at invasion there. But the concentration of German naval and air power in the North Sea was able in the summer seriously to disrupt the Arctic convoy route to Russia, and partly owing to a major miscalculation by Admiral Sir Dudley Pound, the First Sea Lord, one convoy, under the code-name of PQ 17, lost no less than 23 of its 34 merchant ships on the outward voyage alone.[44] All this meant that the shipping situation was as critical as it had been in the worst days of the late winter of 1940-1.

The general public did not know the details of the shipping situation, nor the limitations of the strategic bomber offensive. It was generally assumed that the

42. Bryant, *Turn of the Tide*, p. 363.
43. Roskill, *op. cit.*, ii, 95f.; Doenitz, *Memoirs*, p. 223.
44. Roskill, *op. cit.*, ii, 139-145.

British position in the Middle East was very strong, because the government's excuse for its failures in the Far East had been that it had concentrated its reinforcements upon that area. The fall of Tobruk therefore came as a severe shock, and the government had to face a recurrence, in a more acute form, of the crisis of confidence which it had encountered in February. Even senior ministers doubted the chances of its survival.[45] On June 25th, four days after the supposed fortress fell, a group of backbenchers of all parties led by the Conservative Sir John Wardlaw-Milne placed a motion on the Order Paper of the House of Commons:

> That this House, while paying tribute to the heroism and endurance of the Armed Forces of the Crown, has no confidence in the central direction of the war.[46]

On the same day a by-election took place in the Maldon Division of Essex—a safe Conservative seat. Tom Driberg, a *Daily Express* journalist who stood as an independent against the official candidate, was elected by a substantial majority. 'It was generally agreed', said *The Times* after the announcement of the poll, '. . . that the Maldon result reflects the disappointment felt by electors at the defeat in Libya.'[47] The popularity of the government in the Gallup poll was not tested until some weeks later, but it was significant that support for the government had by then fallen to only 41% of those asked, and even the personal popularity of Churchill as Prime Minister, which people somehow managed to divorce from that of the government as a whole, came down to 78%—the lowest figure it reached during the war.[48] Malcontents were feverishly planning the personnel of rival governments: prominent among them was Beaverbrook, who had been agitating

45. Diary, 21 June, 1942, A. V. Alexander Papers.
46. *The Times*, 26 June, 1942.     47. *Ibid.*, 27 June, 1942.
48. *News Chronicle*, 27 July, 1942.

vigorously for a Second Front in Europe, and had privately urged Sir Samuel Hoare to return home from Madrid (where he was now ambassador) to see what would turn up.[49] He now told Bevin that he was prepared to support him for the Premiership—a suggestion which the sturdy trade-union leader only regarded with contempt.[50]

But the timing of the censure motion did not allow the opposition time to gather its forces and to focus on the weaknesses of the government. Wardlaw-Milne and his colleagues had made a mistake in tabling their motion so quickly; when the debate began on July 1st it was evident that they still had not managed to co-ordinate the line of their criticism. Wardlaw-Milne opened the attack by arguing, not unjustly, that Churchill appeared to be interfering too much in the direction of strategy; but he ruined his case by suggesting that the Duke of Gloucester—who had no experience of wartime command —should be made Commander-in-Chief of the forces. Acording to one member, 'the House roared with disrespectful laughter, and I at once saw Winston's face light up.'[51] Admiral of the Fleet Sir Roger Keyes, who seconded the motion, took the opposite line of attack: in his view Churchill was not allowed enough say in strategy, which was dictated by the Chiefs of Staff. Although Oliver Lyttelton had not yet got the feel of the House and did not put the case very well for the production ministries, Beaverbrook addressing the Lords made a very effective defence of his own record, pointing out that the slow start in designing weapons for land warfare, combined with the need in 1940 for as much equipment as possible, however obsolescent, had held back the mass production of high-quality tanks and guns. The second day's debate in the Commons was marked by a bitter speech from the Labour back-bencher Aneurin Bevan, who suggested that as British generals were no good they should

49. Beaverbrook to Hoare, 12 June, 1942, Templewood Papers.
50. Bullock, *Bevin*, ii, 177.
51. Rhodes James, *Chips*, p. 334.

be replaced by Czechs, Poles or Frenchmen. But no coherence emerged in the criticism of the government; there was no alternative to Churchill as Prime Minister; and so when the debate ended the opposition only mustered 25 votes against 475 for the government. So once again Churchill had his overwhelming parliamentary victory, though not quite so overwhelming as in February. There was some truth in Beaverbrook's view that 'the Coalition's stock of goodwill' was 'nearing exhaustion'.[52] There had to be some victories soon or the opposition would somehow find coherence and real strength.

Life for the civilian population of Britain became still more austere in 1942. Increases in rations which had been made before Pearl Harbour were withdrawn afterwards, and the shipping crisis led in March to an increase in the wheat extraction rate, which meant the end of white bread.[53] Soap, chocolate and sweets joined the list of rationed goods, and biscuits went on 'points'. The basic petrol ration disappeared altogether. New restrictions led to the virtual abandonment of professional boxing and greyhound racing. But the general health of the people continued to improve. It was aided by such paternalistic measures as the supply of orange juice to babies, and of milk to expectant and nursing mothers and to school children. Plans for the introduction of coal rationing were prepared by the Board of Trade in the spring, but the opposition of Churchill himself and of the 1922 Committee of back-bench Conservative MPs led to its being shelved: instead, the government took control of the industry, so as to ensure more efficient production, and created a new ministry, that of Fuel and Power, to supervize the operation of the pits and to allocate supplies.[54]

The public did not seem to be hostile to the measures for tighter rationing—not even to coal rationing, at any

52. Beaverbrook to Hoare, 10 July, 1942, Templewood Papers.
53. Hammond, *Food*, i, 261.
54. For an account of this see Dalton, *Fateful Years*, ch. 27.

rate when it was first mooted.[55] The disasters to British arms in the overseas theatres, and the desire to help the Russians in their desperate struggle, made at least the well-informed citizen willing to accept greater restrictions. Sir Stafford Cripps, the former ambassador in Moscow, touched a responsive chord when he called for greater sacrifices in a broadcast to the nation early in February. In a sample poll taken at the beginning of May, although Eden was still regarded by a large proportion of people (37%) as the most suitable leader 'if anything should happen' to Churchill, Cripps followed very closely behind (34%).[56] A swing to the Left also manifested itself in by-elections, and although Driberg's success at Maldon was the most spectacular, it was only the last of four Conservative seats lost to independent candidates. The independents had rather vague political programmes but they tended to associate with Priestley's 1941 Committee and to advocate more public ownership and greater equality of sacrifice for winning the war.

It may be, however, that this swing to the Left was more a matter of middle-class than of working-class opinion. Feeling in the factories appeared to be characterized more by apathy than by concern for an early victory. Communist shop stewards were now supporting the drive for greater production as vigorously as they had opposed it before the invasion of Russia. But the ordinary worker showed less enthusiasm for the war effort in 1942 than in 1940. Working-days lost in strike action rose from less than a million to 1,527,000, which was more than in several years of recent peacetime experience. One reason for this was that the war was now being fought in distant theatres of the world which people could not visualize, instead of taking place in the skies above their homes. Air attack on Britain in 1942 was on a very much diminished scale, being merely tip-and-run raids and a few deliberate reprisals on non-industrial targets such as Can-

55. *M-O Bulletin*, Sept., 1942.
56. *News Chronicle*, 11 May, 1942.

terbury, Bath and Exeter—the 'Baedeker raids' as they were called. The worker had time to think about life after the war was over—and he did not like the prospect, for he thought at once of the unemployment of the interwar years. For all these reasons, there was a lack of enthusiasm and sense of urgency in the factories.

There would have been more enthusiasm, no doubt, if a higher proportion of British troops had actually been engaged with the enemy at this time, or if those who were engaged had been winning their battles. Much the most inspiring news of 1942 came from the Russian front, where in the summer Stalingrad on the Volga was under heavy attack but was being defended with a tenacity reminiscent of the French at Verdun in the First World War. For a period of eight weeks, from July to September, Stalingrad figured in the main headlines of the popular newspapers almost every day. In Britain countless amateur strategists and left-wing politicians—aided powerfully by Beaverbrook and his newspapers and more surreptitiously by the Russian ambassador[57]—demanded a 'Second Front Now' to relieve the pressure on the Russian front. Churchill felt acutely the embarrassment of being unable to do more to help his Soviet ally, with whose foreign minister he had in May signed a twenty-year military alliance.

After much deliberation with the Chiefs of Staff, Churchill still thought that the best practical operation in the course of 1942—given the acute shortage of landing craft and the lack of trained American divisions—would be an invasion of French North Africa (Operation Torch as it came to be called). The American military view was different. General Marshall and his staff held that a direct attack on the continent from England was the one ultimately decisive operation, and even if this was not practicable in 1942, it would be a pity to delay its accomplishment in 1943 by action in a different theatre. But President Roosevelt was willing to undertake Torch if no

57. Avon, *Reckoning*, pp. 323, 340.

other operation was practicable in 1942, for he hoped for some sort of success in time for the mid-term elections in early November. The result was that in late July the American chiefs reluctantly committed themselves to Torch, and Roosevelt nominated General Dwight D. Eisenhower, who had already established a planning headquarters in London, to take charge of the joint enterprise.[58] In August a large-scale raid on the port of Dieppe, which was carried out by 5,000 Canadian troops and 1,000 British Commandos, provided some evidence of the difficulty of attempting a landing in France: Canadian casualties (including prisoners) amounted to 68% of the numbers engaged.[59]

The planning of Torch was based on the assumption that if American troops led the invasion the Vichy French forces would put up only token resistance, and that the Allied troops would be well-established before the Germans could react with strength. In the meantime, it would be necessary for the British Eighth Army, which was still facing Rommel's forces at El Alamein, to attack and if possible destroy their opponents before the new landings took place. Early in August Churchill and General Brooke visited Cairo and decided to replace Auchinleck with Alexander, who had conducted so skilful a retreat in Burma. They appointed General W. H. E. Gott, one of the Eighth Army's Corps Commanders, as its new Army Commander, but Gott was killed in an enemy attack on his plane and it became necessary to bring out from England General B. L. Montgomery, who had commanded a division at Dunkirk. Meanwhile, the Eighth Army received far more in the way of new equipment than the enemy forces were able to secure. Immediately on hearing of the fall of Tobruk Roosevelt had ordered the despatch to Egypt of 300 Sherman tanks—a highly mobile new type— and a hundred self-propelled guns.

58. Butler, *Grand Strategy*, iii, 636; Matloff and Snell, *op. cit.*, pp. 279-284.
59. Roskill, *op. cit.*, ii, 250.

Montgomery's attack began on October 23rd. It was a set-piece assault, beginning with a heavy artillery barrage, and designed to clear a way through enemy minefields. Once this was done the tanks could go through to cut off the enemy positions. When the enemy counter-attacked he was held by heavy bombing attacks from the air; and furthermore as Alexander reported 'our tanks and anti-tank guns could engage him with longer range.'[60] After twelve days of heavy fighting the armour had pushed through, and Rommel had been obliged to order a full retreat. The main elements of Rommel's Afrika Korps escaped encirclement, but 30,000 prisoners, mostly Italian, were taken, and more than five-sixths of the German tanks were destroyed.[61]

A few days later, on November 8th, the landings in French North Africa began. The transports had all evaded enemy submarines; the troops landed safely on or near their correct beaches; complete surprise was gained and French resistance though strong in places could only last a few days. By the middle of November all of French North Africa, save for Tunisia which the Germans and Italians were hastily occupying, was in Allied hands. On November 11th Churchill spoke at the annual City of London banquet at the Mansion House. 'The bright gleam of victory', he said, 'has caught the helmets of our soldiers and warmed and cheered all our hearts'. In this new situation, he felt it was time to reply to the critics of British imperialism, both at home and in America: 'I have not become the King's First Minister in order to preside over the liquidation of the British Empire.'[62]

60. Churchill, *Second World War*, iv, 531.
61. Playfair and Molony, *Mediterranean and Middle East*, iv, 78f.
62. *The Times*, 21 Nov., 1942.

# 7. Mediterranean Victory

In November 1942 it seemed possible that the North African campaign would be concluded in victory within a few weeks. If it had been, it would have been a triumph of surprise and bluff rather than of real power. Since the destruction of the French fleet at Oran in 1940, the French North African commanders were usually thought to be hostile to the British; and so they were informed by Robert Murphy, the American consul-general, that the invasion force was wholly American, and that it amounted to about half a million men.[1] In fact the assault troops, some of whom were British, amounted to only about 65,000 men. It was to be built up to something like Murphy's figure within a month, but almost half the troops would then be British. But the bluff served its purpose, and the landings met only patchy resistance, though for a few days there was fierce fighting in places. Admiral Darlan, one of the most important of the Vichy regime's leaders and the man largely responsible for the growth of the modern French navy, happened to be visiting North Africa at the time of the invasion, and he was persuaded to order a general cease-fire on November 10th.

Hitler responded by ordering the occupation of Vichy territory in mainland France, wherupon Darlan appealed to the French naval forces at Toulon to sail for North Africa. A few submarines managed to escape, and the remaining ships were scuttled by their crews. Thus Darlan's prompt action had been very helpful to the Allies, and provided the justification for allowing him to remain in authority in North Africa. But the decision was very

1. Murphy, *Diplomat Among Warriors*, p. 165; Playfair and Molony, *Mediterranean and Middle East*, iv, 126, 167.

unwelcome to General de Gaulle and his Free French supporters, who had no part in the bargain; and it caused a sharp reaction in Britain, especially in left-wing circles, where the leaders of the Vichy regime were regarded as little better than Nazis.

Nevertheless Darlan's support enabled General Eisenhower to begin the next phase of the operation, which was a rapid advance into Tunisia in order to prevent the Germans and Italians from seizing Tunis and Bizerta as a firm base for the retreating Afrika Korps. This task was to be the responsibility of the so-called British First Army under General K. A. N. Anderson, whose troops, consisting in fact of hardly as much as two divisions even by December, had been landing at or near Algiers. It was over five hundred miles to Tunis from Algiers, and although the troops pushed ahead quickly, they arrived to find that the Germans had occupied the vital airfields and defences without opposition from the French. The French army commander in Tunisia soon transferred his support to the Allies, but his troops were poorly equipped and could provide little assistance at first. An American corps joined Anderson's line in southern Tunisia, but early in December the Germans counter-attacked strongly, gaining ground to safeguard the lines of communication into Tripolitania where Rommel's forces were still holding the Eighth Army.

Meanwhile Rommel after his defeat at El Alamein had been falling back rapidly to avoid being cut off by Montgomery's advance. His retreat from one good defensive position to another was conducted with great skill. Late in November he was holding El Agheila, which was more than half-way back from El Alamein to the Tunisian border; and by the time that Montgomery had summoned up sufficient strength to mount an attack, he was in retreat again to a position two hundred miles further west at Buerat. As a fresh assault by the Eighth Army began in mid-January he retreated into Tunisia, abandoning the port of Tripoli and, with it, the last remnant

of the former Italian territory in Africa. But Hitler had
decided that Tunisia should be held by Axis forces
throughout the 1943 campaigning season, so as to deny
the Mediterranean route to the Allies, to save Italy from
defeat and to ensure that there would be no Anglo-
American invasion of Europe before he had had a fresh
chance to crush the Russians.

This was a time for the Allied leaders to reconsider their
future strategy. Churchill and Roosevelt wished to arrange
a tripartite meeting with Stalin, but Stalin refused to
leave Russia while the operations near Stalingrad were as
yet unresolved. A Russian counter-offensive there had led
to a German army being cut off, and by the beginning of
February it was completely destroyed, with the loss of a
quarter of a million men. This was a disaster for German
arms on a considerably greater scale than the loss of the
battle of El Alamein. When Churchill and Roosevelt met
at Casablanca in January, these developments were clearly
impending: and so in spite of the stiff German resistance
in Tunisia the atmosphere could not but be one of optimism. All the same, there were sharp differences on what
should now be done to strike at the enemy. General
Marshall wanted the conference to place a limit on the
Allied commitment in the Mediterranean, so that the
cross-Channel operation might be undertaken in 1943.
But American military opinion was not unanimous on this,
and in the end the President accepted the British view
that Sicily, as well as the North African coast, would
have to be captured.[2] The case for this, in short, was
that the Mediterranean could not be opened for Allied
shipping until Sicily was clear of the enemy; and the
continuing critical shortage of merchant ships, owing to
the successes of the U-boats in the early part of the year,
made this course highly desirable. General Eisenhower,
who had been one of the keenest advocates of a cross-
Channel invasion not later than 1943, was now prepared
to admit that such a highly complex operation as would

2. Matloff, *Strategic Planning*, pp. 25f.

be required could no longer be thought of before 1944.[3] But in the meantime, a powerful joint Anglo-American bomber offensive against Germany was to be mounted from airfields in Britain.

The Casablanca conference also saw an attempt to secure co-operation between the rival factions of Frenchmen. Admiral Darlan had been assassinated in December, and his successor was General Giraud, an officer with little political capacity or indeed ambition. The sentiment of the French population in North Africa clearly favoured de Gaulle, and after a period of equal association between Giraud and de Gaulle power gradually moved to the latter. But it may have been in large part as a result of the animosity generated by the recognition of Admiral Darlan that Roosevelt suddenly proclaimed at a Casablanca press conference that the Allied aim was the 'unconditional surrender' of the enemy powers. Churchill at once endorsed this phrase, which did not in itself necessarily imply harsh treatment of the enemy although it did rule out a negotiated peace.

After the conference things did not go uniformly well on the North African front. The withdrawal of Rommel's forces into Tunisia provided the opportunity for a sharp German attack on the comparatively weak and raw troops, largely American and French, who were holding the southern sections of the front under Anderson's command. This attack caused the loss of the Kasserine Pass and a considerable widening of the corridor of enemy-held territory between Tunis and Bizerta in the north and Rommel's forces in the south. But the two Allied Commands were now united; General Alexander, Commander-in-Chief of the Middle East forces, became Eisenhower's deputy with strategic command over all Allied troops operating against the enemy in Tunisia. It was his task to co-ordinate the operations of the First and Eighth Armies and the American and French troops fighting with them. First of all he eased the difficulties of command

3. Playfair and Molony, *op. cit.*, iv, 262f.

at lower levels by separating the different nationalities, which had been somewhat intermingled since the landings. Then he ordered Montgomery to bring the Eighth Army northwards into Tunisia, aiding its operations by pressure from the First Army on the enemy flank. Early in March Rommel himself left Africa for Germany on sick leave. He was never to return, for Hitler did not want to lose one of his most popular generals. The end was approaching: the Allies had overwhelming naval and air superiority and could take an increasing toll of reinforcements and supplies from Italy. The Eighth Army forced the Mareth Line in southern Tunisia in late March, and by mid-April the enemy was enclosed in a tight ring around Tunis, Bizerta and the Bon Peninsula. A final assault, principally by the First Army, led to the capitulation of enemy forces on May 12th and 13th. The success was on a scale comparable with that at Stalingrad, for a quarter of a million prisoners were taken, over half of them German. For the first time British troops had the welcome spectacle of Germans surrendering on a large scale. British and Imperial casualties inside Tunisia were less than 40,000; American less than 20,000.[4]

The North African campaign had enabled the Allies to learn many lessons in warfare, perhaps particularly in coalition warfare. Eisenhower had shown great ability in the task of welding together the staffs of different nationalities, but the British and American troops who landed in French North Africa were less trained and experienced than those of the Eighth Army, and suffered some unnecessary setbacks and losses. It was as well that they fought their first battles in Africa and not in France. Italian equipment and morale were both poor, but the Germans fought with astonishing toughness and flexibility until their essential supplies ran out. They still had at their disposal some forms of equipment which the Allies could not equal —for instance, the Tiger tank which appeared in small

4. *Ibid.*, 460.

numbers in Tunisia. Against such opponents, the prospects of final victory still seemed distant.

But at home in Britain the successes of the autumn of 1942—the beginning of the fourth year of the war—seemed to offer the promise of an early conclusion to the war. Men of all political parties turned their minds to the problems of the post-war world and decided that the government, which had learnt the rudiments of planning for war, should now plan for peace as well. *The Times* declared that 'The African triumphs have brought new force to the demand for timely and well-planned reconstruction.'[5] Yet the first political change that followed the victories in North Africa was the resignation of Cripps from the War Cabinet. Cripps disliked Churchill's way of conducting business, divorcing military from civil policy, and dominating the former himself while largely ignoring the latter. He favoured instead a collective leadership by a small group of ministers free of departmental responsibilities more or less on the lines of the Lloyd George Cabinet of 1917-18. Under pressure from Churchill and other colleagues, Cripps agreed to delay his resignation until after the African offensive, and he then accepted a transfer to the post of Minister of Aircraft Production, which was outside the War Cabinet. He had not been a successful Leader of the Commons—he lectured the back-benchers too much for their liking—and his public standing had gradually declined. Nevertheless, he was one of the few men at the top who had publicly declared his interest in planning for a better postwar world; and it was not clear who would now press for action on these lines by the Cabinet. Herbert Morrison, who replaced him there, was burdened with major departmental responsibilities at the Home Office and Ministry of Home Security. According to Dalton, it was Kingsley Wood, the Chancellor of the Exchequer, who was the major obstacle to the adoption of

5. *The Times*, 23 Nov., 1942.

proposals for reconstruction.[6] But a good deal of the responsibility lay with Churchill himself, who was so far not at all interested in post-war problems, and who as Attlee said 'always closes everything down' when discussion arose on such questions.[7]

One major concern at the time was for the planning of the rebuilding of the cities, which had been so knocked about by the enemy bombers. But the rebuilding of homes could not be separated from the question of the location of industry, and this, according to a Royal Commission which reported just at the outbreak of war—the Barlow Commission on the Distribution of the Industrial Population—needed supervision by a central authority which would aim at a balanced development of all regions of the country. Two departmental committees appointed by the Minister of Works, Sir John Reith, examined the questions of land use and land values and urged increased state planning powers. One of them, the Uthwatt Committee, reported in September 1942 that the State should take over development rights in land near built-up areas, and should have powers of compulsory purchase of built-up land at pre-war values. The other was the Scott Committee, which considered the future of the countryside, and recommended in August 1942 the establishment of a national authority to plan land use there as well. Late in 1942 the government decided to set up a Ministry of Town and Country Planning, but the degree to which it proposed to implement the Barlow, Uthwatt and Scott Reports still remained in doubt.

Yet none of these questions aroused anything like the degree of controversy that was sparked off by the Beveridge Report on Social Insurance. When Greenwood had been in charge of post-war planning studies as a member of the War Cabinet in 1941, he had asked Beveridge to chair a committee of civil servants from different departments 'to undertake . . . a survey of the existing national schemes

6. Diary, 2 Nov., 1942, Dalton Papers.
7. *Ibid.*, 17 Nov., 1942.

of social insurance and allied services . . . and to make recommendations.'[8] Beveridge, who had now retired from the civil service, had been as he put it 'reflecting on the terms of a new crusade'[9] and it soon became clear that he was pushing his colleagues into conclusions which, as civil servants, they could not adhere to in public. It had therefore to be arranged that the report should appear under Beveridge's name only.

The most remarkable advances in social thinking embodied in the Beveridge Report are to be found in its initial 'assumptions', rather than in its conclusions. Beveridge started off by taking it as accepted that the government would secure a high level of employment in the postwar world, that it would introduce family allowances, and that it would devise a comprehensive health service for all instead of the existing patchwork of services. The 'Plan for Social Security' which he drew up in the main body of the report was no more than a rationalization of the financial arrangements, so that in return for a single weekly contribution, wage-earners and self-employed persons, and also their families, would receive old-age pensions and sickness benefits, and wage-earners if unemployed would receive unemployment pay. Beveridge proposed precise figures for the contributions and allowances, and calculated that the whole scheme could be introduced at an initial cost to the Treasury of £86 million a year.

Before the Report was published on December 2nd, 1942, there were numerous leaks to the press about its contents, with suggestions that it was sure to be controversial. These leaks seemed to be devised to prevent any attempt to hold up publication. To be sure, ministers were worried about its implications and impact. Cherwell told Churchill that acceptance of its proposals might endanger the prospects of getting Lend-Lease after the end

8. Report on Social Insurance and Allied Services, *P.P.* 1942-3, vi, 119ff.

9. Beveridge to Frances Stevenson, 4 Mar., 1942, Lloyd George Papers.

of the war, as Americans 'might be told they were being asked to pay for social services in the UK far in advance of their own.'[10] Following this line, Churchill asked Sir William Jowitt, the minister who was supervising the reconstruction studies formerly looked after by Greenwood, to go slow in approving measures of post-war policy until financial arrangements had been made with the United States.[11] After a further general warning had been given to ministers the War Office took steps on December 21st to withdraw a favourable summary of the Report which had been circulated to army units for discussion purposes only two days before.[12] But by this time public interest had been aroused and there was widespread approval of the Report;[13] many people thought that because it was a White Paper it must already be government policy;[14] and the Ministry of Information, which had realized that it served excellently to refute German propaganda about British indifference to social welfare, had worked hard to publicize its details both at home and abroad.[15] Churchill appeared to be unaware of the unfavourable impression that the government's attitude was giving, not only to Liberal and Labour supporters, but also to Conservative back-benchers. On January 12th, 1943 he told his colleagues in a general memorandum: 'A dangerous optimism is growing about the conditions it will be possible to establish here after the war.' He argued that the loss of foreign investment, export difficulties, and the need to develop the Empire as well as to maintain larger armed forces, part of them serving as occupation forces, would all make Britain's post-war economic position hazardous. He urged a cautious approach: 'Ministers should in my

10. Cherwell, 'Notes on Beveridge', 25 Nov., 1942, Cherwell Papers Box 2.

11. Churchill to Jowitt, 3 Dec., 1942, Cherwell Papers Box 45.

12. J. Beveridge, *Beveridge and His Plan*, p. 132.

13. See, e.g., Intelligence Report, Scotland, 19 Dec., 1942 and 27 Feb., 1943, Beveridge Papers.

14. Mass-Observation, 'The Public and Beveridge', *Spectator*, 29 Jan., 1943.

15. J. Beveridge, *op. cit.*, pp. 130f.

view be careful not to raise false hopes as was done last time by speeches about "Homes for Heroes" etc.'[16]

Although Ernest Bevin might have been willing to accept this view, the other Labour ministers were not inclined to do so. Morrison thought that the post-war armed forces could be financed partly by borrowing, and that other countries could probably be persuaded to take over many of the occupation duties in Germany. Dalton believed that 'cheap money' would ease the financial load, and that a capital levy was also a possibility.[17] In any case, he maintained, full employment was quite attainable, especially if there was a firm control of the location of new industrial development. Attlee replied rather sharply to a note of Churchill's, in which the Prime Minister had argued that a Parliament elected as long ago as 1935 should not 'tie the hands of future Parliaments in regard to social matters':[18]

> The doctrine set out in your note seems to me to destroy all hope of this country playing an effective part in carrying the world through the difficult period of transition.[19]

Even Cherwell swung round and now told Churchill that there was 'nothing particularly novel or revolutionary' about Beveridge's proposals and that although they would be expensive particularly in the long term, it would be a practical error to start making 'detailed reservations at this stage'.[20] And Keynes submitted some notes to show that in his view 'our economic position . . . is (to my thinking) the least of our worries'. This was because of the industrial progress which Keynes perceived as taking place in the course of the war, and also because there seemed

16. Churchill, *Second World War*, iv, 861.
17. Dalton to Morrison, 24 Jan., 1943, Dalton Papers.
18. Churchill, *op. cit.*, iv, 862.
19. Attlee to Churchill n.d., Attlee Papers (C).
20. Note, 11 Feb., 1943, Cherwell Papers Box 2.

to be good export opportunities in the post-war period, with Germany and Japan 'knocked out' and American costs too high.[21]

The Beveridge Report was not debated in the House of Commons until mid-February. In the meantime a certain amount of partisan feeling had appeared over Bevin's Catering Wages Bill. Bevin had managed to get Cabinet approval for this measure, which was certainly a piece of permanent legislation, designed to improve conditions in a rather depressed occupation; but no less than 116 Conservatives showed their hostility to what they regarded as an infringement of the basis of the Coalition by voting against the Second Reading. When, a week later, the Beveridge debate opened, Churchill was ill and the government's main spokesmen were Anderson, whose skill as an orator hardly went beyond the ability to read out a civil service brief, and Kingsley Wood, who as Chancellor of the Exchequer had formed a pessimistic view of the expense of the scheme. After listening to these two, and in spite of the fact that Anderson announced the government's acceptance of all Beveridge's 'assumptions', the Parliamentary Labour Party decided to put down an official amendment to the government motion, and when the House divided this secured 121 votes. The supporters of the revolt were only a few more than those of the preceding week's Conservative rebellion, but there were two differences: this was an official party attack on the government; and it was supported by the overwhelming majority of the back-benchers of that party. As Beaverbrook put it: 'The Tories have been for a week-end to Brighton. But the Socialists decided that they wanted to leave home altogether.'[22] Bevin was much put out by the behaviour of his colleagues on the Labour benches. He was lukewarm about the Beveridge Report anyway owing to the fact that it cut across trade-union interests; and he believed that

21. Keynes, 'Rough Notes for the Prime Minister', 11 Mar., 1943, Cherwell Papers Box 45.
22. Beaverbrook to Hoare, 5 Mar., 1943, Templewood Papers.

the party back-benchers owed the same loyalty to Labour ministers as trade-union members owed to their officials. He had threatened to resign from the Parliamentary Labour Party if there was a major revolt, and now he nearly did so. He accused the back-benchers of wanting to 'commit suicide', apparently thinking that their action might precipitate a general election.[23] Certainly the vote threatened the foundations of the government; but if an election had taken place, the Conservatives would have found difficulty in explaining to the general public why the Labour revolt was more damaging than their own attack on the Catering Bill; and the Labour Party had now managed to identify itself with what had become a popular cause in the country, the implementation of the Beveridge Report.

After the clearing of the enemy from the North African coast, the future course of the Anglo-American campaign in Europe had to be determined. The invasion of Sicily had already been decided upon at Casablanca, but it was not yet clear what would be done after this. Churchill saw great opportunities arising from the invasion of the Italian mainland: Italy was the 'soft underbelly' of the Axis crocodile, and heavy blows against her might force her out of the war.[24] Then the Germans would have to take over Italian occupation duties in the Balkans and in various Mediterranean islands if they were not to lose important strategic positions. The German armed forces would become seriously over-extended and would have to draw in reinforcements from other fronts. But the American military planners did not accept the desirability of continued Allied activity in the Mediterranean. They suspected Churchill of political ambitions in the Balkans and felt that any more Mediterranean operations would divert troops, landing-craft, aircraft and supplies from the much more important task of preparing a landing on the north

23. Bevin to Charles Dukes, 26 Feb., 1943, Bevin Papers.
24. Churchill, *op. cit.*, iv, 433 and 586.

coast of France. Compared with this task, everything else was in their jargon 'unremunerative scatterization' or 'periphery-pecking'.[25] They urged Roosevelt that he should no longer be the neutral arbiter on this matter but should withstand Churchill's blandishments at the next meeting of the heads of government.

The result was that when Churchill visited Washington in May, he could not persuade the President to make any definite commitment to invade Italy. Eisenhower was henceforward to be limited to a total of twenty-seven divisions, and seven experienced divisions were to be withdrawn from his command for use in the cross-Channel attack in the spring of 1944 (an operation now known by the code-name of 'Overlord'). Eisenhower was, however, to have discretion to invade Italy if circumstances were favourable, and he was to do what he could to defeat Italy and to 'contain the maximum number of German forces.'[26] Churchill was not happy about the idea of leaving the military commander to determine such important questions, which was not the British practice; and he insisted on visiting Eisenhower at once in order to try and reach a decision. Roosevelt consented to this step on the understanding that General Marshall should also go as his own deputy; and to the disappointment of the Prime Minister, Eisenhower, with Marshall's backing, refused to commit himself until he saw how the invasion of Sicily was going.

The first landings on Sicily took place on July 10th. They provided valuable experience for the Allies in the conduct of amphibious warfare, being the largest such operation yet to take place. Although Eisenhower was in supreme command, British and American land forces participated in equal strength under the operational control of General Alexander. Montgomery's Eighth Army, now including a Canadian division, landed on the southern tip of the island and then moved northwards towards Catania;

25. Matloff, *Strategic Planning*, p. 74.
26. Churchill, *op. cit.*, iv, 724.

Patton's Seventh US Army entered on the left flank and was soon able to clear all western Sicily. After about ten days Eisenhower felt that sufficient progress was being made for him to agree to an early invasion of the Italian mainland. Then on July 25th the situation was transformed by a *coup d'état* in Rome: Mussolini was dismissed, and a new government under Marshal Badoglio prepared to seek an armistice. In the meantime Italian resistance in Sicily slackened still further and the German troops who already formed the backbone of the defence were forced to retreat to the Messina Straits, whence under strong anti-aircraft cover they largely escaped to the tip of the mainland. The Sicilian campaign lasted thirty-eight days in all.

In Washington the American military planners continued to be worried about the extent of the Mediterranean commitment, while in London the prospects in that area seemed far too good to let slip. Churchill persuaded Roosevelt to meet him in Quebec in August for a further discussion of strategy. On this occasion it was agreed that the Allied army should establish itself 'in the Rome area and, if feasible, further north', but that the main object should be to ensure the success of Overlord, which was provisionally timed for May 1st, 1944.[27] Preparations were to be made for a landing in the south of France as a diversion at the time of Overlord, but operations in the Balkans were to be limited to commando raids, bombing, and the supply of guerillas. The Far East was also discussed, and there was some feeling on the American side that the British and Indian forces on the India-Burma frontier had not done as much as they should have done to open up communications with China. Churchill therefore suggested the creation of a new command—the South-East Asia Command—to be given to the young and vigorous Chief of Combined Operations, Admiral Lord Louis Mountbatten. The Americans welcomed this appointment, but there was still no agreement about what operations

27. Ehrman, *Grand Strategy*, v, 9.

might prove feasible in this area when there were so many other demands on Allied resources.

Meanwhile Eisenhower and Alexander had already shaped their plan of attack on the Italian mainland. The Eighth Army under Montgomery was to move directly across the Messina Straits, and shortly afterwards the American General Mark Clark, commanding the Fifth Army containing one British and one American division, was to land farther north at Salerno, near Naples. The operations were scheduled for early September. Then on August 15th the Italian government began armistice negotiations. Terms were signed on September 3rd, but there was no public announcement until five days later, as the Allies hoped to prevent any rapid German reaction before the Salerno landings. The German command, however, had already made its preparations for an Italian collapse, and there were strong reinforcements moving into Italy from the north. When the Allied troops landed at Salerno on the night of September 8th/9th, they were met by heavy opposition. The only major advantages accruing immediately to the Allies from the Italian surrender were, first, the elimination of the Italian fleet, which sailed to internment at Malta, and, secondly, the capture of the port of Taranto, at the southern end of the Italian Adriatic, which German troops had not managed to reach. Nevertheless after a few days' stiff fighting in the Salerno beachhead it proved possible for the Allied Armies to link up and to capture the important airfields at Foggia. On October 1st Naples was occupied. After this, however, progress became very slow. Hitler had determined to prevent the loss of Rome, and the number of German divisions in Italy had risen from six in July to nineteen in October.[28]

Although events had not turned out quite as the Allies had hoped, it would be a mistake to discount the importance of the Italian collapse on the global strategy of the war. Hitler had launched his last great offensive on the Russian front early in July, but it had not gone well, and

28. Jackson, *Battle for Italy*, pp. 41, 333.

after a few days he called it off. One reason for his decision was the need to transfer divisions to the south. As Churchill predicted, it was necessary for him not only to reinforce Italy but also to replace Italian garrisons in the Balkans. The Communist guerillas in Yugoslavia, under the self-styled Marshal Tito, suddenly became a powerful army when they secured the equipment of several Italian divisions. In addition, small British forces were moving into the Aegean, occupying islands which had previously been held by the Italians. Churchill wanted to mount an assault on Rhodes, which was already held by German troops in some strength, but this meant running counter to the Quebec decisions, and Eisenhower, faced with heavy opposition in Italy, could not spare anything for this operation. Hitler was not to know this, however, and in his fear of a Balkan invasion he sent strong reinforcements down to the Aegean, where they at least had the satisfaction of eliminating the advanced British outposts. It had been Churchill's hope that Turkey might now come into the war, but the demonstration of German power virtually on her front doorstep in the Aegean was not an encouragement.

The disagreements between the British and American leaders over the Rhodes and Aegean operations brought out the contrasts of their strategic thinking. The British were still worried by the dangers of the Overlord operation and wished to do everything possible to secure a diversion of enemy strength before it took place. Keeping a close watch on European developments, and conscious of the flexibility provided by their command of the sea, they wished to take advantage of opportunities in the Eastern Mediterranean, where, technically at least, Turkey was an ally and might be persuaded to enter the war. The British view of strategy was summed up by the Chiefs of Staff who said that the object should be to

stretch the German forces to the utmost by threatening as many of their vital interests and areas as possible and, holding them thus, we should attack wherever we can do so in superior force.[29]

This was not the strategy favoured by General Marshall or by the War Plans Division of the American Army. They believed in concentrating the maximum amount of force at what seemed to them to be the decisive point on the enemy perimeter—the northern coast of France, which was close to England and could be dominated by Allied air power. The preparations for such an assault had to be undertaken many months in advance and required careful co-ordination with all the other demands upon the Allied war machine. In particular, Admiral Ernest J. King, the Chief of Naval Staff and Commander-in-Chief of the US Navy, who was largely conducting the war in the Pacific, had to be persuaded that the European operations were sufficiently important to deserve allocations of scarce supplies which might otherwise be used in the war against Japan. The fact that Churchill was so much more fully involved in the shaping of British military thinking than Roosevelt was in American made the Americans all the more suspicious that the British concern for the Eastern Mediterranean was due to some long-term political design, such as a desire to prevent the Russians controlling the Balkans after the war.[30] But Churchill and his colleagues had no such long-term political designs. If they had they would not have supported the Communist guerillas in Yugoslavia. The Americans also misjudged the Russian attitude at this stage of the war, and were startled to find some indications that Stalin actually favoured an increase of Anglo-American activity in the Balkans.[31] The fact of the matter was that both Churchill and Stalin wanted to

29. C. O. S. Memorandum, 11 Nov., 1943, quoted Ehrman, *op. cit.*, v, 110.

30. Harrison, *Cross-Channel Attack*, p. 92.

31. Diary, Sept., 1943 (conversation with Maisky), Dalton Papers; Matloff, *op. cit.*, pp. 302f, 306.

strike at Hitler wherever he was most vulnerable; but neither of them was as much interested in the post-war fate of the Balkans as in that of Poland.

In the late autumn of 1943 the Italian campaign was going very slowly, but Churchill was still pressing for operations in the Aegean and for fresh attempts to bring Turkey into the war, even if it meant delaying Overlord until July. Stalin had been very disgruntled in the summer of 1943 when he learnt that there was to be no large-scale Second Front in 1943; but his feelings improved somewhat in later months, as he found that the Eastern Front was receiving some tangible benefits from Anglo-American pressure in the Mediterranean. He at last consented to meet Churchill and Roosevelt outside the Soviet Union, as protocol demanded, though he was not prepared to go any further than Teheran, the capital of Iran. The Teheran conference at the end of November was Roosevelt's first opportunity to meet the Russian leader, and it was agreed that Stalin should be asked to adjudicate between the two proposed strategies of the western powers: should the main Anglo-American effort be concentrated on Overlord and the divisionary operation in the south of France; or should they be delayed if necessary so as to spare resources for Aegean operations and for strengthening Turkey, to enable her to join in the war? To the great satisfaction of the Americans, Stalin favoured Overlord and the invasion of the south of France as soon as possible; he was not against bringing Turkey into the war but now thought that there would be little advantage in the effort to persuade her. In the course of the more detailed Anglo-American discussions which followed at Cairo, it became clear that the landing-craft which would be held in the Mediterranean for the landing in the south of France could be used beforehand for new outflanking operations in Italy. This pleased the British Chiefs of Staff, who hoped to carry on the Italian campaign with vigour; and they also derived some satisfaction from the fact that the global shortage of landing-craft ruled out for the time being any major operations on the coast of Burma, which they regarded as of little strategic importance.

The winter of 1943-4 therefore saw an ever-increasing build-up of forces and supplies in Britain for the spring invasion across the Channel. Roosevelt sought to persuade Churchill to agree to a supreme European Theatre Commander who would control both the Mediterranean and the cross-Channel operation. For this command he proposed to designate General Marshall. But Churchill and the British Defence Committee could not accept the idea of giving so much authority to a single military leader. In the upshot, it was agreed that an American should command Overlord, as the bulk of the troops to be employed in north-west Europe would be American; and General Eisenhower was chosen for the task. Montgomery was to have command of the British component of the Allied armies and to co-ordinate both the British and American land forces' strategy in the early stages of the campaign. Eisenhower's responsibilities in the Mediterranean were now to be transferred to a British commander, as most of the forces remaining there would be British or British-supplied. The officer chosen for this task was the capable if unspectacular General Maitland Wilson. General Alexander continued to command the armies in Italy, which now consisted of the American Fifth Army under General Mark Clark and the British Eighth Army under General Oliver Leese, who had been one of Montgomery's Corps commanders.

Alexander thus had the difficult task of pressing on with the offensive in the rugged country of central Italy, knowing that his forces and supplies were limited by the needs of the Overlord operation. In mid-January he began a fresh offensive, and on January 22nd he again attempted a left hook with a landing at Anzio not far from Rome. The landing was effected by the Fifth Army, which though mostly American included a British division. Instead of exploiting his opportunity—for the landing was largely unopposed—Mark Clark allowed the troops to dig in and

wait to be attacked. The Germans soon brought up reinforcements and succeeded in containing the beachhead,
while at the same time holding up Alexander's main
thrust at the Monte Cassino Monastery, a dominating
feature which was heavily bombed on February 15th but
whose ruins still provided cover for a determined resistance. Bad weather prevented the Allies from exploiting
their advantage of air superiority. The offensive therefore petered out, and although the beachhead was firmly
established it was clear that it was going to remain as a
beachhead only, and that Rome could not be captured
before the spring. To the troops involved, the Italian
campaign was a disillusioning experience. There seemed to
be no 'soft underbelly' as Churchill had suggested, but
on the contrary a harsh resistance, aided by mountainous
terrain and by cruel winter weather which people from
Britain hardly imagined to be possible in a Mediterranean
country. From the wider viewpoint, however, Churchill's
metaphor was not inappropriate, and the surprising element in the strategic picture was Hitler's refusal to cut his
losses in southern Italy when a more farsighted commander
would have preferred to sacrifice some ground in order
to have reserves for the more important campaigns of the
summer of 1944.

In the winter of 1943-4 the Allies knew that they had
dangerous battles still ahead of them, and that the climax
of the war had yet to come. But earlier, in the late summer
of 1943, it had seemed for a time that there might be a
sudden German collapse, such as had followed the Bulgarian and Turkish armistices in the autumn of 1918. This
had had its effect even upon Churchill, who had so far
done little about post-war reconstruction except to 'show
willing' by talking about a 'four-year plan' shortly after
the Beveridge debate. In the early autumn, however, he
reckoned the odds of a German collapse within six months
at 6-4 against; and he therefore gave way more or less
good-humouredly to urgent representations from Attlee

that something must be done about the transition to peace:
as he put it, he had been 'jostled and beaten up by the
Deputy Prime Minister'.[32] On October 21st he circulated
a memorandum to ministers on 'War-Transition-Peace',
and two days later devoted a Cabinet meeting to the
subject, at which according to a witness he

> . . . elaborated, with great dramatic detail, how we
> should prepare a great book, the Book of the
> Transition, like the War Book, running to perhaps a
> thousand closely printed pages, or taking the form
> of a number of Reports and precise plans contained
> in drawers, one above another . . . All parties in
> Parliament, the country, our returning soldiers, the
> whole world, would be filled with admiration if we
> were able to display a series of neat plans . . .[33]

Churchill's colleagues soon convinced him that War Book
procedure did not quite fill the bill; but it was agreed
that detailed plans and if necessary legislation should be
prepared at once, and that as soon as Germany collapsed
the first phase of the transition to peace could begin. The
Japanese war was still expected to continue for at least
two years after the end of German resistance, but it was
obvious that Britain would not need to deploy any large
proportion of her manpower in the Far East, and so
demobilization and the transformation of the economy to
peacetime purposes could proceed during the final stages
of the war.

The change in the tempo of preparation for post-war
reconstruction was marked by the Prime Minister's decision to appoint a powerful senior minister to co-ordinate
the planning by the various ministries. Churchill's colleagues were at first alarmed by the possibility that
Beaverbrook might be appointed to this task. This was
because Beaverbrook, whose mercurial personality the
Prime Minister had missed since he had left the govern-

32. Diary, 23 Oct., 1943, Dalton Papers.   33. *Ibid.*

ment early in 1942, was now brought back to fill the
non-departmental post of Lord Privy Seal. The vacancy
had occurred owing to Kingsley Wood's sudden death in
September, 1943. Churchill replaced Wood with Anderson,
and in the reshuffle, affecting various posts, the Privy Seal
became vacant. At the same time, the major policy difference dividing Beaverbrook from the Cabinet—the question
of an early Second Front—had disappeared owing to the
commitment to Overlord. Bevin claimed to have told
Churchill that he would resign if Beaverbrook was put in
charge of reconstruction;[34] Attlee also had 'quite a row'
with the Prime Minister on the matter;[35] and other
ministers appear to have made known their concern, for
Churchill grumbled to his Parliamentary Private Secretary, G. S. Harvie Watt, that he surely still had 'the right
to appoint some of his colleagues'.[36] But he wisely chose
another man for the task of Minister of Reconstruction—
Lord Woolton, who had been a successful Minister of
Food and who had no formal party allegiance. Woolton
joined the War Cabinet; and Beaverbrook remained outside its ranks but was available for certain special tasks
such as the preparation of policy for post-war civil avia-
tion. More significantly, he rejoined the 'midnight follies'
—the free-wheeling discussions of policy which took place
in the Prime Minister's circle after formal business was
concluded.

There was one major piece of legislation which had
already been prepared—in fact, by a Conservative minister,
R. A. Butler. This was a bill for the reorganization of
education, and as it did not involve any considerable
immediate expenditure, the Cabinet allowed it to go
forward at once. The bill, which was the product of much
negotiation with the special interests involved—in particular, the churches—was primarily designed to reduce
the anomalies which had been caused by the development
of secondary education within the existing 'dual system',

34. *Ibid.*, 29 Nov., 1943.        35. *Ibid.*, 3 Nov., 1943.
36. *Ibid.*, 11 Nov., 1943.

whereby so many of the schools were 'voluntary' schools maintained by the churches and not directly controlled by the state. The voluntary schools were lagging behind the state schools in the provision of accommodation and teaching for the older pupils.[37] This was the result of a gradual decline in the sectarian enthusiasm of the Protestant churches and in particular of their middle-class laity. Butler offered a compromise whereby the state would obtain a greater control of standards in the schools, especially in the single-school areas, in return for higher grants. Religious instruction and worship were to become obligatory in all schools, though parents would retain their right to withdraw children from it. But the main object of the bill was to achieve secondary education for all up to the age of fifteen in the first instance (the existing school-leaving age was fourteen). Scholarships to maintained grammar schools were to be abolished and instead all the places were to be free. In practice, there was no question of eliminating the differences between the various types of maintained secondary schools, and entry to the grammar schools remained sharply competitive. But these distinctions did not appear in the bill. Provision was also made for mandatory part-time education up to the age of eighteen in 'county colleges'.

The Education Bill was introduced into the Commons in December 1943 and found its way to the statute book without undue difficulty in August 1944. Many of its provisions came into force in 1945, but the raising of the school-leaving age to fifteen was delayed until after the end of the war. Like the Fisher Act of 1918 and the reorganization of Scottish education at that time, it benefited from the weakening of partisan animosities in time of war. But as victory approached, the sense of rivalry between the political parties was already getting much stronger. Beaverbrook noticed in November 1943 that

37. Cruickshank, *Church and State in English Education*, p 138.

Among the rank and file of both the Socialist and Tory parties, hostility grows greater as the prospect of victory becomes more clear.[38]

It was not merely that by-elections were almost invariably contested by independent candidates, but also that at a time when the government's prestige stood very high owing to the turn in the tide of war, these candidates secured large votes. Sir Richard Acland's Common Wealth party, which had developed out of the 1941 Committee, won a seat at Eddisbury in April 1943 and another at Skipton in January 1944. Common Wealth was more like a revivalist movement than a political party, for it had little organization and the greater part of its finances came out of the pockets of two men—Acland himself and a company director called Alan Good.[39] Members of both the Liberal and Labour parties, chafing under the electoral truce, thought that Common Wealth's success indicated a groundswell of political opinion towards their respective viewpoints. A 'Radical Action' group in the Liberal Party sought to ensure the party's adoption of a left-wing programme and a plan to put up a large number of candidates at the next general election; but Sir Archibald Sinclair, the official leader of the party, was more cautious and wanted to explore the possibility of re-union with the National Liberals who had supported Baldwin and Chamberlain.[40] As for the Labour Party, its annual conference in 1943 saw a renewal of the pre-war 'Popular Front' idea with a debate on the application of the Communist Party to affiliate. The Communist Party was enjoying a period of popularity in Britain as a result of the successes of the Red Army, and in May 1943 Stalin's decision to abolish the Communist International removed one of the main arguments of the opponents of the party—

38. Beaverbrook to J. A. Farley, 18 Nov., 1943, quoted Young, *Churchill and Beaverbrook*, p. 256.
39. Common Wealth *Conference Report*, 1944, p. 30.
40. *The Times*, 19 July, 1943.

namely, that it was under alien control. But many of the unions had already committed their delegations to vote against the application before Stalin's decision was announced; and so it was defeated by almost three to one.[41]

Meanwhile the Gallup poll had begun to ask people how they would vote 'if a general election were held tomorrow'. The results confirmed Labour, rather than Liberal, hopes. While only 9% of the samples declared support for the Liberal Party, Labour had a clear lead over the Conservatives amounting to over 10%. The Communist Party was at the level of 3 or 4%, but Common Wealth, in competition with the other left-wing parties, fell to only 1 or 2%.[42] Political leaders did not attach anything like as much importance to opinion polls in those days as they do now; but in any case, the Conservatives had reason to believe that Churchill's advocacy of their cause at a general election would transform the situation. His personal popularity as the wartime Prime Minister had reached a peak in June 1943, after the Tunis victory, when no less than 93% of those polled said that 'in general' they approved of him.[43] Furthermore, Anthony Eden's popularity as his potential successor as leader of the Coalition became quite unrivalled in 1944 (55%). All the Labour ministers lagged badly behind him, and Attlee (4%) was actually below Cripps and Morrison (5% each).[44] Cripps had lost most of the phenomenal popularity that he had had in the months after his return from Moscow. Morrison also ran into a bad patch when in November 1943 he released Oswald Mosley, the Fascist leader, from detention owing to serious ill-health. Angry deputations descended upon Westminster, and once again a revolt of the Parliamentary Labour Party took place, though this time only on a small scale. Bevin even threatened to resign from the government on the issue and was only won back by

41. Labour Party *Report*, 1943, p. 168.
42. *News Chronicle*, 23 Aug., 1943.
43. *Ibid.*, 1 July, 1943.       44. *Ibid.*, 24 Apr., 1944.

skilful pleading on the part of Brendan Bracken.[45] But Bevin's own reputation suffered somewhat owing to his failure to deal with unofficial strikes in the coal industry, which were mostly due to dissatisfaction about piece rates. Bevin attributed much of the trouble to the agitation of a tiny Trotskyite group called the Revolutionary Communist Party. In April 1944 he introduced a new Defence Regulation, 1AA, which made it an indictable offence to 'instigate or incite' a stoppage of essential work. This caused another sharp conflict within the Labour Party, for some of the Labour back-benchers sided with the strikers, and Aneurin Bevan launched such a bitter attack on Bevin and the trade-union leadership that he almost found himself expelled from the party as a result. It looked as if the electoral popularity of Labour might easily be spoiled by quarrelling and by the absence of effective leadership.

In the fourth year of the war the country had achieved its maximum mobilization, and the 'manpower budget', rather than the financial budget, was decisive in determining the government's priorities. About a third of the working population was in the armed forces, in Civil Defence or in the munitions industries, as against 28% in 1918.[46] Those in civil employment were still working long hours: in the engineering and allied industries average weekly hours had risen from 48 in 1938 to 54.1 in 1943 for men, and from 44.2 to 46.9 for women.[47] Over half a million women were in the armed forces or in Civil Defence, and many more had gone into industry; and about a million men and women over the age of sixty-five were in paid employment.[48] While those industries which served essential needs had been virtually eliminated, even inessential industries had been cut to the bone and basic services

45. Bracken to Bevin, 30 Nov., 1943, Bevin Papers; Bullock, *Bevin*, ii, 286.

46. Hancock and Gowing, *British War Economy*, p. 455n.

47. *Ibid.*, p. 454n.      48. *Ibid.*, p. 454.

such as the railways had been deprived of the capital investment which was necessary for their continued efficiency over the long term. Miscalculations as to future trends sometimes proved costly, for it was very difficult to revive an industry which had been deliberately contracted. An unexpected rise in the birthrate, for instance, caused a famine of perambulators and children's footwear.[49] An ageing labour force in the coal industry led to a continuing shortfall of production, which, as we have seen, it was the object of the new Ministry of Fuel and Power to prevent. The difficulties here might have been avoided if miners had not been allowed to volunteer for the forces in 1940. At the end of 1943 it became necessary to introduce a system of compulsory service in the mines by the employment of a small number of conscripts selected by ballot from the usual intake to the forces: they became known as 'Bevin boys'. Agriculture was more of a success story: the government's policy of greater production so as to save food imports had resulted in the acreage under the plough going up from less than 12 million in 1939 to almost 18 million in 1944. Improved efficiency was encouraged by the supervision of farms by County War Agricultural Executive Committees, manned largely by farmers themselves; and the shortage of labour was overcome by increased mechanization, by the use of women workers of the Women's Land Army, and in the closing stages of the war by the employment of Italian prisoners of war.[50]

The general health of civilians was surprisingly good, and although mortality rates had gone up in 1940 and 1941, they declined thereafter.[51] No doubt the government's welfare schemes played a part in this. The main subjects of popular complaint were the blackout and transport difficulties.[52] It became increasingly obvious, though,

49. *Ibid.*, p. 496; Dalton, *Fateful Years*, p. 415.
50. Murray, *Agriculture*, pp. 59, 188, 371.
51. Titmuss, *Social Policy*, pp. 517ff.
52. *M-O Bulletin*, Apr., 1944.

that the major problem of the future would be the housing shortage. The building of new houses had virtually stopped at the outbreak of war, and since then many had been destroyed or damaged in air raids. The damaged houses had for the most part only received emergency repairs. The early months of 1944 saw a renewal of enemy air raids on London, which although not on the scale of 1940/1—it was known as the 'baby Blitz'—was nevertheless an aggravation of the problem.[53] In addition to this, much accommodation had been requisitioned for military use or other essential purposes. Most people had aspirations to improve the quality of their accommodation as soon as circumstances allowed:[54] but they could not do much about it while the war lasted. Indeed under existing circumstances there was little enough to spend money on, apart from beer and cigarettes which for reasons of morale were not allowed to fall short of demand. For the rest, income tax now hit at a large proportion of manual workers: it included an element of compulsory saving in the so-called 'post-war credits' which had been introduced in 1941. Looking ahead to the period when war production would ease off and overtime earnings would drop, the government decided in 1943 to introduce a system of immediate payment of taxes—Pay As You Earn, or PAYE. This was started without serious difficulty in 1943.

In spite of a great extension of factory canteens and other types of industrial welfare, sponsored by the Ministry of Labour, the relations of management and labour did not seem to be as good as in the more exciting days of 1940. In 1943 there were more stoppages of work recorded than ever before, and more working days lost than in any year since 1936. In 1944 things were even worse. Among factory workers in general, there was a good deal of apathy. A study of women factory workers found that

53. Collier, *Defence of the U.K.*, p. 328.
54. Gallup Poll, *News Chronicle*, 18 May, 1944.

The majority of them are so little interested in the war that they do not care whether their work is important to it or not.[55]

And those who were more interested in the hopes of victory could not see how their own work could contribute to it. This attitude could be overcome to a certain extent by propaganda: in the armaments and munition factories, the most effective way was to arrange for visits by servicemen who had successfully used in action the armaments or munitions concerned: but this method was relevant to only a section of the industrial population.

Of course it could not be expected in any case that war production would expand very much after 1942. The country was already fully mobilized and there were few reserves of unused capacity. The great industrial achievements of this stage of the war were in Germany, where desperation, coupled with the genius of Albert Speer, Hitler's Minister for Armaments, was resulting in an effective but belated mobilization of resources; and, on a much larger scale, in the United States, where the vast 'Victory Programme' of military production was now reaching fruition. American military output, which had caught up with the British in the second quarter of 1942, was by the end of 1943 four times, and in 1944 getting on for six times as large.[56] From its prodigal bounty, the United States could provide Lend-Lease assistance to Empire countries which amounted in 1942 to 12.2% of all their munition supplies, in 1943 to 24.5%, and in 1944 to 27.2%.[57]

All this, together with the increased deployment of the United States armed forces, and the success of the Russians on the Eastern Front, explains why Germany was thrown on to the defensive in the military sphere. The Battle of the Atlantic, after a final difficult phase in the spring of

55. Mass-Observation, *War Factory*, p. 45.
56. Postan, *British War Production*, p. 244.
57. Hancock and Gowing, *op. cit.*, p. 373.

1943, turned decisively against the U-boats thereafter. This was in large part a matter of improvements in submarine hunting equipment, in particular the use of escort carriers and very long range aircraft supplied by America, as well as advances in the technique of radar devised by the British. From October 1943 Portugal was persuaded, by virtue of the ancient alliance with Britain, to agree to the use of the Azores as a base for the protection of Atlantic shipping. The shortage of merchant shipping was eased by the transfer under Lend-Lease of a number of 'Liberty ships', which had been made by mass-production methods in the United States. Late in 1943 the convoys to Russia were resumed, and after Christmas an attempt by the German battle-cruiser *Scharnhorst* to interfere with this traffic ended abruptly in her being sunk by the Home Fleet. The battleship *Tirpitz*, which was also in Norwegian waters, was kept out of action, first by midget submarine attack in September 1943, and then by air attack in late December. The battleship era was evidently drawing to a close—a development which was even more obvious in the Pacific, where carriers and aircraft dominated the scene.

In the strategic bombing exchange, also, the enemy was almost entirely on the defensive. One of the major decisions of the Casablanca conference in January 1943 had been that both British and American bombers should build up a sustained offensive against Germany, with the intention of weakening her in the months before the cross-Channel invasion. Bomber Command of the RAF, under Air Chief Marshal Sir Arthur Harris, expanded its policy of heavy area bombing of German industrial towns by night. An élite 'pathfinder' force was used to mark the targets for the main force of bombing aircraft. Occasional raids took place against precision targets, such as the spectacular attack in May 1943 on the Moehne and Eder dams, but the bomber crews for these operations had to be carefully chosen and specially trained. The American Eighth Air Force, which now became established on bases in England, pursued a different strategy—daylight attack on selected targets of industrial importance. This policy very nearly ended in disaster owing to heavy losses from enemy fighters; but a supply of long-range fighters to protect the bombers over enemy territory enabled them to turn the tables early in 1944.

Although the area bombing policy was never fully explained to the British public, careful observers came to learn how it operated in practice—sometimes from neutral sources. Among them was the Bishop of Chichester, Dr G. K. A. Bell, who raised the question in the House of Lords, pleading for the limitation of bombing to targets of a purely military character. Lord Cranborne, who answered the Bishop on behalf of the government, did not of course explain that navigational difficulties at night prevented the bombers from locating their targets with precision. Instead he argued for a more comprehensive definition of legitimate military targets—a definition that went far beyond that which the Chamberlain government had made:

> The great centres of administration, of production, and of communication are themselves targets in a total war. You cannot escape that fact . . . It may well be . . . that those great German war industries can only be paralysed by bringing the whole life of the cities in which they are situated to a standstill, making it quite impossible for the workmen to carry on their work.[58]

This was probably the most detailed public explanation of the Harris-Cherwell policy that was ever given by the government. It came, however, at a time when Harris was being forced to abandon it, at least temporarily. Both he and General Spaatz, the American commander, received a directive from the Combined Chiefs of Staff which obliged them to concentrate on precision targets chosen

58. Hansard (Lords) 130, 752 (9 Feb., 1944).

for their importance in securing the elimination of the German Air Force.[59] Not long after this, the efforts of the two air commands were again diverted, this time to the destruction of the French communications system, which Harris hardly believed his pilots could manage. But this task was regarded as essential for the success of Overlord in the late spring, and Air Chief Marshal Sir Charles Portal, the Chief of the Air Staff, insisted on compliance.[60]

Although the attacks in France were to be precision attacks, large numbers of French civilians were likely to be killed, and Churchill showed some concern lest this should turn French opinion against the Anglo-American invaders. The matter was discussed very seriously at the highest level, but in the end it was decided to go ahead with the attacks more or less as planned. Harris's bombing crews found that after all they could cope with precision targets in France, which were usually less strongly defended than targets in Germany; and the French population showed little sign of hostility as a result. A more dangerous threat to relations between Britain and the United States on the one hand and France on the other was posed by Roosevelt's unwillingness to accept de Gaulle's provisional government as the civil authority in mainland France as it was liberated. In order to prevent leakage of information, it was not until a few days before the invasion that de Gaulle was informed of its date and place, and when he discovered the arrangements already made for the administration of French territory he at first refused to record a broadcast to the French people, and withdrew his civil liaison officers from the Allied armies. It was only in the very last hours as the troops were embarking that he was persuaded to associate himself and his supporters with the launching of Overlord.[61]

If the political side of the invasion plan was somewhat

59. Webster and Frankland, *Strategic Air Offensive*, ii, 84.
60. *Ibid.*, iii, 27f.
61. Woodward, *British Foreign Policy*, pp. 262-6.

B.A.S.W.W.

G

disorganized, the military preparations were by contrast exceptionally carefully thought out. Detailed planning had been going on for almost eighteen months, and the experience of recent combined operations in the Mediterranean was drawn upon. Early in 1943 the British General F. E. Morgan had been put in charge of a combined planning staff in London, and he at once carefully examined the continental coastline for places suitable for a large-scale landing. There had to be firm beaches largely sheltered from the weather, and they had to be located close enough to Britain to be covered by short-range fighter aircraft.[62] The possibilities were soon reduced to two: the Pas de Calais area and the beaches of Normandy in front of Bayeux and Caen. The advantages of Normandy over the Pas de Calais were that its defences were not so strong; that it left a larger area immediately to the East where communications could easily be attacked from Britain; and that, although not offering the availability of a major port immediately on landing, it did open up the prospect of the capture of Cherbourg within a few days. In 1943, planning proceeded on the assumption that the supply of landing-craft would allow an assault by only three divisions in the first wave. But since a simultaneous landing was being planned for the south of France, it was hoped that the enemy build-up of reinforcements would be slow.

When in January 1944 General Eisenhower was appointed to command the operation, these plans were accepted as the basis of the operation, but both Eisenhower and Montgomery insisted on more landing-craft and a more substantial landing on a broader front.[63] It was therefore decided to delay the attack on the south of France by several weeks and to use the extra landing-craft for Overlord. Churchill and the British Chiefs of Staff wanted to cancel the attack in the south altogether, so that all efforts in the Mediterranean might be devoted

62. Morgan, *Peace and War*, pp. 163f.
63. Eisenhower, *Crusade in Europe*, p. 253.

to further exploitation of Alexander's advance north of
Rome.[64] But since most of the troops available for this
operation were French it was desirable to employ them in
the liberation of their own country as soon as possible. At
any rate, the delay in the Mediterranean operation meant
that landing-craft were now available for a five-division
assault on the Normandy coast. On the left flank three
divisions of the British Second Army, including a Canadian
division, were to be put ashore on the beaches which had
attracted General Morgan's attention; and on the right
flank two American divisions were to land even closer to
Cherbourg. Airborne troops consisting of one British and
two American divisions were to be dropped on the
flanks to secure key points and to prevent the beach
defences from being reinforced. To bring ashore the heavy
equipment that would be needed before Cherbourg was
taken and brought into use, two special artificial harbours
known as 'Mulberries' were devised by British experts
for temporary use. Finally, the date of the first landings—
known to the planners as 'D-day'—was provisionally
fixed for June 5th, when the conjunction of moon and
tide would be most suitable.

As June approached, Alexander's troops in Italy began
a new offensive. The main force at last relieved the Anzio
beachhead, and after heavy fighting Rome was captured
on June 4th—just in time to provide a lift for the morale
of the troops embarking on the south coast of England. But
the long-delayed Second Front was held up for one further
day by bad weather, and so it was June 6th, 1944 that
came to be the day that is remembered as 'D-day'.

64. Matloff, *Strategic Planning*, p. 423.

# 8. Victory in Europe

Shortly after midnight on June 5th/6th 1944 British and American parachute troops, followed by airborne forces in gliders, began to land at key points close to the Normandy beaches. An invasion armada of several thousand ships was already crossing the Channel; and as dawn approached warships made a heavy bombardment of coastal defences. This was followed by the landing of assault troops—infantry, tanks, and engineers—on the various beaches, covered by fighter and fighter-bomber attacks on targets close inland. On the three beaches between Arromanches and Ouistreham where landings were controlled by the British Second Army, British and Canadian forces on the first day pushed inland between four and six miles on a broad front, linking up with the airborne elements on the eastern flank. The landing of American troops on the Cotentin coast was equally successful, but their other landing closer to the British western flank (Omaha, as it was described in the Allied code) encountered a mobile division of the German army on manoeuvres and for several hours was held at the beach by withering fire. Yet altogether it proved possible to put 156,000 troops into Normandy before the day was over;[1] and in most places the 'Atlantic Wall' of defences, of which Hitler had boasted, had been very effectively penetrated. German reaction from the air and at sea was totally ineffective—a clear indication of the degree of superiority in these elements that the Allies had already obtained.

The next few days saw the linking-up of the Allied beachheads and a struggle on both sides to reinforce their respective fronts. The *bocage* country limited the move-

1. Ellis, *Victory in the West*, i, 223.

The Invasion of France 1944

ment of armour and slowed up the Allied advance. But the enemy found that it was impossible to bring up reinforcements in daytime owing to air attacks, and it was difficult even at night owing to damage to road and rail inflicted by air attack and by French partisans. The result was that Rommel, the German army group commander, found that he had to commit his entire strength, including tanks, to the task of plugging gaps in the defences, and so could not build up a reserve for counter-attack. In addition, Hitler, who maintained personal control of strategy from his headquarters near the Eastern Front, still feared a fresh landing in the Pas de Calais area, for which elaborate deception plans on the Allied side had provided a good deal of plausible evidence.[2]

Meanwhile Montgomery's aim was to hold as much as possible of the enemy strength in the area of Caen, which he had not yet captured, while the Americans on the right flank broke across the Cotentin peninsula and then cleared Cherbourg. Bad weather hindered the build-up of Allied strength in mid-June, and severely damaged the two artificial harbours or 'Mulberries'; but the amount of stores that could be landed afterwards over open beaches

2. *Ibid.*, pp. 322f.

astounded the planners. On June 17th American troops cut the Cotentin peninsula and turned northwards to attack Cherbourg, which was occupied on July 1st. By this time about 875,000 men, with a slight preponderance of Americans, had been landed on the beaches or by air. There had been just over 60,000 Allied casualties, two-fifths of them British or Canadian and three-fifths American. German casualties amounted to about 80,000.[3] Many of the German dead were the victims of the devastating 'bomb carpets' put down by Allied bombers as the prelude to every major advance.

Montgomery continued to keep up the pressure on Caen and on July 9th the town, now virtually destroyed, fell to the Second Army. Field Marshal von Rundstedt, who was the German Commander-in-Chief, appealed to Hitler to allow him to withdraw from the Caen area, but Hitler refused and soon replaced him with Field-Marshal von Kluge, who had orders to hold fast. Under these circumstances, renewed American pressure on the western sector could lead to a decisive break-through. While the British and Canadians continued to attack south of Caen, a strong American thrust which began on July 25th resulted in a rapid advance southward, and this enabled an armoured spearhead to push into Brittany. Hitler ordered a counter-attack against this spearhead, but adequate forces were not available and the only result was to delay an orderly withdrawal. Montgomery now directed the American columns eastward towards Paris and the Seine. There was a real chance of cutting off the main enemy formation in a pocket which could be closed in the Falaise-Argentan area.

This plan did not entirely work out. The First Canadian Army, now constituted on the left flank as one of the two armies in Montgomery's 21st Army Group, encountered fierce resistance in the advance on Falaise, which did not fall until August 16th. Meanwhile the rapidly-moving American forces had come within a few miles of Argentan

3. *Ibid.*, pp. 307f.

on August 10th, but had then swung eastward. General Omar Bradley, who commanded the American 12th Army Group, had received no orders to move closer to Falaise, and apart from the dangers of a head-on collision with the Canadians, he appears to have thought that the pressure of the German retreat would be too great to enable his armoured columns to hold their ground.[4] Still, the upshot was that the German forces, consisting of the whole of the German 7th Army and nearly half the 5th Panzer Army, had to escape, if at all, through a narrow fifteen-mile gap. The pocket was finally closed on August 21st, but before this, Allied troops and planes had taken a heavy toll of the enemy. Realizing the extent of the defeat, Hitler had replaced von Kluge on August 17th with Field Marshal Model, and von Kluge had committed suicide. Rommel had been badly wounded on July 19th and later also committed suicide to avoid trial for conspiracy against Hitler.

In the last ten days of August the Allied armies, led by the Americans, pushed rapidly up to the Seine and secured bridgeheads across the river. The retreating Germans found themselves obliged to cross the Seine below Rouen, where they again suffered severely from Allied air attack. Troops under General Bradley's command, including a French armoured division, entered Paris on August 24th and 25th, to find the capital comparatively undamaged. Meanwhile the Allied landing long planned for the south of France had taken place on August 15th—having survived criticism on strategic grounds from Churchill and the British Chiefs of Staff almost to within a week of the actual assault. This new assault force, consisting predominantly of American and French troops, met only weak opposition; Toulon and Marseilles were soon captured and southern France was cleared within a few weeks. On September 15th the force came under the control of General Eisenhower, who had now moved his headquarters from England to France.

4. Bradley, *Soldier's Story*, p. 377.

Even among the troops in Northern France, the preponderance of the Americans over the British was rapidly increasing, and it was natural that strategic control of the Allied armies should be claimed by the stronger partner in the alliance. On September 1st Eisenhower assumed this responsibility, and although an agreement to this effect had been made before the landings began, Montgomery was distinctly disappointed when it happened. He was also disturbed to find that Eisenhower believed in an advance on a wide front, rather than a single thrust. It was now Montgomery's view that there should be a strong punch through Belgium towards the Ruhr, and that virtually all the Allied supplies should be concentrated on this. After some argument he obtained agreement for something rather less than this—that the advance of his 21st Army Group on the left flank should have a degree of priority for supplies and that it should have the use of three airborne divisions now held in reserve.

At first, the rapid progress of mid-August was continued. After crossing the Seine Montgomery's armoured divisions found themselves in open country which aided their advance. The Somme bridges at Amiens were seized on August 31st; Brussels fell on September 2nd and Antwerp on the 4th. But enemy garrisons remained in the Channel ports, and Antwerp could not be used until both coasts of the Scheldt estuary had been cleared. Instead of concentrating on the clearing of the Scheldt—which was really the most important task unless the enemy was already in a state of collapse—Montgomery gambled on a thrust northwards into Holland, in the hope of winning a bridgehead across the Rhine which he could exploit on the open country of North Germany (Operation 'Market-Garden'). On September 17th the two American airborne divisions were dropped ahead of the British Second Army to secure the aproaches as far as Nijmegen, and the British division was dropped still further forward to cover the Rhine bridge at Arnhem. The American drops were successful and the troops were soon relieved by a rapid British

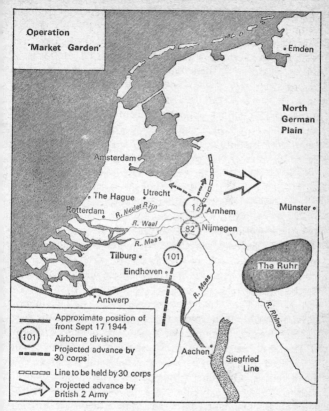

Operation
'Market Garden'

Emden •

North
German
Plain

Amsterdam •

The Hague •      Utrecht •

Rotterdam •    R. *Neder Rijn*     16  Arnhem     Münster •

R. *Waal*    82   Nijmegen

R. *Maas*

Tilburg •       101

Eindhoven •                    R. *Maas*       The Ruhr

Antwerp •                                      R. *Rhine*

————    Approximate position of
         front Sept 17 1944

( 101 )   Airborne divisions

- - - -   Projected advance by
         30 corps                   Aachen •    Siegfried
                                                  Line
□□□□□    Line to be held by 30 corps

⟹       Projected advance by
         British 2 Army

advance up the main road; but the Arnhem force met
strong opposition, failed to secure the Rhine bridge and
after suffering heavy casualties had to be withdrawn across
the river.

It now became clear that enemy resistance was stiffening
and could not be overcome until the supply position was
improved by the opening of the port of Antwerp. The
best campaigning season was over and the chances of
ending the war in 1944 were rapidly fading. While the

Second Army held its salient, Montgomery directed the
Canadian Army to the now increasingly difficult task of
clearing the Scheldt. The southern coast of the estuary was
occupied in October, and on November 1st an invasion
of the island of Walcheren was launched. But the first
convoy of supply ships was not able to enter the port of
Antwerp until November 28th. And although the Allied
armies were pressing against the enemy along the German
border down to Switzerland, shortages of supply prevented
them from mounting any major offensive before the New
Year. In spite of the great victories which had been won,
the chance of ending the German war in 1944—perhaps in
reality never a very substantial chance—had slipped away
in the critical days of mid-September.

Exactly a week after the launching of the assault on the
Normandy beaches—in the early hours of June 13th—a
small pilotless plane or flying bomb with a tongue of
flame from its exhaust, 'making a noise like a Model-T
Ford going up a hill',[5] crossed the Channel from France
and exploded at Gravesend. Three other similar bombs
arrived that night, but only one of them caused casualties.
But this was the beginning of a new type of bombardment
of England, which became more and more severe: soon
a hundred flying bombs a day were being recorded by
the defences. On June 18th one of them hit the Royal
Military Chapel at Wellington Barracks between Whitehall and Buckingham Palace, at a time when a service was
in progress, and 121 people were killed.[6] It was rare for
a single bomb to claim as many victims as this, for people
learnt to take cover when the engine cut out and the bomb
began its rapid descent. But the blast effect of the explosion was severe, and the many bombs which fell in
South London—particularly Croydon, Wandsworth and
Lewisham—caused a great deal of damage to housing. In
July and August about a million school-children and

5. Collier, *Defence of the U.K.*, p. 370.   6. *Ibid.*, pp. 377f.

mothers migrated or were evacuated from London and the South-East, mostly to safer areas in the West, the Midlands and the North.[7]

But this was no unexpected assault, at least so far as the government was concerned. Intelligence reports of the manufacture and testing of this weapon—the V.1 as it was called by Hitler—had enabled preparations to be made for dealing with it, and a series of concrete installations in Northern France which were designed as launching ramps had been heavily attacked by the RAF from December 1943 onwards. Now that the bombardment had begun, the air defences of London were redeployed towards the coast, so as to intercept the bombs over the sea or over open country, where they were likely to do little damage as they fell and exploded. While many were shot down by fighter aircraft, it was reasonable to expect the best results from predicted anti-aircraft gunfire, as the bombs flew on a set course. By late August, with the aid of advanced radar, improved predictors and shells with proximity fuses, some two-thirds of the bombs that were notified were being shot down from the ground.[8] By early September, when there was a lull caused by the overrunning of the bases originally used for launching, about nine thousand flying bombs had been despatched against England. Only about two-thirds of them performed sufficiently well to come within the range of observation in England; and slightly over half of these were destroyed by the defences.[9]

After mid-September the bombardment was resumed from bases in Germany, but as the range of the bombs was limited they had to be launched from aircraft. In the ensuing four months about 1200 bombs were launched, of which little more than half were so much as observed in England. Again a high proportion were shot down, and

7. Titmuss, *Social Policy*, p. 427.
8. Collier, *op. cit.*, p. 384.
9. *Ibid.*, p. 385.

so too were several of the launching aircraft. In March a few bombs capable of longer range were launched from ramps on the ground in Holland; but the offensive was now very weak and petered out before the end of the month. In spite of the casualties and damage that it had inflicted in England, the flying bomb had had little impact on the course of the war. It had caused some diversion of air striking power from the task of bombing Germany into defeat, but it had not retarded the progress of the armies on their way to the invasion of Germany.

But Hitler had a V.2 as well as a V.1, and this second 'secret weapon' was a long-range rocket, with a warhead of about a ton of explosive. The existence of this weapon was also known to British intelligence well before it was first used, but until a test rocket landed by accident in Sweden in mid-June 1944 there was much doubt about its capabilities. The first to land in England fell at Chiswick on September 8th. It was fired from Holland, and was the first of twenty-seven whose arrival was recorded in England, all in or near London, in the next ten days.[10] Casualties were not heavy, and for the time being no announcement was made about the new form of attack, which of course could not be observed before the explosion, except by reconnaissance of the launching pads. Some temporary dislocation of this new offensive took place owing to the rapid advance of Montgomery's forces into Holland in mid-September. But in October rocket explosions were occurring in the London area at the rate of two or three a day; and the rate increased later in the month and early in November. After the Germans had announced the existence of the new weapon, it was publicly confirmed by Churchill. The rocket attack went on throughout the winter, and on several occasions more than a hundred people were killed in a single explosion. Yet the casualty rate was never sufficiently large to cause any new exodus from London—on the contrary, the flying bomb evacuees were constantly trickling back to their homes. Fighter-

10. *Ibid.*, pp. 406f.

bomber attacks were made on the launching pads, with
a certain degree of success in reducing the scale of the
offensive. The last rocket to reach England fell on March
27th, when the rocket troops were withdrawn from Holland
to avoid capture. There had also been a few raids by
piloted aircraft on British airfields in the course of March;
but the last attack from the air against British soil was that
of the last flying bomb on March 29th. In total, the
flying bombs had killed 6184 civilians and the rockets
2754. These formed proportions of 10% and 4.5% res-
pectively of all British civilians killed in the war by
air attack or long-range bombardment.[11] It was reckoned,
though, that whereas all earlier air attack had resulted in
a cumulative total of three million houses destroyed or
damaged, the V.1 and V.2 offensives had increased this
total by about half.[12]

The missile attacks thus brought back to Londoners
many of the rigours of the Blitz, and more generally
exacerbated some of the major problems that it had left
behind. They also provided a sharp lesson on the vulnera-
bility of Britain to new forms of attack, just at a time
when the armed forces were at the peak of their strength
and superiority over the conventional forces of the enemy.
It was lucky indeed that the enemy had got no further in
the development of his devices, and that their deployment
could be so much hampered not only by air attack but
also by the progress of the Allied armies through northern
France and into Belgium and Holland.

Late in the summer of 1944 it seemed quite possible that
there would be a sudden collapse of German resistance.
The British Joint Intelligence Committee in fact expected
this to happen, but Churchill was less sanguine, noting
early in September 'the probability of a lull in the magnificent advances we have made.'[13] At this time he was
on his way to Quebec for another meeting with Roosevelt.

11. *Ibid.*, p. 528.      12. Titmuss, *op. cit.*, pp. 328f.
13. Ehrman, *Grand Strategy*, v, 402.

Whatever might happen in Europe, there were urgent decisions to be taken about the future course of the war in the Far East.

So far the British contribution to the war against Japan had not been on a large scale. The South-East Asia Command under Admiral Lord Louis Mountbatten was a British responsibility, but its priority for scarce equipment and supplies was low, and Mountbatten also suffered from the disadvantage of not having full control of all the Allied forces in the area. This was largely because of the differing aims of Britain and the United States. The Americans sought to re-open the Burma Road to China, so that China might play a more effective role in the war against Japan. The British on the other hand did not want to become too heavily involved in large-scale land warfare in the interior of Burma, arguing that it would be better to hold a line on the Indian frontier and to proceed to an offensive by sea against Singapore and Malaya. It was not the British view that much was to be gained by trying to strengthen China, a country racked by civil war and corruption.

The main forces in the region early in 1944 consisted of the British Fourteenth Army, under General Sir William Slim, a veteran of the Burma retreat, and a number of Chinese divisions more or less under the command of the American General Stilwell. Mountbatten had hoped to co-ordinate operations by these two forces under General Sir George Giffard, his land forces commander; but Stilwell who was Chiang Kai-shek's military adviser and hence partly under his orders refused to accept this arrangement, though he undertook for a time to take directives from Slim.[14] The air forces in the theatre, mostly British to begin with but also containing a substantial and increasing American contribution, were effectively integrated under British command, except for the US Transport Command planes used for the air ferry to China.[15]

14. Slim, *Defeat into Victory*, p. 207.
15. Kirby, *War against Japan*, iii, 439f.

But Mountbatten found that there were serious difficulties even in controlling the British forces, for as usual the Admiralty maintained its direct responsibility for the operations of the fleet against the enemy navy.[16]

The Fourteenth Army consisted mainly of Indian or African divisions with British officers, but it had two entirely British divisions and also some special Long Range Penetration groups under General Orde Wingate, whose unorthodox ideas about tactics had won Churchill's support. The army was a very different force from that which had had to face the first Japanese impact in 1942. Carefully trained by Slim in jungle warfare, and far better equipped than before, it had already gained an important success when in the spring of 1944 the Japanese attacked Imphal and Kohima, inside the Indian border, in the hope of cutting the existing lines of communication to China and raising the standard of revolt in India. Slim was not sorry to have the opportunity of fighting the Japanese on home ground; and with the aid of air transport he could deploy his forces with great flexibility. His garrison at Imphal was cut off for some time, but there was no difficulty about supplying it from the air, while the Japanese faced increasing supply problems of their own. When the monsoon began in the summer the battle had been won, and the Japanese Fifteenth Army—in reality, of about corps strength—had lost over half its effectives and fallen into a state of disintegration.[17]

Meanwhile Wingate's force—the Chindits as they were called—had been operating in support of Stilwell's Chinese divisions, which were advancing south through northern Burma with the object of opening up a new overland route of supply to China. Wingate's well-publicized exploits against the Japanese were in reality very expensive in casualties, but they had done much to improve the morale of British troops in the theatre.[18] It was therefore a great shock when Wingate was killed in an air crash in the

16. Ehrman, *op. cit.*, p. 144.   17. Kirby, *op. cit.*, p. 372.
18. *Ibid.*, p. 222.

course of these operations. But by early August the objects of Stilwell's campaign had been accomplished. The dual victory—Slim's and Stilwell's—opened up the prospect of clearing the whole of Burma more easily than had previously been thought. But future policy both in Burma and more generally in the Far East and the Pacific was still to be determined when the Allied leaders and their staffs met at Quebec in September.

Churchill was anxious that British forces should play a major part in the defeat of Japan. Political considerations certainly entered into his calculations in this theatre—perhaps because he could not take the Japanese quite so seriously as an enemy compared with the Germans. In February 1944 he had warned his colleagues on the Defence Committee that if American arms were alone responsible for expelling the Japanese from Malaya and the East Indies, the United States might demand 'a dominating say in their future', and also claim the control of the oil.[19] He favoured a British attack on Sumatra as a first step, but this was hotly opposed by the Chiefs of Staff, who eventually put forward an alternative proposal for an advance north-westwards from bases in Australia. All this, however, was outdated by the rapid American progress in the central Pacific. In spite of the standing agreement of the Combined Chiefs of Staff that the main Allied effort was to be directed against Germany, Admiral King had managed to secure sufficient resources to maintain a series of simultaneous offensives in the Pacific; and in the main thrust the Mariana Islands were captured in July and an assault on the Philippines was impending. The consequence was that Churchill had to abandon the idea of an advance from Australia, but instead decided to demand of the Americans a share for the British fleet in the main advance in the Pacific.

On the opening day of the Quebec conference, therefore, Churchill announced that 'the British Empire was ardent to play the greatest possible part' in the defeat of Japan.

19. Ehrman, *op. cit.*, p. 442.

He offered 'the British main fleet to take part in the major operations against Japan under United States Supreme Command.'[20] But although the offer was at once accepted by Roosevelt, it was apparent that King was distinctly reluctant, arguing that the bases available were inadequate even for the Americans, and evidently fearing that Churchill would demand a say in the strategy of the campaign. When the Combined Chiefs met to discuss the proposal, there was a rather curious exchange in which the British First Sea Lord thrust upon Admiral King a fleet of four battleships, five or six large and twenty small aircraft carriers, only to find that the American was 'not prepared to accept a British fleet which he could not employ or support . . . It would be entirely unacceptable for the British main fleet to be employed for political reasons in the Pacific and thus necessitate the withdrawal of some of the United States fleet.'[21]

All this was in any case only to take effect after the end of the war in Europe. In the meantime, there arose the question of what to do with the forces in Burma. The British Chiefs of Staff now felt that it was desirable to wind up the campaign as soon as possible. The Japanese forces had already been greatly weakened, and moreover the losses of the British Fourteenth Army from sickness were so heavy—they were running at seven times the level of battle casualties—that it was imperative to bring them out of their present positions as soon as possible. The British thought the campaign could best be completed by an air and sea assault directly on Rangoon; but the Americans preferred a continued movement southward by the land forces in northern Burma, to which a combined operation on Rangoon would be merely an adjunct. The American view prevailed, and Mountbatten was instructed to proceed with an advance southward by way of the Irrawaddy and Sittang valleys, and to prepare for a co-ordinated air and sea landing near Rangoon.[22]

20. *Ibid.*, p. 518.     21. *Ibid.*, pp. 520f.
22. *Ibid.*, pp. 500-503.

For the success of the ensuing campaign in Burma much of the credit must go to Slim, who was certainly one of the ablest field commanders thrown up by the experience of war. He completely outmanoeuvred the Japanese troops defending the Irrawaddy, forcing the river barrier by improvised means at points much farther south than where his attack was expected. Although the Fourteenth Army had complete air superiority—an invaluable boon both for reconnaissance and supply—it was short of engineering equipment and had also lost the collaboration of the Chinese divisions, which had been withdrawn for the defence of their homeland. As the Army pushed rapidly ahead it secured a degree of assistance from the Burma National Army, a body formed by the Japanese but now willing to change sides, for the Japanese had not endeared themselves to the native population.[23] As the monsoon approached, the Japanese evacuated Rangoon in order to safeguard the road into Siam. On May 2nd Rangoon was re-occupied peacefully by newly-landed forces and a few days later they made contact with the troops moving southwards from the Sittang valley. Thus before the end of the war in Europe virtually the whole of Burma had been freed from the Japanese.

As the ring of armies tightened the noose around Germany it became more and more necessary for the Western Allies to make firm agreements with the Russians, both about the strategy of the concluding phases of the war, and about the allocation of political responsibilities. There could be no autumn meeting of the three leaders along the lines of the Teheran conference, as Roosevelt was engaged in a new presidential election; but Churchill particularly wanted to meet Stalin to discuss the future of Poland and the Balkans. Poland was a country of special interest to Britain, for it was on Poland's behalf that Britain had entered the war, and Polish forces of about 150,000 men were fighting under British control. A Polish

23. Slim, *op. cit.*, pp. 484f.

government recognized by the Western Allies had been
established in London since 1940. But when the Russians
entered Polish territory, they established a Polish 'committee' of their own at Lublin. Relations between Russia
and the London Poles, which had never been friendly, became even worse when early in August the people of
Warsaw rose in revolt against the Germans. The Russians
not only failed to do anything to help them even by air, but
actually refused to allow British or American aircraft to
land in Russian-held territory after dropping arms or
supplies. The struggle in Warsaw went on for more than
sixty days, but it ended in the massacre of the resistance
fighters after bitter house-to-house fighting. The impact
of this news in Britain was, temporarily at least, considerable: Harold Nicolson noted in his diary that 'distrust
of the Russians is universal, and by no means confined to
the right or middle wings.'[24] It may be that part of the
explanation lay in a Russian desire to divert the weight
of the attack to a different part of the front. Certainly
the Red Army now began to make rapid gains in the
Danube area: aided by a revolution in Rumania and by
a change of sides by the Bulgarian army, it was able to
advance into Hungary, make contact with Tito's Yugoslav partisans and force a German withdrawal from
Greece.

The British interest in Rumania and Bulgaria at this
time was slight, but the Greek government in exile, like
the Polish, depended on Britain for support and had forces
serving under British command. Furthermore, British
troops had fought in Greece in 1941, and Britain therefore
had a claim to regard the country as within her sphere.
As for Yugoslavia, the problem was not so easy. It was
clear that Tito's partisans formed much the most effective
resistance to the Germans; and the British government had
done what it could to assist them, in spite of Tito's hostility to the exiled King Peter, who was in England. But
Tito was a Communist, and now that he was in touch with

24. Nicolson, *Diaries*, ii, 404.

the Russians on the eastern flank he made it his business to co-operate with them more closely than with the British or Americans.

Churchill's first move when he visited Stalin in Moscow in October was to come to terms on the allocation of responsibilities for the Balkans. Although he was now worried about Russian expansion,[25] he was not seeking to determine a permanent division of spheres of influence for the post-war period, but to make an interim arrangement so as to safeguard the respective interests of the great powers in the concluding phases of the war. Churchill jotted down on a half-sheet of paper his ideas of the relative degree of control by the great powers in the Balkans as follows:

| | |
|---|---|
| Rumania: | Russia, 90%, The others, 10% |
| Greece: | Great Britain (in accord with USA) 90%, Russia, 10% |
| Yugoslavia: | 50-50% |
| Hungary: | 50-50% |
| Bulgaria: | Russia, 75%, The others, 25% |

Stalin 'took his blue pencil and made a large tick upon it.'[26] In this way Churchill, whom some historians have supposed to have had major strategic interests in the Balkans, himself proposed to limit the area of effective British control to Greece, and acknowledged Russian predominance in both Rumania and Bulgaria, with a half share in Yugoslavia and Hungary.

But when it came to the question of the future of Poland no agreement could be achieved. It was clear that the Lublin Poles were as Churchill wrote after meeting their leaders 'purely tools', who 'recited their parts with well-drilled accuracy'.[27] Mikolajczyk, the leader of the London Poles, who had been summoned to Moscow, could not come to terms with them for the formation of a joint

25. Ismay, *Memoirs*, p. 367.
26. Churchill, *Second World War*, vi, 198.  27. *Ibid.*, p. 209.

government, though he promised to try to persuade his colleagues that the eastern frontier of Poland should be, as the Russians demanded, the Curzon Line drawn up in 1919. But when Mikolajczyk returned to London he found that he could not get his colleagues to agree even to this. The Polish question thus remained without a solution.

Meanwhile the Germans were pulling out of Greece, and as soon as the withdrawal began British and Greek troops of the Allied Mediterranean Command moved in to occupy key points in the Peloponnese and to establish, under General R. M. Scobie, a headquarters in Athens. This became a major commitment for British troops, owing to a threat of a *coup d'état* by Greek Communist guerillas of an organization called ELAS. The guerillas had harassed the retreating Germans, and naturally won British approval for this, but they now sought to seize control of Athens. Churchill, having made his agreement with Stalin, had no hesitation in ordering Scobie to resist any such attempt, telling him emphatically to 'act as if you were in a conquered city where a local rebellion is in progress.'[28] The message somehow got into the American press and raised a storm of criticism. The new American Secretary of State, Edward Stettinius, linked Greece with Italy in a statement declaring that the United States expected newly liberated countries 'to work out their problems of government along democratic lines without influence from outside.'[29] And at home, much to Churchill's annoyance even *The Times* took a critical line, saying that

> It is inconceivable that the British liberation armies . . . should be asked to coerce or conquer a section of a liberated and allied people which, only a few weeks ago, was engaged in active and gallant resistance to the Germans.[30]

28. *Ibid.*, p. 252.
29. Stettinius, *Roosevelt and the Russians*, p. 56.
30. *The Times*, 14 Dec., 1944.

Eden was in favour of a compromise whereby the King of Greece would not return to Athens but would appoint a regent to form a coalition government, including ELAS representatives. Churchill would not at first agree, but at Christmas he flew out to Athens with Eden, accepted the idea of a coalition government under Archbishop Damaskinos, and held a conference of all parties.[31] A truce was arranged, to be followed by a demobilization. Throughout the entire crisis the Russian newspapers had uttered no word of criticism of Churchill's conduct, and no Russian aid had been given to the Greek Communist guerillas.

Roosevelt had not been happy about the Churchill-Stalin meeting in his absence, for, as he wrote to Stalin at the time,

> There is in this global war literally no question, either military or political, in which the United States is not interested.[32]

He therefore hoped for an early meeting of the big three leaders as soon as the presidential election was over; and in due course this was arranged for February 1945. Since Stalin refused to leave Russia, on the grounds that he had personally to direct the Red Army's winter campaign, the meeting had to be held in the Crimea, at Yalta. Here, among 'the villas and palaces . . . of an extinct imperialism and nobility', as Churchill put it,[33] the heads of the three nations met to dispose the fate of the world.

It is sometimes maintained that at Yalta the Western Allies made undue concessions to the Russian point of view, and so rendered the post-war settlement of the world, and particularly that of Europe and Asia, more

31. Woodward, *British Foreign Policy*, 361f.; Dixon, *Double Diploma*, pp. 129f.

32. Sherwood, *White House Papers*, p. 825.

33. Churchill, *op. cit.*, vi, 314.

difficult than it might have been. To be sure, the Russians were in a strong position at this time. The armies of the Western Allies had lately been on the defensive in Europe, while the Russians were sweeping forward rapidly in their winter offensive. In the Far East, the Americans were very anxious to commit Stalin to taking part in the war against Japan, and were willing to make territorial concessions to her at Japan's expense. Finally, Roosevelt was no longer in good health and it was at least possible that he would make dangerous errors in the course of the negotiations. But in fact Stalin seemed to show a spirit of compromise, and so far as the formal agreements of the conference are concerned, they indicate an attitude of give and take by the Russians as well as by the British and Americans.

The conference reviewed the proposals for a post-war peace-keeping organization, which had been drawn up at a conference of representatives of the three powers at Dumbarton Oaks, near Washington, in the late summer and early autumn of 1944. It had been agreed that the great powers—that is, Russia, the United Kingdom, and the United States, with the possible addition of France and China—should have the right of veto on any proposal to enforce a collective decision in an international dispute. This was in line with Roosevelt's view that there was a sharp distinction to be drawn between the great powers, which were strong enough to undertake peace-keeping operations, and the other powers which were not. But disagreement developed over a Russian proposal which went even further in asserting the supremacy of the great over the small. The Russians demanded that the veto should be available for use by a great power even in disputes in which it was directly involved. They also claimed separate representation for all the sixteen republics of the Soviet Union, because they understood that all the British Dominions and also India, which was not self-governing, were to be represented. At Yalta Stalin gave some way on both these questions. The veto was not to apply in places where the great powers were directly involved, unless it was proposed to resort to force. As for the representation of the Soviet republics, it was agreed that two of them only —the Ukraine and Byelo-Russia—should be given places in addition to that for the Union of Soviet Republics.[34]

So far as the future of Germany was concerned, the conference accepted in general a plan for occupation zones which had been drawn up by a Commission of the great powers sitting in London, but it also agreed that the French should be assigned a zone, to be carved out of the territory to be allotted to the British and Americans. It was really the British who were insistent on the allocation of a zone to France, and Churchill's concern about this question was heightened by a remark of Roosevelt's to the effect that he did not expect American troops to stay in Europe for more than two years.[35] All four powers were to share in the occupation of Berlin, but for the rest the western powers were to be confined to western Germany, with Britain occupying the northern part, including the whole of the Ruhr and also the North Sea coast, with the exception of an American enclave for supply purposes at Bremen. Churchill and Roosevelt accepted the Russian demand that Germany should pay reparations, and were quite willing, in view of the devastation of the Soviet Union by the invaders, that the lion's share of these should go to Russia; but they avoided committing themselves to any particular figure, remembering the difficulties that had arisen as a result of this after the First World War.

It was with the question of Poland that the conference had most difficulty. Almost all of pre-war Poland was now in Russian occupation, and the western powers were in a weak position to make a bargain. They accepted the Curzon Line as the eastern border of Poland, which meant transferring Lvov, undoubtedly a Polish city, to the Russians. Churchill was already committed to the Curzon Line, which had after all originally been drawn

34. Stettinius, *op. cit.*, pp. 261f; Hull, *Memoirs*, 1701, 1705.
35. Churchill, *op. cit.*, vi, 308.

by a British Foreign Secretary. But neither Churchill nor Roosevelt could agree to a Russian proposal that Poland's western frontier should run along the western Neisse river, which meant the transfer to Poland of a very large slice of Germany. The matter was left undecided, though the western leaders indicated that they did favour some concessions to Poland at the expense of Germany's eastern provinces. So far as a new Polish government was concerned, they tried to ensure that it should contain a fair representation of non-Communist Poles, and that it should not simply be an enlargement of the Lublin government. Stalin finally agreed to accept the word 're-organization' rather than 'enlargement' in the communiqué, and he accepted that free elections should take place as soon as possible. More than this, Roosevelt and Churchill could not obtain; and it was obvious that the future freedom of Poland would depend on Russian good faith.

Finally, Russia promised to enter the war against Japan in 'two or three months' after the German surrender, and in return the western powers agreed to Russian acquisition of the Kurile Islands, to the north of Japan, and to the restoration of all the gains taken from Russia by Japan at the end of the Russo-Japanese war in 1904-5. These were the most important concessions made by the western powers; they were made on American initiative and with the object of shortening the Pacific War, which was still expected to last some eighteen months after the end of the war in Europe.[36]

The western leaders left Yalta with the feeling that they had laid the basis of genuine three-power co-operation after the war. Their main misgivings were in respect to Poland. Churchill indeed had a difficult passage in the House of Commons on this question, for 25 members, mostly of the Conservative right wing, went into the lobbies against him, and a junior minister, H. G. Strauss, resigned from the government. Nor did it take more than a few weeks for the fears then voiced to receive confirma-

36. Ehrman, *op. cit.*, vi, 237.

tion. In Poland and elsewhere in Eastern Europe the Russians refused to proceed even in accordance with the letter of their commitments at Yalta. On April 12th Roosevelt wrote to Churchill to say that while many of the problems that arose in relations with Russia could easily be solved, 'we must be firm'.[37] But the Anglo-American collaboration suffered a grievous blow on the same day when Roosevelt suddenly died of a cerebral stroke. His successor, Vive-President Harry S. Truman, had had no part in the higher conduct of the war and had not even met either Churchill or Stalin. It was by no means clear that in the future western policy towards Russia would pursue a definite and consistent purpose.

In the early stages of the invasion of Europe, British public opinion was too much concerned with the outcome of the battles in France to pay much attention to domestic politics. The successes of Allied arms muted criticism of the government's conduct of the war. But the flying bombs and rockets, although they were regarded as Parthian shots from an enemy already doomed to defeat, had the effect of drawing attention to the housing shortage, which more and more people came to realize was the gravest of Britain's domestic problems. Already a good deal of labour was devoted to repairing bomb damage; some requisitioning of property in London took place; and in heavily damaged areas people were accommodated in temporary huts. In November Churchill put his energetic son-in-law, Duncan Sandys, in charge of the Ministry of Works in the hope that he could do something to speed up plans for prefabricated houses as an emergency measure; and early in the New Year limited supplies of such houses were actually imported from the United States. But it did not seem to be possible to envisage that more than 300,000 permanent houses could be built or building within two years of the end of the war in Europe.

To ensure that houses were built in the right places, a

37. Stettinius, *op. cit.*, p. 278.

Town and Country Planning Act was passed through
Parliament in the summer and autumn of 1944. Its purpose
was to enable local authorities to direct the rebuilding of
towns in accordance with the general convenience. Compulsory purchase of 'blitzed', 'blighted' (i.e. slum), and
'overspill' areas was authorized. Arrangements for compensation caused controversy more or less on party lines,
but it was finally agreed that pre-war prices should be
taken as the basis, with the concession of certain increases
in special cases. Late in 1944 a plan for Greater London
drawn up by Professor Patrick Abercrombie was published.
It showed what could be done in the way of planning for
development. He envisaged a 'Green Belt' of open land
around London beyond which some eight to ten 'satellite
towns' would be built to house the surplus population from
overcrowded inner districts.

The Town and Country Planning Act was a piece of
legislation that had been in gestation for a long time. But
a spate of White Papers in 1944 showed that Woolton's
Ministry of Reconstruction was speeding up the pace
of policy decisions. In February a plan for a national health
service was published: under its terms, a number of
regional Joint Hospital Authorities were to be set up,
consisting of groups of local authority hospitals. The
voluntary hospitals were to be invited to join, but not
forced to do so. These proposals met with a generally
warm welcome on all sides, though the doctors were doubtful about their status in the new system. In May a White
Paper on Employment Policy announced Treasury conversion to Keynesian ideas about the use of fiscal means
to avoid cyclical unemployment. This document also proposed that areas subject to structural unemployment
should be encouraged to develop new industries, along
lines suggested by the Barlow Report of 1940. In September a White Paper on Social Insurance was published. It
followed the Beveridge Plan more closely than public
opinion—influenced by the government's critics—had been
led to expect, proposing slightly higher rates for old age

pensions but rather less for family allowances. A separate paper issued at the same time dealt with Workmen's Compensation, accepting Beveridge's proposal that compensation for industrial injuries should henceforth be a public responsibility rather than, as it had been since 1897, that of the employer. A Ministry of National Insurance was to be set up, and Sir William Jowitt was designated as the first minister.

By the end of the summer it looked as if the war in Europe would soon be over, and this had the effect of quickening interest in the prospects of a general election and party politics generally. In October the Prime Minister announced that unless all parties in the Coalition wished it to continue until after the end of the war with Japan, a general election would be held soon, but not too soon, after the end of the war in Europe. The Executives of both the Liberal and Labour Parties had already announced that they intended to fight the election independently; and their annual conferences, held in the winter, endorsed the view that the election must take place shortly after Germany's defeat. The Labour Party conference, which took place in December while the Greek embroglio was at its worst, was as Dalton remarked 'surprisingly quiet',[38] though a resolution demanding a wide extension of public ownership was passed against the wishes of the Executive. It was the general feeling that the Coalition should end fairly soon, but nobody seemed to want to break it up immediately.

In the early months of 1945 there were several instances of partisan speech-making by ministers, which certainly presaged the return of conflict between the main parties. Churchill, speaking at a Conservative Party conference in March, criticized the Labour Party for adopting, 'much to the disgust of some of their leaders', a programme of nationalization, and he went on to say that he would hope to have in his reconstructed government, after the withdrawal of the other parties, 'men of goodwill' of any

38. Dalton, *Fateful Years*, p. 431.

party or no party.[39] This seemed to be a bid for the
support of Ernest Bevin, who was known to hold the
Parliamentary Labour Party in contempt. But Bevin
replied to this early in April with a vigorous attack on the
Conservatives and a pledge to stand by the Labour Party.
His speech was almost immediately answered, for the
Conservatives, by Brendan Bracken.[40] With ministers
delivering onslaughts against each other in this way, it
was time that the Coalition dissolved. But the final signal
had to come from the battlefields of Germany.

At the beginning of the winter the area of Nazi control
in Europe had declined considerably from its high peak,
but it still included, besides Germany and Austria, the
whole of Norway, Denmark and Czechoslovakia, most of
Holland and half of the Baltic States, Poland, Hungary
and Yugoslavia, together with northern Italy, where the
Allied command had been weakened by supplying troops
for the invasion of southern France. In the west, the loss
of France and Belgium meant that targets in Germany
could now be attacked far more easily from the air, and
when the strategic air offensive was resumed by RAF
Bomber Command, by the Eighth US Air Force and, from
bases in Italy, by the Fifteenth US Air Force, it surpassed
all records for intensity and weight. In the last three months
of 1944 Bomber Command alone dropped more bombs
than in the whole of 1943, and three times as many as in
the whole of 1942; and in the course of twenty-four hours
it dropped as heavy a bomb-load on the town of Duisburg
as had fallen on London throughout the war. Improved
bomb-aiming methods also meant much greater accuracy,
and with adequate fighter cover Bomber Command increasingly emulated the Americans in attacking by day.

Until the summer of 1944 the German war effort had
apparently suffered surprisingly little from air raids:
indeed, until July production steadily rose, coaxed by the

39. *The Times*, 16 Mar., 1945.
40. *The Times*, 9 and 10 Apr., 1945.

managerial skill of Albert Speer. Under interrogation after the war, Speer maintained that the British bombing made little difference because it built up only slowly, which allowed people to get used to it, and because it concentrated on area bombing, rather than on key industrial targets. The Americans, on the other hand, were more successful because they went for synthetic chemical plants, ball-bearing plants and other vital industries.[41] But both Air Chief Marshal Harris of Bomber Command and General Spaatz of the US Strategic Air Forces were now receiving directives which ordered them to give first priority to the attack on oil, which was an obvious weakness of the German war machine after the loss of Rumania. The trouble was that Harris still did not believe that anything but area bombing could win the war. Relying upon his close association with the Prime Minister, he continued to follow his own policy and defied Portal, the Chief of Air Staff, to relieve him of his command.[42] All the same he did attack some oil targets; and this, with Spaatz's contribution, had the effect of crippling the Luftwaffe and increasingly weakening the German Army's ability to wage mobile warfare. Harris was also obliged to agree to put into effect a plan drawn up by Air Chief Marshal Tedder, on behalf of General Eisenhower, to destroy communications in the Ruhr area as a preparation for the final advance across the Rhine.

Probably the most controversial of Bomber Command's raids was that on Dresden on February 13th, 1945. Dresden was not an industrial target, but it was a large city and as such figured on Harris's list of those whose working population had eventually to be 'de-housed'. But it was Churchill personally who insisted on the bombing of this and other targets in eastern Germany on the eve of his trip to Yalta, probably so that he could indicate to the Russians that the Western Allies were doing all they could to aid their winter offensive. Dresden, which was also attacked

41. Webster and Frankland, *Strategic Air Offensive*, iv, 383.
42. *Ibid.*, iii, 79f and 93.

heavily by the Americans, was at this time only fifty miles behind the German lines, and it could reasonably be argued that it was an important communications centre. But such military assistance as the Russians received from the bombing was won at an appalling cost in civilian lives. In the course of the raids it is estimated that some 135,000 people died.[43] Reports of the raids caused Churchill to experience a feeling of revulsion against area bombing. In a minute to the Chiefs of Staff late in March (which he later withdrew) he spoke of it as raising 'a serious query against the conduct of Allied bombing', and he deplored 'mere acts of terrorism and wanton destruction.'[44] But by April, owing to the collapse of German resistance, there was no longer any need to continue the strategic air offensive.

Meanwhile the Allied forces on the Western Front had not had much reason during the winter to feel that the enemy was on the point of defeat. In mid-December Field Marshal von Rundstedt, who had been re-appointed to command of the armies facing Eisenhower, on Hitler's orders began an offensive in the Ardennes. Aided by bad weather, which limited air reconnaissance, his armoured forces broke through the weakly-held positions of the First US Army, and moved towards the Meuse. But the shoulders of the bulge were firmly held, and Bradley was able to throw in some mobile reserves to hold key points such as the crossroads at Bastogne. On December 19th Eisenhower temporarily transferred the command of the First and Ninth US Armies to Montgomery, who quickly re-grouped the forces north of the break-through area; but by December 24th the enemy had reached the limit of his resources. The weather now improved, allowing heavy air attack; and soon the battered remnants of all the German armoured reserves were in retreat to their start line.

Now that his supply position had improved, Eisenhower

43. Irving, *Destruction of Dresden*, p. 7.
44. Webster and Frankland, *op. cit.*, iii, 112.

was planning to resume his advance with, first of all, a clearance of the Rhineland so as to secure the river line as a defence against counter-attack; and then a two-pronged advance north and south of the Ruhr, with the intention of surrounding and capturing the entire industrial complex of that area. It was his idea to make the more northerly of these two thrusts his principal effort, and this meant allowing Montgomery to retain control of the Ninth US Army as well as of the Second British and First Canadian. The campaign began on February 8th, with an advance by the British and Canadians eastward from the Nijmegen salient. Two weeks later the Americans joined in, and in a few days the entire Rhineland was cleared and, by a stroke of good fortune, a bridgehead across the Rhine was secured at Remagen, where the retreating enemy failed to blow the bridge.

At this point it was clear that the enemy resistance was weakening. On the Eastern Front rapid advances were being made by the Russians, and Warsaw and Budapest had fallen. On the night of March 23rd/24th Montgomery's troops crossed the Rhine at Wesel, with a British and an American airborne division dropping ahead to seize key points. Enemy resistance was comparatively weak, and on March 29th largely gave way, enabling a rapid advance on to the North German Plain. American troops encircled the Ruhr, joining hands with the southern spearhead at Lippstadt on April 1st; Field-Marshal Model with a third of a million German troops were cut off inside this trap. At the same time the Canadians moved north to cut off enemy forces in Holland and the British Second Army headed for Hamburg.

The end was now very near. Churchill thought that political advantages would accrue if Eisenhower made straight for Berlin and entered the city before the Russians. Eisenhower, however, would not agree to any departure from his planned course of operations unless the American Chiefs of Staff concurred—which they did not.[45] He was

45. Ehrman, *op. cit.*, vi, 136-145.

concerned about the possibility of continued enemy resistance in the mountains of south Germany, though in the event this turned out to be a false alarm. Bradley's troops therefore advanced south-east, keeping the line of the Elbe on their left, while Montgomery went to Hamburg and across the river as far as Lübeck, partly in order to seal off Denmark from any possible Russian advance.

The first major surrender, apart from that of Model's encircled forces, came on the Italian front, where a new offensive had begun early in April. By April 20th the Allied advance had reached the valley of the Po, and the German troops, without petrol for their vehicles, were in a hopeless plight. Italian anti-fascists took control in many areas and on April 28th seized and shot the former dictator, Mussolini. The German commander, General von Vietinghoff, on April 29th signed an act of unconditional surrender, to take effect on May 2nd. On April 30th Hitler, beleaguered in Berlin, shot himself, having named Admiral Doenitz as his successor. On May 4th a delegation from the Admiral surrendered the German forces in North Germany, Holland and Denmark to Montgomery; and on May 7th General Jodl for the German High Command, signed an instrument of surrender at Eisenhower's headquarters. This was formally ratified at another surrender ceremony in Berlin on May 9th, but already in Britain May 8th had been officially designated as 'VE Day'—the day when victory in Europe had been achieved and could be celebrated.

# 9.   The General Election and the Defeat of Japan

The end of the war in Europe meant a very great relief to the people of Britain. The rigours of life under the bombing, the V-weapons and the submarine blockade could now be regarded as things of the past, and the toll of casualties in the struggle against Germany came to an end. The war against Japan remained, but it was, for Britain, a war conducted at a very great distance and consequently in a less intense way. The distinction was recognized by the Whitehall planners, who spoke of the new phase as 'Stage II': they saw it as a period of gradual reconversion to a peacetime economy, for only a relatively small proportion of the nation's manpower could now be employed for the actual fighting, and the manufacture of munitions could be substantially cut. Provided Lend-Lease were continued at a moderate level, a certain improvement could be made in living conditions in Britain, and a start could be made on the capital re-equipment of the country's basic industries, which had gradually become worn out in the preceding five and a half years.

On Lend-Lease the United States Treasury largely accepted the British arguments, which were ably presented by Keynes in negotiations that followed the Quebec conference of September 1944.[1] It was agreed that aid should continue to the extent necessary not merely to maintain existing levels of consumption in Britain, but also to allow the levels to be somewhat raised. The supply of munitions under Lend-Lease would continue, primarily but not exclusively for the purposes of the Japanese War, and the British export trade, previously severely restricted, would be gradually resumed. But American policy began to

1. Blum, *Morgenthau Diaries*, iii, 319; Sayers, *Financial Policy*, pp. 470ff.

change as circumstances and personalities changed. After Roosevelt's death and the actual ending of the European War the American administration seemed to become much more aware of its Congressional critics; and this was reflected in a stricter interpretation of existing commitments. Only munitions directly required for the Far Eastern war continued to flow across the Atlantic. Supplies for other purposes, on which the British ministries had been basing their plans, unexpectedly failed to arrive, and when Churchill took the matter up with Truman he received only a vague response and a request to 'be patient'. This was disconcerting, not only for the immediate future, but also for the prospects of any sort of continuation of Lend-Lease in 'Stage III'—that is, the period after the Japanese war was over. But Stage III still seemed comparatively remote, as the Japanese were expected to continue their resistance through 1945 and almost to the end of 1946.[2]

Meanwhile the plans for partial demobilization, which the Ministry of Labour under Ernest Bevin had carefully drawn up, were put into operation in June. Age and length of service were the sole criteria for early release of able-bodied servicemen, except for a special category, not to exceed ten per cent of the total, of men with skills regarded as especially valuable for peacetime purposes—in particular, building workers and underground miners. Remembering the dangerous military unrest that occurred in 1919, the government was anxious to ensure that those who had to 'soldier on' this time should regard the system of demobilization as fair and reasonable. In June it was also decided to cut the maximum period of overseas service in the South-East Asia Command to three years and four months. This created considerable operational difficulties in the Command, where Mountbatten was planning a seaborne landing on the Malayan coast for September, and where in any case there was an acute shortage of transport to bring the men home.[3] But it was clear that the 'Forgotten Army' as it was sometimes called had to be

2. Ehrman, *Grand Strategy*, vi, 237.    3. *Ibid.*, pp. 249-251.

treated more generously in this matter than the forces stationed nearer home.

In Britain the Home Guard had been stood down in December 1944. Fire-watching duties had been abandoned in March 1945, and the black-out, which had been re-laxed in September 1944, was altogether lifted after the German surrender. The enemy garrison of the Channel Islands, which had been by-passed by the Normandy invasion, belatedly accepted the general surrender, and British troops took over the islands, finding to their relief that the remaining civilian inhabitants were in relatively good health. The Home Secretary was now able to revoke many of the Defence Regulations which had been in force since 1939 or 1940: among them were 18B and 18D, which gave him special powers for the detention of 'suspected persons' without trial.

The ending of the German war was also the signal for the ending of the Coalition Government itself. Churchill's Conservative Party advisers urged him to fight an election as soon as possible while his prestige as the architect of victory was at its height.[4] The course that he personally favoured however was to maintain the Coalition until after the end of the war against Japan. He therefore invited the Labour and Liberal leaders to accept one or other of these alternatives. Attlee was away at San Francisco attending the foundation conference of the United Nations Organization, which was being set up to keep the peace along the lines agreed at Yalta. But Morrison on Attlee's behalf suggested to Churchill that the Coalition Government should continue until the autumn, by which time a new and more accurate register of electors could be prepared, but not beyond the autumn, as it would not be seemly to pass yet another Prolongation of Parliament Act.[5] Tactically, this would have suited the Labour and Liberal Parties very well; and for the same reason, it did not appeal at all to Churchill. When Attlee returned from San

4. Churchill, *Second World War*, vi, 511.
5. *Ibid.*; Morrison to Attlee, 11 May, Bevin Papers.

Francisco a few days later, therefore, Churchill presented him with a letter which formally gave the Labour Party the choice of an immediate election or a continuation of the Coalition until after the defeat of Japan.[6] Attlee was personally inclined to favour the continuation of the Coalition, and he advised the National Executive of the Labour Party in this sense. But only three trade-union representatives were willing to support him,[7] and the Executive issued a recommendation to the Labour Party Conference, then in session at Blackpool, that Churchill's offer of a continuation of the Coalition should be rejected. Since Attlee did not publicly reveal his own attitude, the recommendation appeared to be a unanimous one and the conference had no difficulty in accepting it. Thus the extra-parliamentary organs of the Labour Party—the National Executive and the Conference—played their part in dismantling the Coalition government, as they had done in its establishment.

The Labour Party's decision was taken on May 21st. On May 23rd Churchill submitted his resignation to the King and thus formally terminated the life of the Coalition Government—a government which had taken office at a moment of impending disaster and which now broke up at a time of victory and impending victory. In place of the Coalition, Churchill formed a 'Caretaker' Government consisting of Conservatives, National Liberals, and such non-party men as were prepared to serve in the interim before the election. A Cabinet of sixteen members was constituted —a change from the War Cabinet of only half that number —but it contained very few newcomers to Whitehall. One of the few was Harold Macmillan, who had served with distinction as Minister of State in North Africa and Italy, and who now became Secretary for Air. Eden remained Foreign Secretary; Anderson continued as Chancellor of the Exchequer; and Bevin's place at the Ministry of Labour was taken by R. A. Butler. It was announced that

6. Churchill, *op. cit.*, vi, 515.
7. Diary, 19 May, 1945, Dalton Papers.

a general election would now take place on July 5th, which was the earliest possible date that could now be decently arranged.

There were considerable inaccuracies in the register on which the general election was fought, as the Labour Party was quick to point out. It had been compiled in January, but the work had been done by an inadequate staff; probably it could have been done again, and more accurately, in time for an autumn election. Nevertheless, even an autumn election would have suffered from the difficulty that many servicemen would still have been abroad, and many people would have been changing their residence within Britain as the gradual conversion of industry took place. Arrangements would have had to be made then, as they were in July, for servicemen to vote either by post or by proxy. Perhaps a larger proportion of them would have been registered, and a larger proportion of those registered would have been able to vote. In the July election it is apparent that the service vote was a good deal lighter than it should have been.[8] This was in spite of the fact that the count was held up for almost three weeks after polling day—from July 5th to July 25th—in order to ensure that the ballot papers could be sent in from the many service units overseas. Since the count was delayed, it was also possible to make special arrangements for constituencies in Britain where works holidays had already been arranged at election time. Polling for some twenty-two seats was delayed for this reason until July 12th, and for one seat until July 19th.

The Conservative election programme was entitled *Mr Churchill's Declaration of Policy to the Electors*. It emphasized the need for continuity of leadership at a time when the country was still at war and faced with formidable problems of reconstruction. For the rest, it outlined a policy of social reform along the lines of the White Papers already published by the Coalition Government. Labour's

8. McCallum and Readman, *Election of 1945*, p. 43.

manifesto, largely drafted by Morrison, was called *Let Us Face the Future*. It made no mention of Attlee, or any other leader; but it offered, in addition to a roughly similar programme of social reform, a stern policy towards 'bureaucratically-run private monopolies'; and it indicated a number of industries which, for one reason or another, it was proposed to take into public ownership—fuel and power, inland transport, iron and steel and the Bank of England. Iron and steel would probably not have been included if it had not been for the emphasis on 'heavy industry' in the resolution of public ownership carried against the Executive at the Labour Party Conference of 1944. As for external policy, there were few practical differences between the proposals of the two parties, but the Labour manifesto argued that before the war 'the Tories were so scared of Russia that they missed the chance to establish a partnership.'

It might be supposed that ministers and MPs who had for so long been in collaboration would have found it difficult to conduct a vigorous campaign of mutual criticism. Even among the electorate at large there was a considerable degree of support for the maintenance of Coalition government: a Gallup Poll held at this time found that people were about equally divided on the merits and demerits of its resumption after the election.[9] But Churchill himself took the view that the best means of securing the future of his government was to attack the Labour Party; and this he did at once, in his first election broadcast on June 4th. He declared roundly that Labour's commitment to Socialism would end, sooner or later, in the establishment of a political police like the Gestapo, 'no doubt very humanely conducted in the first instance'. This was an astonishing attack, so soon after the revelation of the worst atrocities of the Nazi regime; and Attlee, following him on the radio the next evening, invited the electorate to draw a distinction between Churchill the war leader and Churchill the party leader whose speeches

9. *News Chronicle*, 4 June, 1945.

were drawn up by other men: 'The voice we heard last night was that of Mr Churchill, but the mind was that of Lord Beaverbrook.'

Ten days later the Conservatives were able to take up another line of attack, and one which seemed to have much more substance in it—thanks partly to an indiscretion by the chairman of the Labour Executive, Professor Harold Laski. Churchill had invited Attlee to accompany him to the forthcoming three-power meeting at Potsdam, which was due to begin before the election results were known; and Laski at once published a statement to the effect that under the Labour Party constitution, Attlee would have no power to make any commitments for the future. Certainly the Labour Party constitution, as revised after the 1931 split, did seek to restrict the power of the party leader and required him to submit himself for re-election by the parliamentary party at the beginning of every session. Laski thought that Morrison would be a better party leader than Attlee and hoped to see the change as soon as Parliament re-assembled. But the Conservatives now had an opportunity of drawing the attention of the electorate to the possibility that Attlee would not be master in his own house, even if he won the election. Beaverbrook, however, went on to try to make Laski into a scapegoat, and accused him of aiming at 'the destruction of the Parliamentary system' and of seeking to establish 'the dictatorship of something commonly called the National Executive'.[10] Beaverbrook's newspaper the *Daily Express* also picked on a remark of Laski's at an election meeting which suggested that he favoured the use of force if Labour could not get what it wanted by constitutional means. Laski took out a writ against the *Daily Express*; and Attlee sought to develop a counter-offensive against Beaverbrook himself—a man, he said, with 'a record of political intrigue and instability' and with 'an insatiable appetite for power'.

10. *Daily Express*, 20 June, 1945, quoted McCallum and Readman, *op. cit.*, p. 148.

In spite of these polemics at the national level, the campaign in the constituencies was comparatively quiet. A Gallup poll showed that by far the most important issue, in the view of the electors, was Housing (41%). After this came Full Employment (15%), Social Security (7%) and Nationalization of Industry (6%).[11] A perceptive Labour candidate in the industrial Midlands remarked that

> Abstract questions such as controls versus freedom and complicated stories like the Attlee-Laski incident seem terribly far away in the streets and factories here. What people want to talk about is 'redundancy', housing, pensions and what will happen to ex-Servicemen after the war.[12]

Heckling at meetings was mostly directed against Conservative speakers; but Churchill himself received great ovations on a tour of the country, and only ran into noisy opposition when visiting East and South London just before polling day. From these surface manifestations and such other evidence as was at their disposal, the election managers found it difficult to judge what the outcome would be. Churchill told the King, no doubt on advice from Conservative Party agents, that he expected a majority of 'between thirty and eighty'.[13] The Labour leaders expected defeat, or a situation like 1929 in which no party had a clear majority.[14] Many people, and not only Liberals, predicted a considerable Liberal revival. The only accurate forecast was that of the Gallup poll published in the *News Chronicle*, which continued to suggest, as it had done for years, that an election would produce a Labour majority, and that the Liberals and minor parties would fare badly.

11. *News Chronicle*, 11 June, 1945.
12. *New Statesman*, 30 June, 1945.
13. Wheeler-Bennett, *George VI*, p. 635.
14. Williams, *Prime Minister Remembers*, p. 3; Dalton, *Fateful Years*, p. 466.

Since no important politician or journalist, not even anybody on the staff of the *News Chronicle*, paid serious attention to the Gallup poll, everyone was taken by surprise when the results began to flow in on the night of July 25th. By the afternoon of the next day Labour had a clear majority, and in the evening Churchill went to the Palace to resign. The King at once sent for Attlee, who arrived at 7.30 p.m. looking 'very surprised'[15]—as well he might, considering the hazards that might have prevented him from receiving this invitation. Morrison, who was a rival candidate for the party leadership, aided by Ellen Wilkinson, his most loyal supporter, and Laski, the party chairman, tried to insist on a new election for the leadership before Attlee accepted the Royal Summons;[16] and indeed, as we have seen, they had the letter of the party constitution on their side. But Attlee had to weigh this against the expectations of the country and the needs of the international situation, for Truman and Stalin were waiting impatiently at Potsdam for the resumption of the conference of the three powers. Showing the capacity for quiet decisiveness which was to be characteristic of his premiership, Attlee ignored Morrison's request and drew up a first list of senior ministers—including Morrison himself, who at once gave way and accepted the second place in the administration as Lord President of the Council. Bevin was to be Foreign Secretary; Arthur Greenwood returned to Whitehall as Lord Privy Seal, in charge of the social services; and Dalton became Chancellor of the Exchequer. Attlee had originally intended to make Bevin Chancellor and Dalton Foreign Secretary, but at the last minute he changed his mind. This was partly the result of advice from various quarters, including the King, who wanted Labour's strongest man to be at what he thought would be the post of danger.[17] But Attlee's main reason for the switch was his conviction

15. Wheeler-Bennett, *op. cit.*, p. 638n.
16. Dalton, *Fateful Years*, p. 467.
17. Wheeler-Bennett, *op. cit.*, p. 638.

that Morrison and Bevin 'must be kept apart' owing to their mutual animosity.[18]

A few days later, after the final stages of the Potsdam Conference—at which an official of the Foreign Office noted little change in the policy of the delegation but a change in its style from 'the gay regime of the Stuarts' to 'Hanoverian'[19]—Attlee returned to England and completed his Cabinet-making. The new Cabinet consisted of twenty members, four more than that of the Caretaker government; but it was Attlee's intention to reduce it when the Japanese War ended by excluding the heads of the three service departments and appointing instead a Minister of Defence—a responsibility which for the time being, following Churchill's example, he retained for himself. Among the members of the new Cabinet were the leading Labour critics of the Coalition government, Emanuel Shinwell (as Minister of Fuel and Power), and Aneurin Bevan (as Minister of Health). The final results of the election were now complete and the Labour Party had won 393 seats as against 213 for the Conservatives and their allies, 12 Liberals and 22 Independents. The new government thus had an overall majority of 148. The Independents included two Communists and one member of Common Wealth, the wartime movement of the Left which largely lost its *raison d'être* when the Labour Party went into Opposition in May.

The defeated Conservatives joined with the newspaper analysts in an attempt to account for their defeat, the worst they had experienced since 1906. The first reaction of *The Times* and the *Manchester Guardian* was to blame Churchill himself for the type of campaign that he had conducted. According to *The Times*, he had been at fault in 'emphasizing the narrow animosities of the party fight'.[20] The *Guardian* believed that his broadcasts and his 'attempt to turn the election into a personal plebiscite did him

18. Diary, 27 July, 1945, Dalton Papers.
19. Dixon, *Double Diploma*, p. 173.
20. *The Times*, 27 July, 1945.

immense harm.'[21] Naturally, this interpretation did not appeal to Churchill himself or his more loyal supporters. It was his personal view that the Conservatives had suffered because their organization was weaker than that of the Labour Party, whose stalwarts, he argued, were not on active service abroad like their Conservative counterparts but were relatively undisturbed by the war, as they were mostly industrial workers.[22] These short-term explanations ignore the fact that the electorate had been showing a persistent bias toward the Left at least since 1942. The campaign probably made little difference to this bias, except perhaps slightly to reduce it. The political transformation seems in general to have been a result of a general reaction against the years of Conservative rule, combined with a vague idea that Socialist planning had something to be said for it if the Russians could fight so hard and, in the long run, so successfully. The same leftward swing was apparent in other western European countries, where the Communists, already a major element in the resistance movements, tended to obtain much of the political advantage which in Britain went to the Labour Party. The new Labour MPs, though by no means predominantly a body of elderly trade-union officials as they had been in previous Parliaments, were yet for the most part devoid of genuinely revolutionary sentiments. But it was not entirely inappropriate that when Parliament re-assembled on August 1st, they should have sung the *Red Flag* in the Chamber of the House of Commons.

To those in the retiring Cabinet and the Foreign Office who had been dealing with increasing evidence of Russian intransigence in Europe and the Far East, this manifestation by the new Labour MPs seemed at best absurd and naïve, at worst a reason for real despondency about the future.[23] Stalin's failure to observe the Yalta agreements, particularly with respect to the establishment of a new

21. *Manchester Guardian*, 27 July, 1945.
22. Churchill, *op. cit.*, vi, 508f.
23. Dixon, *op. cit.*, p. 166.

government in Poland, had already aroused much concern among the western leaders. Churchill, who was inclined to take the initiative in the western alliance now that Roosevelt had died, sought to capitalize upon the fact that Eisenhower's forces had gone deeply into Germany and Austria and were temporarily occupying considerable areas which were allocated to the Russian zone of occupation. In his view, these areas could be used as bargaining counters to ensure that the Russians held to their obligation to provide facilities for the Allied participation in the control of Berlin and Vienna.[24] Churchill also suspected that Stalin had abetted Tito's action in seizing Trieste, the Italian port at the head of the Adriatic, which the Yugoslavs claimed from Italy, but which Field-Marshal Alexander needed to hold as a supply base for the occupation forces of the Western Allies in Austria. Truman joined Churchill in encouraging Alexander to take a strong line against Tito, and in the end the Yugoslav forces withdrew without bloodshed. But Truman made no move to encourage Eisenhower to bargain over the mutual adjustment of occupation forces in Germany and Austria; and the problem was solved when Stalin apologized for the delay and agreed to a simultaneous movement in all the areas concerned on July 1st.

Shortly after this date the Allied commands broke up: Eisenhower became a purely American commander, for the first time in three years, and Montgomery became the British Commander-in-Chief in Germany and the British representative on the four-power Control Commission for Germany. Meanwhile, military government officers were taking over from the fighting troops in the occupied zone, and efforts were being made to establish normal civilian life, by repairing shattered communications, and by repatriating prisoners of war and as many of the other 'displaced persons' as had homes to go to. Leading Nazis and also many German military commanders were detained to answer charges of war crimes: it had already been

24. Churchill, *op. cit.*, vi, 524.

agreed between the Allied governments that they would collaborate in establishing tribunals for this purpose. If anything, popular sentiment in Britain and America had hardened against the Nazis in the last few months as a result of the revelation of torture and genocide in the concentration camps.

By the summer of 1945 a meeting between the heads of government of the three leading Allied powers had become highly desirable. Truman had still not made the acquaintance of either Churchill or Stalin, and there was an immediate need for decisions about the establishment of machinery for drawing up the European peace treaties, and about ways and means of completing the war in the Far East. Truman thought it would be a good idea if he met Stalin informally before the conference began, and this caused some concern to Churchill, who feared that he was planning to make agreements between the two powers which would leave Britain out.[25] But this misunderstanding was soon cleared up and it was agreed that all three delegations should assemble simultaneously for the conference, which was to be held at Potsdam, the old Prussian royal residence near Berlin, beginning on July 15th. In view of the British elections, the conference was to go into recess for a few days on July 25th. The result of the count would determine whether Churchill or Attlee would lead the British delegation in the later stages of the conference.

When the delegations first met it was soon agreed that a Council of Foreign Ministers of the three powers and also France should be set up to meet regularly in the future to deal with the problems of the settlement of Europe. The Council was to meet in London in September for its first session. But on the actual matters which required immediate decision, the early stages of the conference brought no progress except such as could be obtained by a clarification of points of difference. There were sharp disagreements in particular over the Russian

25. *Ibid,* p. 503.

insistence on advancing the Polish frontier to the western Neisse, as compensation for the Russian frontier being moved forward to the Curzon line. Stalin also demanded reparation from Germany to a total which threatened to destroy the possibility of reviving the country's economy. When the recess came, Churchill went off to London planning to have a 'show-down' with the Russians on his return:[26] but instead, he was replaced by Attlee who was not in a position to play any such powerful role. But in any case Truman was anxious not to risk a break with Russia while his military advisers were still placing great importance on a Russian declaration of war against Japan as a means of saving American lives. It was a source of considerable gratification to Truman that Stalin did reassure him that Russia would declare war at an early date.[27]

It was to be expected, therefore, that Truman's new Secretary of State, James Byrnes, should do his best to produce a formula for papering over the differences between the powers which the early stages of the conference had revealed. Since it was apparent that the Russians were already stripping their own zone of Germany of all moveable industrial equipment and wealth, Byrnes accepted the inevitable and proposed that each country should take such reparations as it required from its own zone of occupation, but that the Russian claim for a larger share than that of the other powers should be met by the allocation of a small proportion from the western zones. After much haggling, an agreement was reached along these lines. On the frontier question, Britain and the United States agreed to accept for the time being that Poland should administer the German territory east of the western Neisse, without prejudice to the final settlement, and received certain assurances about 'free elections' in Poland, which were to take place early in 1946. It was also agreed that a first list of German war criminals for

26. *Ibid.*, p. 582.
27. Truman, *Year of Decisions*, p. 341.

joint trial should be drawn up within thirty days. All this was little enough to show for two and a half weeks of discussions among the powers which would control the destinies of the post-war world.

Meanwhile, there remained the Japanese war. The power of the United States was so far predominant in the campaign in the Pacific that there could be no real question of the British Chiefs of Staff taking a major role in the planning of strategy. They did try to assert a claim, but when the American Joint Chiefs refused to concede it, they had to give way.[28] Australian troops were playing an important part in the fighting in Borneo, which was under General MacArthur's command, and of course the forces under Mountbatten were overwhelmingly from British or Empire sources. But the main operation of the War would be the invasion of the Japanese Home Islands; and Churchill and the Chiefs of Staff felt that for political reasons it was essential that Britain should have some part in this. In accordance with the agreement made at Quebec in September 1944 a British fleet was despatched to join Admiral Nimitz's forces in the Central Pacific. It took part in attacks on the Ryukyu Islands, close to the Japanese Home Islands, in March, April and May, and in the summer it operated against the Home Islands themselves. By this time Allied superiority by sea and by air was so great that the fleet was able to operate in close proximity to enemy bases. The only serious danger was from Kamikaze or suicide pilots who flew their planes, loaded with explosives, with the intention of crashing on their targets. Although British warships were hit in this way, none were sunk.[29] For the future, there were plans for the establishment of a British bomber force at Okinawa, the island in the Ryukyus which the Americans had captured in March after several weeks' bitter fighting.

The main commitment of British ground forces, after the

28. Ehrman, *op. cit.*, vi, 271f.
29. Roskill, *War at Sea*, iii, Part II, pp. 346, 352f.

completion of the Burma campaign, was to be in Malaya, and it was hoped that Mountbatten would be able to make a landing in September with the object of clearing the peninsula and recapturing Singapore later in the year. But Churchill and the Chiefs of Staff also wanted the army to play a part in the final operations against the Japanese Home Islands, and their proposal was that a British Commonwealth force of several divisions should take part in the invasion of Honshu, now provisionally set for March 1946. The plan was considered by General Mac-Arthur on behalf of the American Command, and by late July 1945 he had boiled down the Commonwealth contribution to a contingent of three divisions, one British, one Canadian, and one Australian; all three were to be trained in American methods and were to use American equipment and supplies.[30] But further progress in the arrangements was interrupted by the sudden and unexpected collapse of Japanese resistance in August 1945.

The early Japanese surrender was largely due to the heavy pressure of blockade and bombardment that was brought to bear in the late spring and early summer of the year. By July the country's industrial output had dwindled to two-fifths of its wartime peak, and the output of shipyards and air engine factories was down to only a quarter.[31] The damage from bombing was already equivalent to that in Germany, about 40 per cent of the built-up area in some sixty-six cities having been destroyed.[32] A single raid on Tokyo in March killed more people than all the raids on Britain in six years of war. By the end of July the civilian members of the government were already advocating surrender, and only the military were resisting.[33] To be sure, in the prevailing state of Japanese politics the military view continued to be decisive. But it seems fair to conclude, in the words of the United States Strategic Bombing Survey, that 'air supremacy over Japan

30. Ehrman, *op. cit.*, vi, 269.
31. Craven and Cate, *Army Air Forces*, iii, 753.
32. *Ibid.*, p. 751.     33. Feis, *Atomic Bomb*, p. 113.

could have exerted sufficient pressure to bring about unconditional surrender and obviate the need for invasion'. This could probably have been accomplished by the beginning of November, when the landings on Kyushu were due to begin, and certainly by the end of the year.[34]

From the evidence available to the American Joint Chiefs of Staff at the time, however, it seemed that invasion would be necessary to ensure a Japanese surrender unless some psychological shock could be inflicted upon the country which would break the rigidity of the military minds. Henry Stimson, the American Secretary of War, wrote later:

> I felt that to extract a genuine surrender from the Emperor and his military advisers, they must be administered a tremendous shock which would carry convincing proof of our power to destroy the Empire.[35]

These tactics were certainly in tune with the experience of the air war in Germany, where enemy morale had only been severely shaken by air raids which were either unexpected, or unexpectedly heavy, as at Hamburg in 1943 and Dresden in 1945. Stimson therefore favoured the earliest possible use of the Allies' new secret weapon, the atomic bomb, which had been manufactured after some three years' work by scientists and engineers working under the control of his department. The first two bombs, which became available early in August, were to be used against military targets in Japan, but military targets which were surrounded by residential housing.

The atomic bomb was a joint Anglo-American invention. The feasibility of the project had been more or less established in a brilliant paper by two refugee scientists at Birmingham University, Otto Frisch and Rudolf Peierls, early in 1940. But it was largely the fear that scientists

34. Craven and Cate, *op. cit.*, p. 756.
35. Feis, *op. cit.*, p. 57.

in Germany might be engaged in similar work—a fear later shown to be unfounded—that impelled the two governments to explore the possibilities of development.[36] In 1943 it was agreed that there should be a joint project, but that the main engineering works required should be undertaken in the United States and Canada, where greater resources were available and where it would be easier to maintain secrecy from air reconnaissance. British scientists were sent to work in both Canada and the United States, but as time went on the investment of manpower and resources became more and more predominantly American. When the bombs finally became available, Britain retained only a veto power over the use of the weapons, and a promise from Roosevelt, given in September 1944, that 'full collaboration . . . in developing Tube Alloys [the British code-name for the project] for military and commercial purposes should continue after the defeat of Japan unless and until terminated by joint agreement.'[37]

In July 1945, when he was at Potsdam, Truman received word that a test explosion had been successfully conducted. He told Churchill, who was highly encouraged by this strengthening of the power of the Western Allies vis-à-vis Japan—or, if needs be, against Russia. Truman gave a few hints about the project to Stalin, who showed no sign at this stage of appreciating its significance. Truman had little difficulty in deciding that the bombs should be used to effect the termination of the Japanese War; and Churchill readily agreed. At this time General Marshall was predicting that the American casualties in an invasion of Japan might run up to a million:[38] the Japanese casualties would no doubt be at least comparable. The only people known to have expressed their concern about the immediate use of the weapon were some of the American scientists who had worked on the project, and also the Danish pioneer of atomic research Niels Bohr, who tried

36. Hewlett and Anderson, *The New World*, pp. 41-3; Gowing, *Britain and Atomic Energy*, p. 78.

37. Gowing, *op. cit.*, p. 447.     38. Feis, *op. cit.*, p. 12.

to persuade both Roosevelt and Churchill against its use, but without success.[39] The Allied leaders thought the bombs would shorten the war and would thus save lives. They proved to be correct.

It was suggested at the time, and it has been suggested since, that the best course would have been to make a demonstration of the power of the bomb against some isolated target in Japan, so that the enemy leaders could see its potential and draw their own conclusions. But practical problems ruled this out. Only two bombs were available by mid-August, and there was the possibility of a failure in their mechanism. Furthermore, the success of the weapon, as we have seen, was thought to depend in large part upon its psychological effect. Its actual destructive power was not as great as that of a heavy raid with high explosive bombs. Consequently, all that Truman was prepared to do was to issue a solemn declaration from Potsdam, in the name of the American, British and Chinese governments, warning the Japanese that the weight of attack upon their country would rapidly increase if they failed to agree at once to unconditional surrender. Although there had already been certain overtures from Tokyo through the Japanese ambassador in Moscow, there was no indication that the Japanese were prepared to surrender, or that the Potsdam declaration made any difference to their attitude.

The first atomic bomb was dropped on the city of Hiroshima on August 6th. Over 70,000 people were killed in the explosion. The number would not have been so large if the population had realized that a raid was about to take place: but they had got used to single aircraft flying over on reconnaissance missions. Even so, the casualties were less than in the Tokyo fire raid of March: though they amounted to more than all those killed in all the air raids on Britain throughout the war. Two days later the Russians announced that they would declare war upon Japan, and Red Army troops began to invade

39. Gowing, *op. cit.*, pp. 353-8, 374.

Manchuria. It seems likely that Stalin had brought forward his plans in order to ensure that Russia was actually in the Eastern war before it ended: otherwise he could not have claimed as of right the territorial gains for which he had bargained with the Americans. But his action had the important advantage of increasing the pressure on the Japanese leaders at the critical moment. On August 9th the second atomic bomb was dropped, this time on Nagasaki—or rather, as it happened, on an industrial suburb of the city. The casualties of the second bomb were not quite so heavy—about 40,000 were killed.

On August 10th the Japanese Cabinet decided to invite the Emperor to state whether he thought the country should surrender. The Emperor, until now virtually a figurehead in politics, replied in the affirmative and the Cabinet then agreed with him unanimously. After securing details of the precise surrender terms, the final decision to accept was conveyed to the Allied governments through neutral channels on August 14th. Thus under the shadow of the newest and most awesome weapon, but also as a direct result of its use, the Second World War came to an end. Hostilities between China and Japan had been going on for a little over eight years. The United States had been actively involved for three years and eight months. For Britain the surrender of Japan came within three weeks of the sixth anniversary of her declaration of war on Germany.

Japan was not divided into separate occupation zones, as Germany had been. The Americans, who had borne the brunt of the Pacific War, assumed sole authority, and Truman appointed General MacArthur to accept the surrender of the Japanese government and to give orders, through the Emperor, for the future conduct of affairs. The formal authority of the Emperor over civil life in Japan was thus retained, subject to MacArthur's policy directives. The Japanese were saved from the complete political disintegration which occurred in Germany, and also from the division of their homeland into separate states. But the Japanese armies which were spread over Eastern Asia and the islands had to surrender to local Allied commanders; and this meant that Mountbatten's Command took responsibility for Malaya and the Dutch East Indies, and Chiang Kai-shek for the whole of China. Hong Kong fell within Chiang's sphere, and he evidently looked forward to assuming at least temporary control of the island; but he was forestalled by a British naval force which was hastily despatched to restore colonial rule.[40] With the re-occupation of Hong Kong the formal authority of the King-Emperor had been re-asserted over all the territory which had been usurped by his various enemies. But much had changed, in the East no less than in Europe, and peacetime brought more radical alterations in the world's political boundaries than had directly resulted from the ebb and flow of the tide of battle.

40. Feis, *op. cit.*, pp. 153f.

Part Three

# The Lessons and Effects of War

# 10.  Britain's Role in Retrospect

The people of Britain had entered the war without enthusiasm; but they participated in it with a will, especially after it was brought home to them by the Battle of Britain and the Blitz. Generally speaking, those who took a Conservative view of politics had rallied to their country's cause in the traditional way, and those of left-wing leanings were in most cases sufficiently hostile to Nazism to accept that the war was just and necessary, and so undertook, as Louis MacNeice put it, to 'defend the bad against the worse'. Communist and pacifist opposition was active in the early months of the war but was not sufficiently strong to make much impact upon this general support. 'Stop-the-war' candidates at by-elections in the 'phoney war' period sometimes secured fair-sized votes, but were never very close to being elected to Parliament; and after the spring of 1940 their cause was obviously hopeless. A significant index of popular feeling may be found in the proportion of conscripts who were provisionally registered as conscientious objectors. In late 1939 it was over 2% of those registering; but by the summer of 1940 it was hardly more than 0.5% and later it even fell below 0.3%.[1] This was not because conscientious objectors were harshly treated either by the government or by public opinion. On the contrary, the arrangements for hearing their cases were distinctly more liberal than in the First World War, and it was accepted that conscientious objection could exist on grounds other than religious.[2] Furthermore, the attitude

1. Parker, *Manpower*, pp. 488-90. The American proportion throughout the war was 0.4%: L. S. Wittner, *Rebels Against War* (New York, 1969), p. 41.

2. Parker, *op. cit.*, p. 156; Hayes, *Challenge of Conscience*, p. xii.

of the public was much less hostile, partly because the dangers to which civilians were exposed were for a long time not markedly less, and sometimes seemed to be greater, than those which threatened the lives and limbs of servicemen.

As for the Communist Party, its pre-war membership was small—about 18,000—and there is some reason to believe that it lost members rapidly when at the behest of Moscow it decided to oppose the war.[3] Its stalwarts worked hard to get up an agitation against the war effort, especially in the People's Convention movement of 1940-1; but this was not a success. More surprising, in view of the influence of the party in the trade unions, was the complete failure of its attempts to encourage industrial unrest. In 1940 the number of working days lost in strikes and lock-outs was less than in any year since records began. Then in June 1941 after the invasion of Russia the Communists became almost overnight the keenest supporters of the war effort. This might have been expected to reduce the level of discontent in industry; and no doubt it worked that way. But in fact the later years of the war saw a considerable increase in the number of working days lost by stoppages. There were serious demarcation disputes in the shipyards in 1941 and later; and a good deal of unrest occurred among the Yorkshire miners in 1944, owing to the fact that piece rates had failed to keep in line with the rise in the cost of living.[4] Ernest Bevin tended to see political motivation in the strikes, and he thought that a tiny group of Trotskyist agitators was to blame.[5] But the remarkable feature of industrial relations in the Second World War, as compared with twenty-five years earlier, is the relatively small proportion of trouble due to strikes, and the almost entire absence of political motivation in the strikes that did take place.

3. Pelling, *British Communist Party*, pp. 116f.
4. Inman, *Labour in the Munitions Industries*, pp. 96, 394; Court, *Coal*, pp. 267f.
5. Bullock, *Bevin*, ii, 269f.

The dangers to industrial morale arose much less from political feeling than from particular grievances, combined with apathy about the war, due to a lack of comprehension of the issues involved. Many workers saw little need for hastening a victory which, so far as their expectations went, would only mean a return of low wages and unemployment. Probably even more failed to appreciate that their own efforts had any direct relationship to the length of the war. The propaganda of the Ministry of Information was often entirely above the heads of the people working at the bench.[6] Late in 1942 Mass-Observation reported that the 'prevalent feeling' was that after the war 'money will be tight and jobs scarce.'[7] It was clear that people based their expectations on what had happened at the end of the First World War: and on this basis a victory for Britain could amount to a personal defeat for the employee in the war factory.[8] Under these circumstances it is not surprising that a feeling of apathy grew up as the main theatres of the fighting moved away from the shores of Britain.

All this suggests that, given the varieties of social background, education and intelligence throughout the country, the mere fact of political unity could not enable the government to squeeze a quart out of the pint pot of industrial morale. A full sense of community could really only arise at moments of crisis, such as during the Battle of Britain; thereafter, the long years of war replaced urgency with monotony, and so there was an inevitable slackening of enthusiasm. The Ministry of Labour and the other departments of government were at least aware of the problems, and in various ways—such as by encouraging a great expansion of factory welfare and by introducing joint production committees wherever possible—they helped to improve the climate of industrial relations. Considering that in the latter part of the war over half of Britain's

6. Advertising Service Guild, *Change*, no. 2 (1941), p. 75.
7. Mass-Observation *Bulletin*, Nov., 1942.
8. Mass-Observation, *People in Production* (1942), p. 241.

national income was devoted to war expenditure—a figure not surpassed by any of her allies, whose efforts were in any case sustained for considerably shorter periods—it is not surprising that there was evidence of war weariness in industry.

The performance of the armed forces depended primarily upon equipment, training and experience. This meant that only the Navy and the RAF were much good at the beginning of the war, for the regular Army was far too small for its new tasks, and its equipment and training were unsuitable for a continental war. The failures in Norway and France were therefore only what could be reasonably expected. The British commander at Narvik, General Auchinleck, formerly of the Indian Army, rather surprisingly blamed the soldiers under his command: they were, he thought, 'distressingly young, not so much in years as in self-reliance and manliness generally.'[9] They had certainly never been trained for a campaign in the Arctic. The troops who fought in Belgium and France, including a high proportion of regulars, won a reasonable respect from their opponents. According to a report prepared by the German IV Corps, which faced them for some time, the British soldiers were 'tough and dogged' in battle, and after the defeat those taken prisoner discussed the losses of their own side 'with complete equanimity' in the 'unshakeable' conviction that Britain would win in the end.[10] The remarkable feature of this campaign, however, was that so many of the British Expeditionary Force escaped from Dunkirk. According to J. B. Priestley this was a 'sudden democratic improvisation', and a case of the 'free creative spirit of a people taking charge of events.'[11] This is very far from the truth. Although the little ships which were hastily mobilized played a useful part in the operation, the great bulk of the troops evacuated came out on ships

9. Connell, *Auchinleck*, p. 149.
10. Ellis, *War in France and Flanders*, p. 326.
11. J. B. Priestley, *Out of the People* (1941), pp. 7, 8.

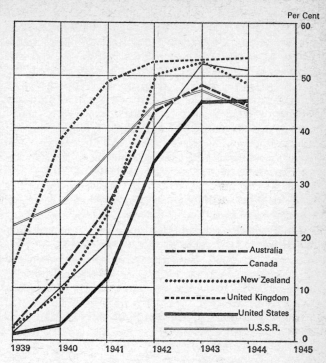

Per Cent

| | Australia |
| --- | --- |
| | Canada |
| | New Zealand |
| | United Kingdom |
| | United States |
| | U.S.S.R. |

1939  1940  1941  1942  1943  1944  1945

War Expenditures in per cent of National Income Taken by permission from W. K. Hancock and M. M. Gowing, *British War Economy* (HMSO 1949)

of the Royal Navy; and the operation was a triumph of skill and training on the part of the Navy, the RAF, and regular soldiers.

It is difficult to find fault with the operational performance of the Navy, although things sometimes went wrong when the Admiralty overruled local commanders, as during the Norwegian campaign or much later, in the unhappy episode of Convoy PQ17 in July 1942.[12] There was also

12. Roskill, *War at Sea*, i, 202 and ii, 145.

a failure to use the most up-to-date methods of coding, with the result that from 1939 until 1943 British naval cyphers were being read by the enemy.[18] Otherwise, British naval skill and equipment were quite the equal of German, and distinctly superior in the later stages of the war, when enemy surface crews had little opportunity of gaining experience in operational conditions. Against the Italians the British Navy had great advantages in equipment, especially radar, and this largely accounted for the successes it won in the Mediterranean. The main fault among naval commanders was a failure to realize the need for close co-ordination of operations with the RAF, and the danger of proceeding without air cover when within range of enemy aircraft. To be sure, the shortage of British aircraft in the early part of the war was bound to involve the Navy in a good many risks in any case; but certainly not as many as it chose to take.

In 1940 the RAF was tolerably equipped and prepared for its primary task, the air defence of Britain, and with the aid of radar its successes were certainly to be expected —though no one would wish to detract from the heroism of the fighter pilots in the Battle of Britain. More susceptible to criticism—albeit marked by at least equal heroism—was the performance of Bomber Command, which for a long time could bomb neither accurately nor heavily enough to make any serious impression on the enemy. Considering that the strategic bomber force was supposed to be a major deterrent to the enemy from the start of the war, this was very disappointing. But throughout the war Bomber Command exaggerated the success of its operations, and when it became clear from air photography that the degree of accuracy of night bombing was very low, an equally mistaken belief in the efficiency of area attack infected its leaders. Although Harris apparently managed to sustain the morale of his pilots with remarkable success, his refusal to adopt a more flexible strategy against key enemy targets was a major folly of the war. But

13. McLachlan, *Room 39*, pp. 76f.

the Chiefs of Staff and the Prime Minister himself must bear some of the blame for allowing Bomber Command to absorb so many scarce resources, when the manufacture of aircraft suitable for use in naval co-operation would have paid greater dividends. As it was, the Fleet Air Arm and Coastal Command both became almost entirely dependent on American aircraft, and the weakness of both arms in the early stages of the war was highly dangerous for Britain's survival.

Nevertheless, it was upon the Army that the critics of the government tended to concentrate their fiercest criticisms, especially after the repeated setbacks in the Middle East and the dismal failure in Malaya and Singapore. In the Western Desert the trouble lay to a very considerable extent in the poor quality of the Army's equipment. Wavell won remarkable successes against the Italians, but these could not be repeated against an enemy armed with superior tanks and artillery. But clearly British generalship was on the whole much less able than German, especially in the handling of armour. Tanks were still largely a novelty in the British army, at least for the officers and men who actually had to employ them. Thus although Auchinleck, Wavell's successor, was himself a general of considerable capacity, his subordinates were of indifferent quality, and Auchinleck failed to see the need to replace them. The defeat in Malaya and Singapore was principally due to lack of air power and to the poor training of the British and Indian troops, who were equipped, as Wavell put it, 'on White Knight principles'.[14] It was quite unnecessary for men operating in the jungle to carry gas masks at all times. Given the way in which the Chiefs of Staff under-estimated the Japanese, defeat was probably inevitable: but it was made much more rapid and humiliating by the incapacity of the officer commanding land operations, General Percival.

14. Connell, *Wavell*, ii, 86. According to Spencer Chapman (*The Jungle is Neutral*, p. 28) they were 'equipped like Christmas trees'.

In Britain there was much heart-searching about the surrender of Singapore and later of Tobruk. Ill-informed people tended to find explanations which fitted in with their existing prejudices. Those on the Left in politics thought that the system of selecting officers by social class was to blame. In fact, somewhat more rigorous methods of selection were being introduced at the time, by the establishment of the War Office Selection Boards: [15] but they could make little difference to the range of senior officers available for service at this stage of the war. Those on the Right felt that the trouble was due to the lack of an old-fashioned discipline in the army. Yet there had not really been much alteration in discipline since the 1914-18 war, except for the abolition of the death penalty for desertion.[16] The fact was that in the circumstances of mobile warfare there is often no alternative to surrender for troops who have been outmanoeuvred, other than to undergo a wholesale and immediate slaughter. The behaviour of British prisoners of war when in German hands did not suggest that there was much wrong with their morale. An SS report on prisoners of war in general in the Klagenfurt area of Germany in August 1943 said that 'the British are the most respected and discussed by the local population.' It was because they were smart, well turned out and self-possessed: 'This, combined with the good impression they give of the nation, influences the German people in a way that should not be underestimated.'[17] Prisoners in Japanese hands were not treated in accordance with the Geneva Convention and it is difficult therefore to make any comparison in their case: to survive at all, after the ill-treatment that they experienced, was often a sign of resilience in itself.

When the tide turned in late 1942 and the Army began

15. Ahrenfeldt, *Psychiatry in the British Army*, p. 23.
16. Nicolson, *Diaries*, ii, 213.
17. Wynne Mason, *Prisoners of War*, p. 270.

to win a succession of victories, talk about the troops' poor morale was largely stilled. Montgomery's greatest contribution was to restore the faith of the ordinary soldier in the quality of leadership. He did this in part by deliberately attracting favourable publicity to himself and by personally addressing as many of his troops as he possibly could. His actual operations were marked by a caution which his ablest opponent, General Rommel, regarded as 'excessive'.[18] But Rommel and other German generals had always criticized the British for their lack of mobility, although, as they admitted, it was accompanied by tenacity in adverse circumstances.[19]

In later operations, the British often worked side by side with the Americans, and could be compared with them. The German General Blumentritt, whose troops faced both the British and the Americans in Normandy, thought that the Americans had a 'keen sense of mobile action' which the British lacked, but that they were quick to fall back when under artillery fire. 'By contrast, once the British had got their teeth in, and had been in a position for twenty-four hours, it proved almost impossible to shift them.'[20] To some extent these impressions may be coloured by the different roles assigned to the British and American armies in this campaign. But there seems no doubt that Montgomery's tactics tended to be cautious and deliberate, compared to those of the American Army Group commander General Bradley. Bradley was very disappointed by the slowness with which Montgomery launched his attack from the north at the close of the Rundstedt offensive in the Ardennes.[21] And Tedder thought that the British and Canadian armies in North-west Europe had become 'drugged' with air power, so that they would never attack unless the German troops in

18. Liddell Hart, *Rommel Papers*, pp. 520f.
19. *Ibid.*, p. 262.
20. Liddell Hart, *Other Side of the Hill*, p. 427.
21. Bradley, *Soldier's Story*, p. 480.

front of them had been subjected to a heavy bombardment from the air.[22]

There was some truth in all this, and there was also a natural explanation. Constant advances, against a determined and skilful enemy, were expensive in casualties, and Montgomery's army was running short of infantrymen. Even if an infantryman managed to avoid being killed or wounded, he was likely sooner or later to break down under the strain of constant action. 'Battle exhaustion' was recognized as a condition which could be treated in forward areas by army psychiatrists, and this enabled many men to be returned to their units after relatively short spells of treatment. But personnel selection had not been undertaken scientifically in the early part of the war, and as the Navy and Air Force had the pick of the conscripts, the army naturally had a high proportion of dull, illiterate or mentally unstable recruits, many of whom were still in fighting units when they went overseas. This tended to increase the number of desertions and breakdowns.[23] Yet in spite of the very high proportion of men whom it rejected from service on psychiatric grounds, the American army appeared to suffer from the same problem and to a similar degree.[24] The difference was that there were considerably more American infantrymen available as reinforcements in the later stages of the war.

If Britain's soldiers won only qualified approval from enemy generals, and if the army's organization and the ability of its senior officers were, at least in the early years of the war, the object of much criticism, a large part of the explanation lies in the very small size of the peacetime army in relation to those of the other major powers, with the exception of the United States. Indeed, Britain's relations with her major allies, other than America, were always marked by some embarrassment about the limited character of her contribution to land warfare. The fact that

22. Tedder, *With Prejudice*, pp. 572, 606.
23. Ahrenfeldt, *op. cit.*, p. 32.   24. *Ibid.*, pp. 172, 281.

in 1939-40 the British Expeditionary Force was so small in relation to the French Army obliged the British government to leave the conduct of strategy for the land war entirely to the French; and Gort, the BEF commander, had to take his orders, not directly from Gamelin, the French Commander-in-Chief, but from a subordinate, General Georges. On the other hand the British took good care to ensure that units of the RAF, including even the air arm of the BEF, were controlled from Whitehall and not from any French headquarters. This led to poor liaison in the early stages of the Battle of France. It was reasonable enough later on that the strength of the British air defences should not be dissipated in a hopeless effort to prevent a French collapse. Dowding knew that his fighters, even with the most modern system of radar defence, could only just about cope with the defence of Britain; and so after seeing his reserves diminish as a result of the despatch of successive reinforcements to France, he 'went down on his knees and thanked God' when he actually heard of the Franco-German armistice.[25]

After the fall of France, British troops did not again re-enter a European campaign until in March 1941 they went to the aid of Greece. The decision to enter Greece was thoroughly unsound on military grounds, as the Germans had overwhelming strength, and the poor quality of the Greek roads made it unlikely that a good defensive position in the mountains could be prepared and maintained. Churchill had his doubts about taking on this new commitment, but its keenest advocate was Eden, who managed to convince Wavell and Dill that the operation was desirable for political reasons. The decision led to another rapid defeat and withdrawal, without great loss to be sure, but once again at the expense of British military prestige and at the cost of a great deal of scarce equipment, which could have been far better used in an effort to clear the remaining Italian troops out of Tripoli, or in securing the island of Crete.

25. Halifax Diary, 8 Feb., 1941, Hickleton Papers.

At this time the prospects of Britain ever defeating the German armed forces seemed exceedingly remote. Yet the Chiefs of Staff committed themselves to the belief that at some not too distant date it would be possible to invade Europe, and, with the help of guerilla movements and resistance among the conquered nations of the continent, to overcome the entire German army. There was of course a historical precedent of a sort for this in the Peninsular War at the beginning of the nineteenth century; but to believe that after over a century of the development of military techniques the German armed forces would be so weakened by guerillas that it could not cope with a coastal landing by a numerically much smaller army, was indeed to make the wish the father to the thought. It was naturally the left-wingers in the government who sought to exploit the possibilities of continental resistance movements. But as time went on, and as Britain acquired new major allies, the idea that this sort of assistance would make very much difference to the outcome of a major land campaign was gradually abandoned. This is not to say, of course, that the limited amount of effort that was put into building up the Special Operations Executive to assist the guerillas was wasted or superfluous.[26]

Another disappointment for the Left in Britain—or at least for most of it—was the government's failure to pursue an effective policy of political warfare against Germany. For this purpose it would have been necessary to distinguish clearly between 'good' and 'bad' Germans and to have encouraged the army and the populace to revolt against the Nazis. Undoubtedly this would have caused the Foreign Office some difficulties, particularly with Spain whose rulers were of a roughly similar political complexion to Germany's. But the real reason why the policy was not adopted lay in differing attitudes within the government. The Foreign Office had its anti-Germans, one of whom, Sir Robert Vansittart, was allowed in late 1940 to broadcast and then to publish (under the title

26. Foot, *S. O. E. in France*, pp. 441f.

*Black Record*) an absurd farrago of evidence to show that the Germans had always been aggressive people ever since Roman times. This was very useful to Dr Goebbels in his work of proving to the German people that the enemy would not try to distinguish between them and their leaders: indeed, he spoke of Vansittart as 'worth his weight in gold'.[27] It was a misfortune for the Left that the one man who might have directly influenced Political Warfare on their behalf—Dalton—was the one prominent member of the Labour Party to be a passionate Germanophobe. Although anti-German feelings in Britain were never as bitter as they had been in the First World War, inevitably the course of the conflict tended to strengthen the support in high places for a more or less Vansittartite viewpoint.

The invasion of Russia transformed the strategic situation in Europe—though only gradually, for, as we have seen, British military opinion was inclined in 1941 to expect an early collapse of Russian resistance. Russia had been an unfriendly neutral for the preceding two years, and although a common hostility to Nazi Germany now linked her to Britain, there was bound to be a good deal of mutual suspicion in the relations of the two countries. The conclusion of a treaty of alliance, signed in May 1942, was held up for some time while the Soviet Foreign Minister, Molotov, attempted unsuccessfully to persuade the British government to agree to Russian absorption of the Baltic States and half of Poland, for whose independence Britain had entered the war. Meanwhile Britain and the United States sent to Russia as much in the way of military equipment as they could possibly spare—or perhaps it should be said, more than they could possibly spare if they had given their own needs complete priority. But what the Russians wanted even more urgently than even the best equipment was the early opening of a 'Second Front' in Europe to take off their shoulders some of the

27. L. P. Lochner (ed.), *The Goebbels Diaries* (1948), p. 267; Bruce Lockhart, *Comes the Reckoning*, p. 158.

burden of the German onslaught; and it was very difficult for Churchill to explain to Stalin that the problems of building up the British and American armies and then organizing them for an opposed landing from the sea were such that it could not be contemplated in 1942 or even, as it later transpired, in 1943. For several months in 1943 the Churchill-Stalin correspondence lapsed and the Soviet ambassadors were withdrawn from London and Washington, ostensibly to report. There were some in the Foreign Office and in the State Department who feared that Stalin might make a separate peace with Hitler.[28]

Later in 1943, however, relations improved. The Russians may have been agreeably surprised by the amount of relief that they obtained from the Italian surrender, and from the movement of German forces, which might otherwise have fought on the Eastern Front, into Italy and the Balkans. Late in the year, at Teheran, Stalin had fresh evidence of the Anglo-American determination to cross the Channel into north-western Europe, and he was even invited to adjudicate upon strategic disagreements between the western powers. For their part, the western leaders formed a favourable impression of Stalin's willingness to co-operate and to make concessions at times to the western point of view. Roosevelt, Churchill, Eden and Cordell Hull all felt that it was possible to reach useful agreements with Stalin, and they did not abandon this view even in private until after the Yalta conference.[29] This was in spite of the fact that the Russian attitude on the future of Eastern Europe, and particularly Poland, was quite obdurate. The callousness of Stalin's reaction to the gallant Polish revolt in Warsaw in the summer of 1944 was especially shocking to the western leaders.

But although it seemed throughout the war that some sort of meeting of minds was possible at the very highest

28. Woodward, *British Foreign Policy*, p. 240; Unpublished Diary of Adm. Leahy, 7 May, 1943.

29. For Churchill see, e.g., Woodward, *op. cit.*, p. 500n; Nicolson, *Diaries*, ii, 437.

level, there was very little effective collaboration between
subordinate officials or staff officers of the two countries.
This was because Russia was a closed country subject to
dictatorial rule. Servants of the dictator did not dare
to engage in give-and-take with agents of another country,
as they had virtually no powers of discretion, and were
conscious that before the war even purely social contacts
with foreigners had been regarded with the utmost suspicion. British officials who tried to follow up the Churchill-
Stalin agreements by liaison at a lower level consequently
had frustrating experiences. It was very difficult to reach
the Russian capital, as British or American planes were
not normally allowed to cross Soviet territory. Those
officials who did arrive in Moscow or Kuibyshev were given
very little information indeed, could conduct virtually no
business, and although sometimes treated to magnificent
official banquets were never informally invited to visit
Russian homes.[30]

Ivan Maisky, Russian ambassador in London in the early
part of the war, later offered the British ambassador in
Moscow, Sir Archibald Clark Kerr, some explanation
of the difficulties in Anglo-Soviet relations at the official
level. It was, he said, because the Russians had an 'inferi-
ority complex'. His view, with which Clark Kerr was
inclined to agree, was that 'You make us look like country
cousins, and we mind because we are.'[31] But the Russians
need never have felt any embarrassment about their
country's relative backwardness if they had not spent a
large part of their time since the Revolution pretending
that the Soviet Union was a sort of earthly paradise.

In spite of all these social and political differences, sheer
necessity might have been expected to lead to some
degree of military collaboration. But what there was
tended to be very one-sided. The British Navy and merchant navy suffered appalling losses in trying to keep
open the Arctic convoy route; but the Navy was not

30. Birkenhead, *Monckton*, pp. 191, 214.
31. Woodward, *op. cit.*, p. 243n.

permitted to establish any medical facilities for the seamen at Archangel owing to the 'active opposition of the Russian government authorities.'[32] Arrangements for the exchange of military information benefited only the Russians: as Air Chief Marshal Sir John Slessor was later to put it, 'It is hardly an exaggeration to say that we knew more from our Intelligence about our enemies than our so-called allies would tell us about themselves.'[33] All this gave Whitehall a very jaundiced view of the Soviet government just at the time when enthusiasm for all things Russian was at its peak among the British public. There was, in fact, by 1945 a dangerous gap between official and non-official thinking on Anglo-Soviet relations.

The association of Britain and the United States was of an entirely different character. The common language and the close peacetime links between the two countries—economic, cultural and political—all combined to make it so. American neutrality in the first twenty-seven months of Britain's war was friendly neutrality from the start; as time went on it became a deep commitment to ensure the survival and if possible the victory of the British cause. The confidential exchange of information between Churchill, as First Lord of the Admiralty, and Roosevelt, himself a former Under-Secretary of the Navy, developed after the summer of 1940 into a close understanding cemented first by the use of Harry Hopkins as an intermediary and then by personal contact, initiated in August 1941 at Placentia Bay, Newfoundland, where the Atlantic Charter was drawn up. In the meantime the United States had become more than just a major source of supply, on a private enterprise basis, of armaments and munitions for the British war effort. By the destroyers-bases agreement of September 1940 the American government had been brought into the bargain; and when in the autumn British dollar resources began to run out, the President sponsored

32. MacNalty and Mellor, *Medical Services in War*, p. 9.
33. Slessor, *Central Blue*, p. 399.

the Lend-Lease arrangements which after enactment in March 1941 enabled Britain to continue to use American industry as her strongest ally.

The intimate relationship established between the British and American governments from the summer of 1940 onwards gradually extended to almost every aspect of the two countries' response to the challenge of war. Before Pearl Harbour, the extent to which American industry was working for Britain is indicated by the fact that in the last eighteen months of American neutrality 40% of the country's aircraft production and about a quarter of its output of other munitions was in fulfilment of British orders.[34] This gave a considerable boost to Britain's military strength, but at the same time it added enormously to the capacity of American industry for war purposes.

The direct military collaboration between Britain and the United States began with informal talks in London in August 1940, when a party of American officers was given an outline of British strategic thinking. This was followed early in 1941 by secret staff conversations in Washington, at which it was agreed that the European theatre of operations should take precedence over the Pacific. In the course of the year there was a gradual development of joint action in the Atlantic, with the American Navy patrolling North Atlantic waters to protect convoys as far as 25° West, and with arrangements for an American force of Marines to reinforce and then to replace British troops in Iceland. By September 1941 the United States Navy was fully committed to a 'shooting war' in the Atlantic. After this, the relative ease with which the Combined Chiefs of Staff and their associated economic organizations were set up after Pearl Harbour was only to be expected.

Anglo-American collaboration in the exchange of new military technology was particularly effective. It began on British initiative in the late summer of 1940. In the contacts that followed both nations gained a good deal, but in

34. Sayers, *Financial Policy*, p. 552.

the short run the Americans who had not yet mobilized their scientists for war work got the better of the bargain.[35] There was above all the resonant cavity magnetron which Professor Marcus Oliphant took over to Washington, and which became the basis of microwave radar: it has been described by an American scientific historian as 'the most valuable cargo ever brought to our shores.'[36] Rapid exploitation of this device took place in both countries: and it proved of special value for the detection of enemy submarines from the air. But the development of the same invention which led to the proximity fuse for use by artillery was undertaken entirely in America, and the British got a good return for their foresight in giving away their own military secrets when in 1944 American proximity fuses in anti-aircraft shells helped to defeat the menace of the V.1. In the case of the atomic bomb, as we have seen, research undertaken in Britain later encouraged the Americans to begin large-scale development work, and it was the vastly greater resources available in the United States and Canada that eventually led to the production of the bombs before the end of the war.

Anglo-American relations differed from Anglo-Russian relations (and also from Russo-American relations) in the degree of intimacy that developed between the partners, not just at the highest level, but also at every other level—military and economic, diplomatic and cultural, official and unofficial. This is not to say that there were no disagreements. Americans tended to be critical of the Empire, were suspicious of the morale of Indian troops, and held the view that nothing would ever be achieved in Burma under British command.[37] British public opinion was much less cordial to the Americans than officialdom was: and the

35. V. Bush, *Modern Arms and Free Men* (New York, 1949), p. 39.

36. Baxter, *Scientists Against Time*, p. 142.

37. 'Draft Memorandum on Military Situation in India' Wendell Phillips Papers.

ordinary soldier's view of the GI on first meeting in England was that he was too well paid, had no respect for British girls, and looked 'slovenly'. Racial segregation in the US Army astonished the British, and the attempt by some white Americans to secure the exclusion of Negroes from certain British hotels caused ill-feeling.[38] But differences such as these did not seriously endanger the collaboration of the two countries. Although the machinery of the South-East Asia Command was somewhat creaky, the American Joint Chiefs respected Mountbatten, the British-appointed commander, and in its various operations, British, Indian, African, American and even Chinese troops worked together in reasonable harmony—which is more than any of them succeeded in doing in any theatre with the Russians. As for the American troops in Britain, they were carefully coached in British customs, and considering that on the eve of D-Day there were over a million and a half Americans in Britain, it is remarkable how little friction there was. The British opinion of the Americans soon began to improve, paradoxically, when they heard of American casualties in action; and on the fighting fronts in Africa British troops soon became impressed with American resilience after initial setbacks.[39]

The great bulk of officials and servicemen engaged in inter-Allied planning and actual operations found it easy to copy the friendly mutual trust which existed between Churchill and Roosevelt. At Washington, Dill established a particularly close relationship with Marshall; and Stimson and Halifax, both former Foreign Secretaries, became intimate friends. In London, Ambassador Kennedy had been regarded with increasing disfavour because of his lack of faith in the British cause; but Winant, his successor, was very popular—although the increasing personal contact between Churchill and Roosevelt reduced the importance of

38. Memorandum 27 Nov., 1943, US Army ETO Admin. Files, Record Group 212.
39. Morale Reports 1943, US Army ETO, *loc. cit.*

the embassy. Above all Eisenhower, after his brilliant achievement as the director of an inter-Allied team in North Africa, proved equally successful in charge of the most important joint operation of them all, the invasion of north-western Europe. He won not only the loyalty but also the affection of those who served with him; and in the differences about strategy that he had with Mont-gomery, he had the support of his British as well as of his American staff officers, both at the time and afterwards.[40]

In the discussions which have taken place since the war about the course of Anglo-American strategy in the years 1941-5, interest has focused on the disagreements which took place between the British and American leaders about the relative importance to be given to the Mediterranean theatre. American spokesmen argued at the time that Churchill in advocating an advance into Central Europe from Italy, perhaps through the so-called 'Ljubljana gap', was allowing political influences to govern military stra-tegy; his aim, it was said, was to establish a new British sphere of influence in the Balkans.[41] After the war, when relations between Russia and the western powers deter-iorated, this ceased to be a reproach to Churchill and became instead an example of his far-sighted statesman-ship.[42] In reality, however, Churchill was slow, by com-parison with Smuts or Eden, to react to the prospect of Russian domination of Eastern Europe. It was a matter of disappointment to Eden that Churchill was for so long unwilling to take any interest in the structure of inter-national relations in Europe after the war. Eden agreed with Smuts that 'Winston's mind has a stop in it at the end of the war.'[43] Churchill's own explanation of his Mediterranean strategy was that he wanted to 'nail down' enemy divisions in the Balkans with the aid of guerillas,

40. F. E. Morgan, *Peace and War*, p. 200.

41. Leahy, *I Was There*, p. 285; Matloff, *Strategic Planning*, pp. 163, 166, 215.

42. Wilmot, *Struggle for Europe*, pp. 12f. Cf. Howard, *Medi-terranean Strategy*, pp. ixf.

43. Avon, *Reckoning*, p. 350.

and thus to cause a dispersal of enemy strength.[44] It was fortunate on purely military grounds that Roosevelt accepted as much of the Mediterranean strategy as he did: for thereby the Allies obtained the experience in combined operations and in land warfare against a skilful enemy without which the invasion of France might easily have been a failure.

Members of the staff of the US War Plans Division were quick to accuse the British of allowing political considerations to dominate strategy because they knew that Churchill helped to formulate the plans of the British Chiefs of Staff, whereas Roosevelt left the American Joint Chiefs to work out their own plans before he entered the debate—acting, as they thought, more as an international referee than as a guardian of American interests.[45] But the US Army staff do not seem to have realized how much their other rival, the US Navy, was managing to modify the original strategic principle that the European theatre should take priority over the Pacific; and this modification could only be due to political considerations of a sort likely to appeal to the American mind—such as, that the American people were, at any rate in 1943, more anti-Japanese than anti-German;[46] that the post-war situation of the United States vis-à-vis both Britain and Russia would be much improved if the war against Japan was well advanced by the time Germany collapsed;[47] and that it was important for American policy in the post-war world that Chiang Kai-shek's regime should be strengthened as much as possible and as soon as possible.[48]

There was not much open debate about these issues in the Combined Chiefs of Staff. The British Chiefs left the

44. Churchill, *Second World War*, v, 324; Matloff, *op. cit.*, p. 302.

45. Harrison, *Cross-Channel Attack*, p. 92; Matloff, *op. cit.*, p. 23.

46. Cantril, *Public Opinion*, p. 776; Wittner, *Rebels Against War*, pp. 104f.

47. Leahy Diary, 14 Apr., 1943.

48. Avon, *Reckoning*, pp. 376-8; Matloff, *op. cit.*, p. 205.

formulation and conduct of the Pacific War very largely to Admiral King, the sharp-tempered and single-minded officer who combined the two posts of Commander-in-Chief of the US Navy and Chief of the Naval Staff. King virtually controlled the assignment of shipping produced by American shipyards; and this included the Landing Ships, Tank (LSTs) which though designed in Britain were all being built in the United States. Since the supply of LSTs was the critical factor in dictating the size and number of assault landings whether in Europe or elsewhere, it was obvious that King, unless overruled by Roosevelt, was in a position of great strength to determine the strategy of the war, at any rate in its offensive phase. When in 1942 Churchill and the British Chiefs placed their veto on a cross-Channel operation for 1943, Marshall gave them a clear hint of what would happen: American interest would be transferred to the Pacific.[49] Dill also warned Churchill: 'King's war is against the Japanese'.[50] Churchill's view, however, was that the American attitude was unreasonable. He complained to Halifax: 'Just because the Americans can't have a massacre in France this year, they want to sulk and bathe in the Pacific.'[51] But King largely had his way, and at the end of 1943 there were as many American servicemen in the Pacific theatre as there were in the European. For 1944, King planned major operations in the Marianas; and so he refused to allocate more than three months' production of LSTs to the European theatre.[52] It was this shortage of LSTs which delayed the landing in the south of France until six weeks after D-Day and was largely responsible for prolonging German resistance through the winter of 1944-5.

American policy in another sphere was also primarily to blame for the fact that in the last winter of the war the German army and people saw nothing to be gained

49. Sherwood, White House Papers, p. 597.
50. Wedemeyer, Wedemeyer Reports!, p. 166.
51. Halifax Diary, 15 July, 1942, Hickleton Papers.
52. Greenfield, American Strategy, p. 39.

by overthrowing Hitler and negotiating a surrender. At the Casablanca conference in 1943 Roosevelt had proclaimed the slogan of 'unconditional surrender', and he adhered to it throughout the war, resisting suggestions from both British and Russian governments, and from General Eisenhower in Europe, that it should in some way be modified.[53] In addition, at Quebec in September 1943 he and Churchill endorsed the Morgenthau Plan to 'pastoralize' the German economy. Both leaders in initialling the proposals acted under the influence of persons not directly associated with foreign policy (Roosevelt on Morgenthau's advice and Churchill on Cherwell's) and both the foreign secretaries, Hull and Eden, worked for the abandonment of the plan. It was in fact soon dropped, but not before, in the course of the battle within the American administration, its terms had been broadcast to the world.[54] Goebbels made good use of it to persuade the Germans that there was no alternative to a fight to the bitter end.

It may thus be seen that, for what may broadly be called political reasons on the American side, the war in Europe was not concluded as quickly as it might have been. Probably a good many more British and American soldiers were killed than was necessary, not to speak of the enemy, and many more people in occupied countries suffered the hardships of another winter of war. Nor would the ending of the Japanese war have been held up for long, if the Mariana operations had been postponed. The Pacific effort in the winter of 1944-5 could have been intensified by the release of manpower and supplies from Europe; and in any case the atomic bomb would have become available at the same time in 1945. But both the British and the Russians would have taken a larger part in the closing stages of the war in the Pacific and might reasonably have

53. Woodward, *British Foreign Policy*, pp. 478-483; *U.S. Foreign Relations, Dip. Papers 1944*, i, 484ff.
54. H. Stein (ed.), *American Civil-Military Decisions* (Birmingham, Ala., 1963), p. 378.

claimed a greater say in the occupation of Japan and in the formulation of the Far Eastern peace treaty. Furthermore, since Lend-Lease would have continued for a longer period after the defeat of Germany, British industry would have completed a substantial part of its reconversion to a peacetime basis before the dollar crisis became acute, and so the burden of debt which the country had to shoulder as a result of the war would have been considerably smaller. But this is to enter upon a discussion of the effects of the war upon Britain's external situation, which can more conveniently be dealt with in a separate chapter.

No discussion of the Anglo-American collaboration during the war should end upon a note of criticism of either of the partners. For after all, on balance, the collaboration was a remarkable success story. Both countries contributed much from the start; but towards the close the American contribution became overwhelmingly the greater, because of the much larger manpower and resources of the United States. The mutual interaction of the experience and skill of the statesmen, the administrators, the military staffs, the scientists and leaders of industry in the two countries was of immense advantage in bringing the war to a victorious conclusion. It was a relationship which had never previously existed between two great countries; which might never be repeated in the future, for the circumstances which brought it into operation were exceptional; but which deserves to be remembered as an episode reflecting no little credit on the common sense and enlightened self-interest of those who furthered it, from Roosevelt and Churchill down to the ordinary soldier and civilian who learned to understand each other through the not altogether transparent medium of a common language.

After almost six years of war, in which for so long Britain's peril had been acute, it was agreeably surprising to find that the cost to the country in dead and wounded was much lighter than in the four years of the First World War.[55] United Kingdom fatal casualties in the armed forces, at about 270,000, were much less than half the number suffered in 1914-18. The number of wounded hardly exceeded that of the killed and was less than a sixth of that in the previous war. To the armed forces totals, however, must be added the civilian casualties, which were higher than previously: 35,000 members of the merchant navy died, as compared with 15,000, and 60,000 civilians were killed in air raids, as compared with 1100. Fatal casualties of other British Commonwealth armed forces amounted to just under 110,000, which was about half the figure of the First World War.

It has sometimes been suggested that the heavy casualties of the First World War deprived Britain of almost an entire generation of potential leaders, and that this accounted for the weaknesses of British foreign policy in the 1930s. It is, however, a mistake to suppose that men in the age-groups which suffered most severely would have been expected to rise to policy-making positions in only about fifteen years of peace. The effect of the heavy casualties of the First World War was much more in persuading people of all ages that the nation should under no circumstances risk such an experience again. This not only led to an unwillingness to re-arm, but also to a reluctance to accept any commitment of ground forces to a continental ally; and even in the course of the war it encouraged an extremely cautious attitude on the part of the Chiefs of Staff whenever the question of large-scale fighting on the continent was broached to them. As the American Secretary for the Army Henry Stimson said, the 'shadows of Passchendaele' formed the background to their deliberations.[56]

But the casualties of the Second World War must not be made light of. Few of the fighter pilots of the Battle of

55. World War II figures from 'Strength and Casualties of the Armed Forces &c, 1939-1945', *P.P.* 1945-6, xv, 89lff.
56. Stimson and Bundy, *On Active Service*, p. 436.

Britain, and still fewer of the pilots of the Fleet Air Arm in the early years, survived the war. The bomber crews of the RAF experienced a rate of attrition quite comparable to that endured a quarter of a century earlier by officers on the Western Front. The Navy and merchant navy had to face continuous exposure to considerable risks, and suffered heavy losses. Even in the army, casualties were serious in infantry and armoured units which bore the brunt of offensive warfare. But in any case, it was little consolation to the families of the dead to know that their own personal loss was not quite so common an experience as it had been twenty-five years earlier.

All the same, people's reactions to events tend to be dictated by their expectations; and whereas in 1914-18 they were shocked by casualties which were enormously greater than in any earlier war, in 1945 they were relieved to discover that the losses were much less than a generation before. Partly for this reason, there was much less desire to put up expensive monuments to the dead. Since both wars had been against Germany as the main enemy, a more practical and less pious generation of civic leaders, with the wartime notions of austerity and utility in their minds, decided in many cases simply to add a second list of names to an existing memorial of the earlier war. The new cemeteries of the dead overseas were taken over and dutifully looked after by what is still called the Imperial War Graves Commission, founded after the First World War; but at home the solemnity of inter-war Armistice Days, when throughout the country all work stopped for the two-minutes silence at 11 a.m. on November 11th, was never revived after 1945.

# 11. Britain's Place in the World after 1945

If it was an agreeable surprise to find that wartime casualties had been very much less than in the First World War, there could be no denying that material losses were greater than in 1914-18. This was the harsh fact that the British people had to face as they assessed the prospects for life in the post-war world. Since the war had lasted six years, there had naturally been a heavier depreciation of the nation's capital equipment. In addition, there had been extensive damage to housing and industrial property as a result of bombing. The merchant fleet was only about 70% of what it had been at the outbreak of war. It was estimated in 1945 that these factors were responsible for a loss of about one-tenth of pre-war national wealth.[1] But external disinvestment was an even more serious matter, and with this taken into account it was reckoned that the loss of national wealth came to about a quarter of the pre-war total. The calculation was originally made to support a request to the United States for post-war aid in the form of a grant or low-interest loan; and it may be that it tends to be unduly pessimistic, not taking into account certain important items on the credit side of the ledger. The expansion of the engineering industry during the war had been substantial, and much of its new capital equipment could be used for peacetime purposes. The efficiency of production had been improved in many ways. In agriculture, for instance, the number of tractors had almost doubled in less than four years.[2] There was much more machinery in the coal-mines, and the output of electricity

1. Hancock and Gowing, *British War Economy*, pp. 548, 551.
2. CSO, *Statistical Digest of the War*, p. 63.

had increased by about half.[3] All this certainly went some way to offset the losses.

But the very high degree of external disinvestment was a serious national burden for the future because of its direct effect on the balance of payments, which had been causing concern to economists since the mid-1920s. In the period from the beginning of the war to June 1945, external disinvestment amounted to a total of £4,198 millions.[4] Only a little over a quarter of this—£1,118 millions—was due to the realization of capital assets, such as the forced sale of investments in the United States in the first part of the war. A much larger proportion—£2,879 millions—was due to the increase in external liabilities, that is to say, new debts assumed by the Treasury, or old ones cancelled, mostly within the sterling area. By mid-1945 Britain had registered a loss of £2,723 millions to the sterling area countries, most of it to India, Burma and the Middle East dependencies. This was largely in payment for the upkeep of Indian and colonial troops on the battle fronts, and for goods and services for the armed forces generally. It was only the white Dominions which normally paid for their own forces on service outside their own frontiers. Other Commonwealth troops were an extra burden for the British taxpayer—an arrangement designed to avoid awkward political repercussions among the non-self-governing peoples, who had after all been pitchforked into the war entirely without consultation of their own wishes. There was a certain rough justice about this, as the Indian and colonial empire was poor as well as dependent; but it hardly fits into the framework of the Marxian analysis of imperial exploitation.

There was rather less justice about the fact that even the relatively wealthy white Dominions imposed a burden upon British finances during the war. To be sure, for some

3. Hancock and Gowing, op. cit., p. 551; London and Cambridge Economic Service, The British Economy: Key Statistics, 1900-1966, p. 6.
4. Hancock and Gowing, op. cit., p. 352.

time they were somewhat remote from the European War. Canada, Australia and New Zealand felt little impulse at first to mobilize their resources to the same degree as Britain; and South Africa was constantly in danger of reverting to neutrality if the standard of living of the Afrikaner population was reduced.[5] Eire of course was neutral and could be expected to make what profit she could out of the needs of war. The British imperial relationship was thus like an old ocean-going steamer, leaking at the joints when subjected to the buffeting of a storm, and making only slow headway, owing to the water she had taken in, when she reached the calmer seas of peacetime.

It is true that the financial relations of the United Kingdom with the United States and Canada were based upon principles more generous to the British Treasury. They had to be, for the British supply of dollars had been on the point of running out entirely. American aid to the United Kingdom in the years 1941-5 amounted to slightly over £5,000 million, against which may be set a total of British reciprocal aid to the value of £1,200 million.[6] These were goods and services exchanged between allies for war purposes (though the United States was still technically neutral when the exchange began), but the balance of contribution was naturally very heavily from the American side. The Canadian government early in 1942 made Britain a gift of $1000 million (£220 million) to facilitate purchases of munitions and other goods, and followed this later by substantial further payments under mutual aid arrangements.[7] Britain, for her part, made gifts of aid to Russia amounting to £312 million and to other countries to the value of £383 million.[8] These figures did not result in post-war indebtedness on either side.

For centuries Britain had been accustomed to strengthening her cause in wartime by providing loans or subsidies

5. Sayers, *Financial Policy*, pp. 293, 320.
6. Hancock and Gowing, *op. cit.*, p. 353.
7. *Ibid.*, p. 375.     8. Sayers, *op. cit.*, p. 535.

to her allies. The United States was now in a much better position to do this than Britain, and in so far as the British armed forces would have been much smaller without American aid, the Americans could be said to have made mercenaries of the British. But whereas the United States actually became richer during the war, Britain became poorer; and as Keynes pointed out, all Britain's allies, as well as her Dominions and dependencies 'ought to figure in the eyes of history as our mercenaries' because Britain ended the war owing money to them all.[9] Clearly this applied less to the United States and Canada than to the other countries. But in whatever direction one looks, British financial relations had deteriorated as a result of the war.

It was obvious therefore that Britain's problem of paying her way in the post-war world was going to be formidable. But as we have seen there were some grounds for optimism. For many years to come it appeared that Britain's principal competitors in the field of industrial exports, Germany and Japan, would be unable to provide an effective challenge. There seemed to be no reason why the country should not resume its pre-war role in the provision of services such as shipping and insurance for the entire world— the 'invisible exports' that helped to make up the balance. The immediate difficulty was to get through the period of re-adjustment to peacetime, estimated at about three years, during which exports would build up only slowly to pre-war levels and beyond. At the end of 1944 the country was so fully mobilized for war that exports had shrunk to only 30% of the 1938 total; now, the target was to be a figure of 75% above 1938.[10] If the war against Japan had lasted as long as the Chiefs of Staff expected, half this period of adjustment would have passed before the final termination of Lend-Lease; and in the meantime,

9. *Ibid.*, p. 484.

10. Hancock and Gowing, *op. cit.*, p. 521; Worswick and Ady, *British Economy 1945-1950*, p. 10.

negotiations for assistance from the United States for the remaining period of adjustment could have been undertaken in the friendly atmosphere that befitted negotiations between allies still at war.

The sudden collapse of Japan, and the termination of Lend-Lease only a few weeks later, jolted the new Labour Government into a realization of its immediate difficulty— that of sustaining the balance of payments in the postwar transition period. In peacetime as in war, there was only one course to follow in the first instance—to seek a grant or low-interest loan from the United States to tide the country over. But the American administration was now in no mood to maintain its wartime generosity of financial aid. The war had ended, the partnership of Roosevelt and Churchill had disappeared, and Congressional critics were on the watch to ensure that no foreign country received special favours at the expense of the American taxpayer. As a result the negotiations, conducted in Washington by Keynes in the autumn of 1945, were marked by much hard bargaining.[11] In the end, the United States government agreed to provide a loan of about £950 million at a low rate of interest; and in return Britain promised to liberalize her foreign trade as soon as possible, to join the International Monetary Fund (which, to be sure, Keynes had had a part in shaping) and, in particular, to restore a measure of sterling-dollar convertibility by mid-1947.

It was only with great difficulty that the American administration managed to get the loan agreement through Congress; but even so, its terms proved too stringent to tide Britain over the period of reconstruction. This was partly because the British balance of payments ran into additional difficulties owing to changes in the 'terms of trade'—that is to say, the relative costs of imports and exports. It was also partly because the British Treasury was unable to control the policies of the other governments in the sterling area, some of which took the first oppor-

11. Gardner, *Sterling-Dollar Diplomacy*, ch. 10.

tunity to convert as much sterling as possible into dollars. When convertibility was restored in July 1947, the result was disastrous. There was a very rapid drain on the remaining dollars in the American credit, and this forced the British Treasury to end the experiment after only five weeks. The effect was to postpone indefinitely the prospect of trade liberalization on which the American government had placed so much hope. For this was not just a British problem: it affected all the countries of the sterling area, and it was equally clear that the countries of Europe as a whole had failed to re-establish their pre-war trading relations, owing to difficulties comparable to Britain's, and because trade between eastern and western Europe was almost at a standstill since the extension of the Soviet sphere.

Fortunately for both Britain and western Europe, by 1947 there had been a sharp change in American public opinion on the question of providing financial assistance to other countries for the purposes of post-war recovery. This was because of the emergence of the Soviet Union as a potential threat to world peace, and the feeling in the United States that it was necessary to find allies to meet this threat. The failure of the Foreign Ministers of the great powers to agree on a German peace treaty, the Russian diplomatic pressure on Iran and Turkey, the Communist guerilla activities in northern Greece and the increasing weakness of the Chiang Kai-shek regime in China all had their effect. The main results, so far as Europe was concerned, were, first, a rapid decision by President Truman to assume the obligation of supporting Greece and Turkey when the British government announced its intention of withdrawing aid from those countries in March 1947; and secondly, a pledge by General Marshall, now Truman's Secretary of State, in June of the same year, that the administration would be willing to sponsor financial assistance to European countries if they could work out a joint plan for recovery.

The European Recovery Programme, which emerged

from Marshall's initiative, together with additional financial assistance for the purpose of re-armament at the beginning of the 1950s, finally effected the restoration of the economies of western Europe, including that of the United Kingdom. But the whole story of Anglo-American financial relations in the post-war years demonstrated clearly that although Britain might still be a 'world power' in the literal sense—was indeed, by reason of the role of sterling as a reserve currency, in a special position for international finance and commerce—she could no longer sustain the range of responsibilities consonant with her imperial past and the role which she had played in the war so lately ended. Many of the reasons for this lay in very long-term factors: after all, the gradual decline in Britain's share in world trade had begun in the late Victorian era. But the substantial disinvestment effected by the Second World War, and the new commitments which resulted from the war, in particular the occupation of a large part of Germany, caused a financial crisis which even with American help could only be surmounted by a drastic reduction in the British political and military presence in other parts of the world. This meant, among other things, the early end of the extraordinary situation whereby a populous sub-continent of Asia was governed in the last resort from an office in Whitehall.

As we have seen, the British 'Commonwealth and Empire' (in Churchill's phrase) was restored in the entirety of its geographical limits at the end of the war. Even Hong Kong, which Roosevelt had dearly wished to hand over to Chiang Kai-shek, and which technically had been within the generalissimo's sphere of command at the moment of Japan's capitulation, had been rapidly re-occupied by British forces before Chinese troops could arrive. The restoration of law and order throughout the British Empire, and the disarmament and repatriation of enemy troops to be found within its borders, were formidable undertakings in themselves. But the burdens of the Chiefs of Staff did not stop at this. Britain had assumed control of substantial zones of Germany and Austria: that of Germany alone contained some twenty-four million people. In addition, British troops were serving as garrisons in Italy, Greece, and North Africa. It was also their task, in the Far East, to disarm Japanese troops in Siam, French Indo-China and throughout the Dutch East Indies. In many of these territories there were substantial nationalist movements, usually relatively well-armed, and invariably strongly hostile to any restoration of colonial rule.

This is not to say that nationalism, nourished by the Japanese occupation, can be regarded as the main catalyst of political change in the British Empire in the East. To be sure, the Dutch position in the East Indies was lost because Holland had not the power and Britain had not (owing to her other commitments) the will to crush the Indonesian nationalists under Sukarno; and in Burma too the movement towards independence was accelerated by the Japanese recognition of independence in 1943, and by the strength of national feeling which this created at the end of the war.[12] Nevertheless, the Dutch East Indies became independent more because Holland was occupied by Germany than because the Indies were occupied by Japan; and the countries of the British Empire which secured independence, including full dominion status, in the immediate post-war years—India, Pakistan, Ceylon and Burma—were those in which the development of self-government had advanced the furthest in the 1930s; only one of them had been conquered by the Japanese. Malaya, Singapore, North Borneo and Sarawak, in spite of having been in Japanese hands for well over three years, were to be restored to British colonial rule for a long period; and Hong Kong continues so to the present day. In practice, the most immediate result of the Japanese conquests upon the unity of the Commonwealth and

12. H. Baudet in J. S. Bromley and E. H. Kossmann, *Britain and the Netherlands in Europe and Asia* (1968), pp. 207ff.; Tinker, *Union of Burma*, pp. 16-23.

Empire was the decision by the Australian and New Zealand governments to look to arrangements with the United States, rather than with Britain, for their future security. The process of re-appraisal which began at the time of the loss of Singapore culminated in the ANZUS Pact of 1951 by which the two Pacific Commonwealth nations formed an alliance with the United States to which Britain was not directly a party.

The independence of India and Pakistan was clearly foreshadowed in the constitutional and administrative changes of the pre-war years, which have already been mentioned. Not only was provision made by the Government of India Act of 1935 for the grant of responsible government at both the provincial and central levels; of equal importance was the fact that the Indian Civil Service—the small élite of officials who controlled the administrative machine—was being progressively Indianized. Under such circumstances, there could be no question of halting the movement towards self-government. The trouble was that the delays imposed by the war, and the fact that the British wartime Prime Minister was a last-ditch opponent of change, threatened to turn what might have been a relatively orderly transition into a bloodbath. Churchill and the Viceroy, Lord Linlithgow, managed between them to maintain a deadlock on constitutional initiatives in the early part of the war, which was only broken when after the loss of Singapore it seemed as if the invasion of India was imminent. Then a combination of criticism within the War Cabinet, pressure from the United States and fears for the internal security of the country led Churchill to authorize the Cripps Mission in 1942. Unfortunately Cripps's proposals could readily be dismissed by the Congress leaders as an insincere offer, dictated only by weakness, and of little intrinsic value. But the Indian government had little difficulty in putting down the widespread disorders which followed the rejection of Cripps's proposals; and neither this nor the Bengal Famine of 1943—a tragic case of administrative failure in the face of an unexpected emergency, which may well have cost the lives of as many as a million and a half people[13]—seem to have interfered seriously with the morale of the Indian troops serving under British command on the Mediterranean and Burma fronts.

It is indeed arguable that British control of India was actually prolonged by the war. Baldwin had said in 1934 that there was 'a wind of nationalism and freedom . . . blowing as strongly in Asia as anywhere in the world.'[14] Certainly the war provided the excuse for the postponement of a response to this, and it also brought to the top in Britain the man (Churchill) who was prepared to make full use of that excuse. The somewhat surprising result was to weaken the Congress Party, whose leaders refused to co-operate with the Viceroy during the war, at the expense of the Muslim League, whose leaders had no such qualms. This tended to strengthen the case of the Muslim League for a partition of the country and the establishment of a separate Muslim state, Pakistan. But of course there was also the fact that the Muslims traditionally contributed a very high proportion of the soldiers of the Indian Army. It is difficult to speak of them as being a 'minority' in any ordinary sense of this term, as they numbered at the 1941 census about 94 millions of the 389 million inhabitants of the Indian Empire.

It was, to be sure, a good deal easier for the new Labour Government than it would have been for the Conservatives, at any rate while Churchill was still their leader, to accept the immediate desirability of Indian independence, and to impose a time limit for the transfer of power. But the time limit was originally suggested by the Viceroy appointed by Churchill, Field-Marshal Lord Wavell,[15] and it was brought forward to an earlier date by another Viceroy, Admiral Lord Mountbatten, who suc-

13. B. H. Bhatia, *Famines in India* (2nd ed., 1967), p. 324.
14. K. Middlemas and J. Barnes, *Baldwin* (1969), p. 713.
15. Diary, 20 Dec., 1946, Dalton Papers.

ceeded Wavell early in 1947 and had plenipotentiary powers to make a settlement. The decisive arguments in favour of a rapid British withdrawal were practical rather than ideological, and it is perhaps not without irony to find them set down in the private diary of Hugh Dalton, a man much given to emphasizing Socialist doctrines in his public utterances, but as Chancellor of the Exchequer now in the best possible position to sense the pressure of administrative necessity:

> If you are in a place where you are not wanted and where you have not got the force to squash those who don't want you, the only thing to do is to come out. This very simple truth will, I think, have to be applied to other places too, e.g. Palestine . . . I don't believe that one person in a hundred thousand in the country [i.e. Britain] cares tuppence about it, so long as British people are not being mauled about.[16]

But when Attlee announced the decision to withdraw all British troops and to acknowledge the two states of India and Pakistan, he received a special message from the National Council of Labour, hailing the decision as 'one of the finest and most courageous ever undertaken by any government'.[17] It was some comfort to a Labour Prime Minister to have at least one of his necessities regarded by his supporters as a virtue.

But to be able to withdraw gracefully, with such a skilful impresario as Mountbatten in charge of the manoeuvre, was certainly very much better than to be so obviously forced out as the Dutch were from the East Indies. As Dalton said, very few people in Britain cared about the Indian connexion, but they did not want to see it dissipated in the bloodshed of their own kin. As it turned out, there

16. Diary, 24 Feb., 1947, Dalton Papers.
17. M. Phillips to Attlee, 26 Mar., 1947, Attlee Papers (U).

was a great deal of bloodshed: getting on for 200,000 people died in the communal disturbances which took place in the Punjab at the time of the transfer of power.[18] But relatively few Britons were directly involved, and British public opinion did not seem to feel that their government was responsible for the slaughter of Indians by Indians as British control ended—although Churchill blamed it on the Labour Cabinet and a good many Indians regarded it as the heritage of imperial rule. What was consoling for the British public was that the new leaders of both India and Pakistan consented to stay in the Commonwealth. This seemed to be a tacit tribute to good government during the years of Empire. In reality it probably owed rather more to the existence of the enormous sterling balances, which the new governments naturally did not wish to jeopardize. But perhaps the sterling balances were, in a way, the result of good government, if only during the preceding six years, and under some pressure from the nationalist movement. The admission of these two large Asian countries to the Commonwealth ended the old dichotomy between the white self-governing states and the non-white non-self-governing dependencies of the Empire. Henceforth the Commonwealth concept would cross the barriers of race; and in Britain, Liberals and Socialists discovered a new virtue in it which they had not seen before.

Meanwhile the neighbouring states of Ceylon and Burma were also proceeding rapidly along the path to independence. The development of responsible government in Ceylon had been a smoother process than in India, and much of it had taken place in the later years of the war. The Soulbury Commission, appointed in 1944, recommended a constitution which provided for considerable advance in self-government. It was brought into effect in 1946, and amended in the following year in such a way as to enable Ceylon to assume full independence. In February 1948 Ceylon followed India and Pakistan into the

18. P. Moon, *Divide and Quit* (1961), p. 293.

ranks of the independent members of the Commonwealth. Burma, as we have seen, was a country which had suffered far more than India from the ravages of war. It had developed a powerful nationalist movement which claimed independence with all the more confidence because it had been ceded by the Japanese in 1943. The British government envisaged a rather leisurely transition towards independence in Burma, with the first post-war elections being held only after some years of reconstruction;[19] but the nationalists soon showed that they were not prepared to wait. The Labour Government found it had to face widespread disorders, or else drastically revise the time-table. It chose the latter course—with little hesitation, for there was no more desire to stay in Burma, now that India was becoming independent, than to stay in Ceylon. The Burmese left the Commonwealth altogether, thinking that their independence would thereby be more complete; but they left, perhaps rather to their surprise, with the goodwill of the British government and with only polite regrets at their unwillingness to maintain a formal link with the Crown.

The independence of India and the neighbouring countries did not mean that Britain ended all her military ties with these countries: Ceylon made a defence agreement which provided for the maintenance of British naval and air bases; and both India and Pakistan continued to employ British officers to help to organize their armed forces. But for Britain, the loss of the Indian Army meant the loss of a valuable reserve of military manpower previously available for her world-wide commitments—although, of course, those commitments had already been considerably cut by the reduction in the size of the dependent empire. Field-Marshal Lord Alanbrooke, the former Chief of the Imperial General Staff, described it as the loss of 'the keystone of the arch of our Commonwealth defence'.[20] Only a few battalions of Gurkhas, who came

19. 'Burma: A Statement of Policy', *P.P.* 1944-5, x, 45f.
20. Bryant, *Triumph in the West*, p. 533.

not from India but from Nepal, were allowed to soldier on under the control of the British War Office.

But with India gone, the case for maintaining a hold on that other arena of British effort during the war, the Middle East, was considerably weakened. The protection of the Suez canal was no longer so important for the sake of communications to India; but Arabian and Iranian oil was a valuable element of the dollar-hungry British economy, and so Britain had an interest in maintaining the status quo in the area. Unfortunately, both Palestine and Egypt were in ferment, and in 1946 there were almost 100,000 British troops in each country. The Egyptians had a right to expect that the British would withdraw into the Canal Zone as soon as the war was over, in accordance with the Treaty of 1936; but they hoped for a new treaty which would end the occupation altogether. At first the Labour Cabinet considered plans which would have satisfied these aspirations: Attlee put forward the idea that there should be a complete withdrawal from the Middle East, and that a new line of defence to protect Central and Southern Africa should be drawn from Lagos to Kenya.[21] But Bevin and A. V. Alexander, the new Minister of Defence, supported by the Chiefs of Staff, managed to defeat this plan.

In 1946-7 it was decided that a major strategical base for the British Army should be established in Palestine.[22] To be sure, the decision provided a path of escape from the Egyptian problem. But this was merely to step from the frying pan into the fire, for the Palestine Jews were in revolt, responding to the desperate plight of their co-religionists seeking to immigrate from Europe, and fortified by a supply of weapons stolen or illegally purchased throughout the Middle East. There could be no simple solution of the Palestine problem, as the Arab inhabitants

21. Bryant, op. cit., p. 531; Diary, 22 Mar., 1946, Dalton Papers.
22. Monroe, Britain's Moment in the M.E., p. 157.

were bitterly hostile to any Jewish assumption of power, and proposals to partition the country, originally put forward by the Peel Commission before the war, hardly seemed likely to establish a viable Jewish state. In 1947 fresh difficulties in the state of the British balance of payments, coupled with the further growth of terrorism, forced a decision which otherwise the Cabinet seemed incapable of taking. In September it was decided to hold on in the Egyptian Canal Zone, but to give up the mandate to govern Palestine, originally derived from the League of Nations.[23] The United Nations Assembly was invited to decide the destiny of the country. Under American influence the Assembly declared in favour of partition, but as this meant in effect siding with the Jews, the British government refused to enforce the decision, and simply withdrew all British troops in May 1948, leaving the Palestinians and their neighbours to fight it out. This was certainly an ignominious end to British rule. The Jews promptly proclaimed the state of Israel, and after some months of intermittent warfare with the Palestinian Arabs and the forces of the neighbouring states of Egypt, Jordan and Syria, they secured an armistice in 1949 which left them with the rather cramped boundaries that nevertheless served them until 1967.

By the end of the 1940s, therefore, Britain was left with an attenuated position in the Middle East. The Anglo-Egyptian Treaty of 1936 was still in force, to the annoyance of the Egyptians, and so Britain could legally maintain the base at the Suez Canal. Cyprus and Aden remained under Colonial Office rule and there were treaty relationships with Jordan and with the Emirates in the Persian Gulf. It was not clear what the value of this limited relationship would be: certainly the hostility of Arab nationalism was not abated as a result. If a crisis were to arise, it was likely to be dangerous for Britain to act alone without the support of the United States. The matter was put to the test

23. Diary, 20 Sept., 1947, Dalton Papers; Monroe, *op. cit.*, p. 165.

in 1951, when the Anglo-Iranian Oil Company was nationalized by the Iranian government. Attlee sounded out Truman on the idea of British intervention with troops, but Truman reacted adversely, and Attlee accepted this, overruling Morrison, who had succeeded Bevin as Foreign Secretary and favoured a British landing.[24] It was obvious that British power in the region would continue to decline; especially as the Anglo-Egyptian Treaty of 1936 ran only for a term of twenty years.

But if Britain's post-war role in the Middle East was a weak and unhappy one, this did not mean that there were very many people in the later 1940s who expected the British colonies in Africa and elsewhere shortly to cut their ties with the Colonial Office. At the end of the war the British government was prepared to tackle its responsibilities to these colonies with new vigour. The old autonomy of the colonial governors now largely came to an end: in spite of its own problems, the home government was determined to assist the social and economic development of the dependencies, in a way not attempted before the war. The staff of the Colonial Office trebled in size between 1938 and 1950. This was not simply the result of having a Labour Government in Britain. A start had already been made by the Colonial Development and Welfare Act of 1940—really the product of the last months of the Chamberlain Government and of the West Indian Royal Commission which reported in 1939. Under this Act, £10.4 million had been spent during the war years. A further Act passed in the first months of the Labour Government provided £120 million for the ensuing ten years—a figure increased in 1950 to £140 million.[25] In addition to this, an Act of 1948 set up two public corporations: one, the Colonial Development Corporation, was to sponsor development schemes of a commercial nature; the other, the Overseas Food Corporation, was to undertake

24. Diary, 27 Sept., 1951, Dalton Papers.
25. Central Office of Information, *Economic Development in the U.K. Dependencies* (1955), p. 7.

the development of the supply of foodstuffs for the British market. The Overseas Food Corporation unfortunately committed itself to an unsound scheme to grow groundnuts in East Africa, and this resulted in a loss of £36 million for virtually no return. But most of the money spent on economic development was wisely spent; and one feature of the post-war years was a considerable expansion of colonial education, including higher education, which helped to provide Africa with a new generation of leaders.

Yet there was so much to be done; and politicians and officials alike, recognizing this, expected the era of colonial rule to extend throughout the foreseeable future in nearly all the territories under their care. Even Malaya, rich though it was, seemed to be too much divided racially to make any rapid advance towards independence. When guerilla activity developed there in 1948 the British government accepted the challenge and after years of effort restored a degree of relative stability. It was not until the late 1950s that a further rapid movement of 'decolonization' occurred, this time mostly in Africa. Admittedly this new movement owed not a little to the example of the early post-war movement in Asia and to the encouragement offered by the Communist and ex-colonial states, now a numerous body, at the United Nations. But this is an extension of the story which takes us well beyond the aftermath of the Second World War.

The obligation to occupy a substantial zone of Germany bulked very large in British thinking about post-war problems. It was largely responsible for the decision to maintain conscription, which had been introduced as an emergency measure in 1939. It has already been suggested that the cost of the occupation, in manpower and in foreign currency, had an important influence on the decisions to accelerate the achievement of independence by the Asian countries. The occupation was undertaken in the first instance to insure against a resurgence of German militarism; but it could be argued that in the new age of missile

292 The Lessons and Effects of War

warfare to which the V.1 and V.2 had been the prelude, it was essential for the protection of Britain to have in friendly hands the whole of western Europe, not just as far as the Rhine but as far as the Elbe. Since the occupation was largely an Army affair, it was natural that the Army staff should be the first to draw this conclusion. The Navy and the Air Force were less readily converted, and when Montgomery shortly after becoming CIGS in 1946 presented his colleagues with a staff paper giving first priority to 'a strong western bloc' and to a British commitment to 'fight on the mainland of Europe, alongside our allies', he at first met with a dusty answer from the First Sea Lord and the Chief of Air Staff.[26]

Gradually however the logic of the situation imposed itself upon both the Cabinet and the Chiefs of Staff. Russia was the one great power with substantial forces in Europe, and the attitude of Russian diplomats was far too inflexible to be re-assuring. No government in Britain was likely, so soon after the failure of 'appeasement', to turn a blind eye to this sort of thing. At first it seemed doubtful whether the Americans could be relied upon for help to western Europe in resisting this threat. But Britain could at least cultivate closer relations with the other western powers, ostensibly in order to form a barrier against a revival of German aggression. In March 1947 Bevin signed a treaty with the French foreign minister for this purpose. After this events moved rapidly, and so did the reactions of peoples and governments. In early 1948, by the Treaty of Brussels, the association was extended to include the Netherlands, Belgium and Luxemburg; and this time the possibility of Russian aggression was covered in the terms of the alliance. Meanwhile, the prospect of military co-ordination with the American forces in Europe in the same event had been explored on a purely military level as early as 1946. The machinery of the Chiefs of Staff Mission in Washington was still in existence, and it was

26. Montgomery, *Memoirs*, p. 436; Leahy Diary, 12 Sept., 1946.

easy enough for contacts to be made through these channels. In the summer of 1946 Montgomery visited Canada and the United States for the first time and was invited by the American Chiefs of Staff to a cruise on the Potomac.[27] Serious discussions took place amid these pleasant surroundings, and it was decided that staff conversations should take place to co-ordinate plans to meet a Russian attack on western Germany. But when the Americans saw the British plan, they did not like it at all. The fact was that neither power had forces adequate to hold a Russian advance. The only real deterrent appeared to be the exclusive American possession of the atomic bomb.[28]

In the absence of adequate documentation on the Russian side, there is bound to be some doubt about the motivation of Stalin's foreign policy in the post-war years. He is generally believed, even by the Russians themselves, to have been a ruthless dictator, and it is likely that he proposed to extend Soviet power as far as he possibly could, short of undertaking a new world war. He was probably banking on an early withdrawal of American troops from Europe, perhaps as a result of the post-war economic depression in the United States which Communists were wont to predict, and which many people in western Europe also thought was likely. But, as we have already seen, he misjudged the American reaction. The Truman doctrine and the Marshall Plan of 1947 showed that the United States government and public opinion now took a very broad view of their responsibilities. The lesson of Munich was a lesson learnt throughout the western world. And so, when in 1948 the Russian screw in eastern Europe tightened still more—in particular by the Communist coup in Czechoslovakia and by the attempt to squeeze the garrisons of the western powers out of Berlin—the American government felt obliged to put its military commitments in Europe onto a permanent basis by means of an alliance with the powers of western Europe. This

27. Montgomery, *op. cit.*, p. 442.
28. Leahy Diary, 12 Nov., 1947.

alliance, signed at Washington in 1949, set up the North Atlantic Treaty Organization. Its founder members included the United States, Canada and the five Brussels Treaty powers, and also Italy, Iceland, Norway, Denmark and Portugal. It was the most comprehensive military commitment ever undertaken by Britain, and the first formal military alliance made by the United States since 1778.

It took some time for the NATO armies to present the appearance of an effective 'military force adequate for the defence of freedom in Europe', as was the announced intention of the signatories of the treaty. In 1952 Greece and Turkey were admitted to the treaty, but this seemed to increase the obligations of the original signatories without significantly increasing their military effectiveness. Although the European powers at once undertook a measure of re-armament, and this was extended when the Korean War broke out in 1950, there was as yet no agreement on an American proposal that Western Germany, already recovering a degree of economic health, should be allowed to make a military contribution of its own. It was natural that the ex-allied countries should still be afraid of German militarism. The French government suggested that one way round the difficulty would be for all the powers of western Europe to form a European Army, with an integrated staff, and then the Germans could take part in this. But the proposal was rejected by the British government, which could not bring itself to make a permanent commitment of its forces for a purely European purpose. There was no significant difference between the main British political parties on this, at any rate when in power. It would have smacked too much of the idea of a supra-national European state, and on this matter, opinion in Britain had not moved forward since 1939. In the end, the West Germans were admitted to NATO with a separate army of their own; but this was not until 1954, by which time Eden, who was once again in charge of the Foreign Office, felt that he could at least give an undertaking that Britain would maintain permanently in Europe the four divisions of troops and the Tactical Air Force which she had already assigned to NATO.

The effect of the war, therefore, was to impose a new pattern upon British policy—a pattern dictated partly by new commitments, partly by fresh limitations upon her economic strength. The country could no longer regard its obligations as primarily imperial and overseas, apart from the traditional concern for the maintenance of the balance of power in Europe. Now there was still an overseas empire to defend, but a much smaller one, mostly in the relatively poor and strategically unimportant continent of Africa. Europe, on the other hand, in a major war would be a battleground for British forces from the start, for a fair proportion of them were stationed there under an American Supreme Commander. British defence expenditure in the late 1940s and early 1950s ranged between 7 and 11 per cent of the gross national product—that is to say, three or four times the proportion that was spent in the early 1930s.[29] Even so, there could be no question of keeping up with the massive military might of the United States and Russia. Yet post-war British governments still drew back from the logical conclusion of this—that Britain would never again be able to fight a major war except as a part of a European federation, or alternatively, with the support of one of the two remaining great powers. The fact was that in the aftermath of victory it was difficult to accept that the war had resulted in a diminution of the country's capacity for an independent role in world affairs.

At the outset of the post-war period, most people in Britain had no doubt that it was wise to be militarily strong. Six years of war against so atrocious an enemy as Nazism had convinced them that in matters of national defence the end justified the means—even to the point

29. Peacock and Wiseman, *Growth of Public Expenditure in the U.K.*, p. 187.

of employing such a weapon as the atomic bomb. Attlee's government, like that of Churchill, seems to have had little difficulty in deciding on the manufacture of nuclear weapons; and when the decision was announced to the Commons in 1948, there were no protests from back-benchers or demands for a debate. The decision was, to be sure, made before the signature of the North Atlantic Treaty, which brought a firm American commitment to the defence of western Europe. But after the treaty had been signed no voices were to be heard calling for the abandonment of the British nuclear defence programme. The first British atomic test took place in 1952, seven years after the first American test and three years after the first Russian. Thus by a curious paradox, the newest weapon in the British armoury, which derived in large part from the effective mobilization of the country's scientific resources in the Second World War, was also the main prop of the most traditional and already perhaps the most unrealistic element of British policy—the belief that, in the last resort, Britain could defy the world alone as she had done in 1940.

# 12.  Inside Britain after 1945

The impact of the war on British domestic history—on the nation's economy, its politics, its social conditions and its cultural life—is extraordinarily difficult to determine, for any attempt to draw up an assessment involves us at once in problems of hypothesis. If the war had not occurred, what would have happened in the six years, 1939 to 1945? The question can have little meaning in reference to Britain's external relations, but there may be some point in attempting to distinguish the long-term trends of change within the country, and then asking whether they were accelerated, retarded, or otherwise affected by the war. Too frequently it was assumed, at the end of the war or shortly afterwards, that changes which had occurred since 1939 were the direct outcome of the war. As time goes by, however, we are able to get a clearer picture of the long-term trends, and in many cases we then discover that what people have ascribed to the impact of war really has more deep-seated causes. All too often the observer has failed to avoid the commonest of historical pitfalls, the fallacy of *post hoc, ergo propter hoc.*

The first question to which we may address ourselves is whether the very great increase in public expenditure, which was such a feature of the war, had a permanent effect in the post-war years. The ordinary taxpayer might think so, as the standard rate of income tax, which had not been above 5s 6d in the pound in the period 1923 to 1939, was never thereafter below 7s 9d. Looking at the matter from the other side, we find that government expenditure in the inter-war period, before the beginning of re-armament, rarely amounted to more than 25% of the gross national product, whereas since the war it has never fallen below 36.5%.[1] On the basis of these figures, the economists A. T. Peacock and J. Wiseman have argued that war has a 'displacement effect, shifting public revenues and expenditures to new levels'.[2] They claim that this is partly because the crisis of war enables levels of taxation to be raised, and it is easier to keep up an existing rate of taxation in peacetime than to raise it for the first time. 'It is harder to get the saddle on the horse than to keep it there.' At the same time, wars are inclined to raise social problems which governments feel they must spend money in solving. Peacock and Wiseman speak of this as an 'inspection effect', which provides the justification for increased government expenditure. A sociologist, Professor S. Andreski, has put the matter in a slightly different way: in his view, modern wars have called for an increasingly large participation by the people as a whole, and as a price for their support the people in one way or another secure compensation in the form of increased social welfare.[3] This concept of a 'military participation ratio' as Professor Andreski calls it has been taken up in recent years by a number of historians.[4]

The main difficulty with such views is that there is no reason to suppose that, in the absence of total war, government expenditure would have remained constant as a proportion of the gross national product. In Britain there was a rapid increase of expenditure in the years 1900 to 1914, and there has been a considerable increase again in the years since 1955.[5] Unfortunately for the supporters

1. Peacock and Wiseman, *op. cit.*, p. 191; A. E. Holmans, 'Growth of Public Expenditure in the U.K. since 1950', *Manchester School*, xxxvi (1968), 318.

2. Peacock and Wiseman, *op. cit.*, p. xxiv.

3. S. Andreski, *Military Organisation and Society* (new ed., 1968), p. 33.

4. R. M. Titmuss, *Essays on the Welfare State*, (new ed., 1963), p. 86; P. Abrams, 'The Failure of Social Reform 1918-20', *Past and Present* no. 24, (1963), p. 45; Marwick, *Britain in the Century of Total War*, p. 14.

5. Peacock and Wiseman, *loc. cit.*,; Holmans, *loc. cit.*

of the theory of the military participation ratio, in neither of these two periods was it assumed by the government that war, if it came, would require the active participation of the bulk of the population. If, instead of looking at all government expenditure, we examine separately the expansion of the social services, we find that the growth of expenditure per head of the population has been remarkably uniform since the beginning of the century.[6] This is partly because commitments assumed by legislation tend to build up gradually as time goes on. Furthermore, as an enquiry into social welfare programmes all over the world has indicated, 'the degree of social security coverage of a nation's population is most powerfully correlated with its level of economic development.'[7] This would no doubt account for Sweden, which has not been involved in any of this century's conflicts, having much better welfare services than Italy, which was heavily engaged in both world wars and in several other wars as well. If we look for an example from within the British Commonwealth, we may notice that the principal extensions of welfare which took place in Britain by legislation in the later 1940s were enacted in New Zealand by the Social Security Act of 1938.[8] On some reckonings New Zealand had a slightly higher standard of living than Britain at that time; but her wars were coterminous with Britain's.

It is generally maintained that the most important single change in the economy effected by the war is the existence of full employment—a condition introduced in Britain (though not in Northern Ireland) by the demands of total

6. Peacock and Wiseman, *op. cit.*, p. 87 (Chart 16).
7. P. Cutright, 'Political Structure, Economic Development and National Social Security Programs', *American Journal of Sociology* lxx (1965), p. 536. A similar standpoint will be found in G. V. Rimlinger, 'Welfare Policy and Economic Development: a Comparative Historical Perspective' in *Journal of Economic History*, xxvi (1966).
8. W. B. Sutch, *The Quest for Social Security in New Zealand* (Wellington, NZ, 1966), pp. 236f.

war, and then maintained in peacetime, so it has been argued, by Keynesian policies of stimulating demand, to which all the British political parties became committed when they accepted the Full Employment White Paper in 1944. There is no doubt about the fact of full employment: between the wars the proportion of the unemployed to the total labour force was rarely less than 10 per cent, whereas since 1945 it has rarely been as high as 2.5 per cent. This has had dramatic effects in strengthening the trade unions, providing far greater opportunities for women's work, and leading to a constant inflation of about 4 or 5 per cent per annum, with an annual 'wages round' as one of its more prominent features. But whether full employment has been entirely, or even largely, the result of the application of Keynesian ideas may be doubted, as the government has been constantly under the necessity of taking demand out of the economy, and has never been able to do any 'pump priming' of the kind that Keynes advocated.

Professor R. C. O. Matthews, who has recently examined the reasons for full employment since the war, has argued that the principal explanation is to be found in the fact that advanced economies tend to have a high proportion of the labour force employed on a permanent or semi-permanent basis.[9] The growth in the size of the public sector also has an effect, and no doubt government encouragement of investment—largely a post-war phenomenon—has played a part in stimulating overall demand. In Britain's case, the Location of Industry Act passed by the Coalition Government in 1945 helped to ensure that at least in the immediate post-war years all regions of Britain got their share of this investment, and so prevented or postponed the re-appearance of 'depressed areas' of the type all too familiar between the wars. This act was really an outcome of the recommendations of the Barlow Com-

9. R. C. O. Matthews, 'Why Has Britain Had Full Employment Since the War?', *Economic Journal*, lxxviii (1968), pp. 555f.

mission, which had completed its work before the outbreak of the war. It may be, however, that the ideas of Keynes had some effect in preventing post-war governments from indulging in harshly deflationary policies in order to correct the recurrent adverse balance of payments.

There are many other changes in the post-war world which appear to be directly related to the existence of full employment. Among them is the increased rate of growth, which for Britain ran at an average percentage of 1.9 in the years 1948 to 1962, as against 1.1 in 1924-37, and even lower figures in earlier periods.[10] Although economists now spend their time trying to account for Britain's relatively slow rate of growth, as compared with that of other countries, it is important to realize that it is historically a very fast rate. The increasing tendency to apply scientific methods to the production process, and to utilize the latest technological advances, has played a part in it, and it is tempting to think that the highly successful mobilization of Britain's scientific manpower for military purposes during the war, and the methods of 'operational research' which they evolved, may have had some impact on the attitude of both sides of industry since the war. But as was pointed out in the report of its wartime activities by the Department of Scientific and Industrial Research, the phrase 'operational research' was 'really a new name for an old and well-tried activity' in industry.[11] Nor did British manufactures in general appear to benefit markedly from advances in technology which the country's scientists had evolved during the war. The great expansion of British exports in the immediate post-war period was in old products as well as new, including even textiles, at a time when the export trades of the ex-enemy countries, particularly Germany and Japan, were still prostrate. Later

10. R. C. O. Matthews, 'Post-war Growth in the British Economy in relation to Historical Experience', *Trans. Manchester Statistical Society*, 1964-5, p. 3.

11. DSIR, 'Report for 1947-8 with review of the years 1938-48', *P.P.* 1948-9, xxi, 68.

on, when the ex-enemy countries recovered and competition became fiercer, it did not seem that Britain got much advantage from wartime technology. It is true that she shared with the United States a lead which had originated during the war in such fields as radio, jet aircraft and atomic energy. But the country which has to pay the costs of pioneering in technological advance does not necessarily make the most profit out of its achievements in the long run. The Italian and Japanese export booms have largely been powered by the sale of goods made on licences from foreign countries. Furthermore, a large proportion of Britain's scientific manpower has since the war been retained on development work for defence; and as Sir Solly Zuckerman, the Chief Scientific Adviser of the Ministry of Defence, has himself suggested,

> the belief that the progress of scientific knowledge is accelerated under the stimulus of military need must be viewed with suspicion.[12]

Here we may have a partial explanation of Britain's relatively slow growth compared with ex-enemy countries. The two industries whose post-war growth has probably made the greatest direct contribution to the British balance of payments—agriculture and oil refining—both owe a great deal to deliberate state encouragement: in the case of agriculture, because of the need to save foreign exchange and the fear of another war in which Britain would again be blockaded: in the case of oil refining, with the object of saving part of the dollar cost of imported oil.[13] But in both cases the technology employed was largely American, and led to a considerable increase in the stake of United States firms in British industry (Ferguson, Ford and Allis-

12. Zuckerman, *Scientists and War*, p. 48.
13. J. H. Dunning and C. J. Thomas, *British Industry* (1961), p. 87; P. Self and H. J. Storing, *The State and the Farmer* (1962), p. 20.

Chalmers in agricultural machinery, Esso and Vacuum in oil refining).[14]

The stresses and strains of war transformed ordinary family life, but it is surprising how little difference they made in the long run. By mid-1944 about 30 per cent of the male working population were in the forces, and for most of them this meant separation from their wives, parents, children, homes. Many civilian families were also split up for long periods, owing to the evacuation of mothers and children from the cities, or as a result of the transfer of labour for which family housing was not available. Women's work also altered the character of family life: comparing 1943 with 1939, about three million more women had become engaged in full-time or part-time work.[15]

Certain changes in official statistics suggested that there were some unfavourable developments as a result. Divorce petitions filed in England and Wales rose from 9,970 in 1938 to 24,857 in 1945, and the rapid increase continued after the war.[16] But the figures do not tell the whole story, for the Matrimonial Causes Act, which came into operation in 1938, had considerably extended the grounds for petition; and in addition, facilities for servicemen and poor civilians to obtain divorce had been considerably extended. The statistics of juvenile delinquency rose by about a half between 1938 and 1944, and this was naturally attributed to the temporary effects of wartime.[17] But the continuance of the rise even in the 1950s has now led to second thoughts on the causation.[18] The spread of venereal disease in war-time can more readily be related to the separation of

14. J. H. Dunning, *American Investment in British Manufacturing Industry* (1958), pp. 61, 65.

15. Ferguson and Fitzgerald, *Studies in the Social Services*, p. 6.

16. *Ibid.*, p. 20.     17. *Ibid.*, p. 21.

18. 'Report of the Committee on Children and Young Persons', *P.P.* 1959-60, ix, 700.

families. Fortunately, new drugs, especially penicillin, greatly reduced the dangers of serious illness or disablement as a result.[19]

Throughout the war the government kept a close watch on the health statistics, realizing that morale both in the forces and in industry would suffer if there were any serious deterioration. The Ministry of Food, with advice from nutritionists, succeeded in providing a system of rationing which would encourage health while economizing on imports. The Ministry of Education sponsored a rapid development of school meals and school milk supplies. The Ministry of Health, fearing epidemics as the result of air raids, developed preventive medicine: immunization against diphtheria began in 1940 and proved a striking success, bringing the death-rate down by two-thirds.[20] But tuberculosis increased early in the war, probably because many patients suffering from the disease had been sent home to make room for air raid victims, and infected other people.[21] On balance, the nation's health was surprisingly good. The death rates did not appreciably increase, and maternal mortality fell markedly. The 1944 infantile mortality rate was a record low figure.[22] Although the government's measures played their part in this, the most important single factor was probably the improvement in family incomes. Considerable credit must also be given to the advances in medical knowledge in the 1930s and 1940s—the use of new drugs such as the sulphanomides and penicillin, and the practice of new techniques such as blood transfusion.

Meanwhile, the institution of marriage became more popular than before, and the birth rate at last began to increase. The average marriage rate for the war years was higher than it had been in the preceding years of peace.[23] A certain proportion of the rise must have been due to the

19. MacNalty and Mellor, *Medical Services in War*, p. 331.
20. Ferguson and Fitzgerald, *op. cit.*, p. 169.
21. *Ibid.*, pp. 253-5.
22. *Ibid.*, p. 172.
23. *Ibid.*, p. 18.

marriage of British brides to American, Canadian and other Allied servicemen: in Scotland the proportion of such marriages was as high as 5 per cent. But for the most part these families did not stay in Britain.[24] On the other hand, the number of young adults at the end of the war, somewhat depleted as it was as a result of military casualties, was reinforced by the admission of some 84,000 'European Volunteer Workers' recruited from the more or less stateless refugees of Central Europe, and another 125,000 members of the Polish armed forces and their dependents who accepted the British government's invitation to them to stay in Britain when they showed great reluctance about returning to their home country, now under Communist rule.[25] With the return to Britain of the great bulk of her own servicemen, some of them with brides, especially from occupied Italy and Germany, the birth rate rose to a post-war peak in 1947—and this in turn produced the so-called 'post-war bulge' of children and later young men and women who packed the schools in the 1950s and early 1960s and then strained the resources of the colleges and universities.[26] Since 1945, the birth rate has remained well above the net reproduction rate and there is no danger of the wartime fears of a declining population being realized. But the change appears to be due more to the better economic conditions and prospects of the great bulk of the population than to any specific acts of social policy, such as family allowances or child welfare.

The story of the development of British political feeling between 1939 and 1945, culminating in the great success of the Labour Party in the 1945 election, may suggest that the swing to the Left was itself a product of the war. It

24. *Ibid.*
25. M. Bülbring, 'Post-War Refugees in Britain', *Population Studies*, viii (1954-5), p. 99.
26. For a table showing the size of annual age-groups, see 'Report on Higher Education', *P.P.* 1962-3, xi, 710.

is certainly true that people's political views were powerfully affected by events closely connected with the war, such as the Munich agreement of 1938, and by the course of the war itself, perhaps in particular the unexpectedly successful resistance of the Russians. Public opinion was so strongly pro-Soviet in 1944 that it was almost impossible to publish a book implying sharp criticism of the Stalinist regime: George Orwell's *Animal Farm* was turned down by Faber and Faber in July of that year by, of all people, T. S. Eliot, who was a director of the firm and who wrote to say that this was not 'the right point of view from which to criticize the political situation at the present time.'[27] As for the earlier swing to the Left, something like it might well have occurred even if there had been no war. The 1935 election had put the Liberals firmly into the position of a small minority, and it was henceforth clear that the National Government's only possible challenger for power was the Labour Party. It was only to be expected that sooner or later—and it might well have been sooner, that is, before 1945—a Labour Government with a clear majority over other parties would have been elected. Its policy would presumably have been something like *Labour's Immediate Programme* of 1937, which proposed to nationalize the Bank of England, the railways, coal, electricity and gas, and, among other things, to extend the school leaving age to fifteen, to improve pensions and to 'extend' health services.[28] This is not very different from the policy of Labour's election manifesto in 1945, *Let Us Face the Future*; but it is evident that the idea of a national health service owed a good deal to official and professional thinking just before and during the war. The chaotic jumble of municipal and voluntary hospitals had been effectively co-ordinated for the first time by the Emergency Medical Service, which the Ministry of Health had fashioned as a flexible instrument for dealing with the

27. T. S. Eliot to G. Orwell, 13 July, 1944, quoted in *The Times*, 6 Jan., 1969.
28. Labour Party *Report*, 1937, pp. 277-9.

flood of air raid casualties which was expected; and all concerned with the service decided that they could not go back to the pre-war state of affairs.

Apart from this, the main difference, so far as the

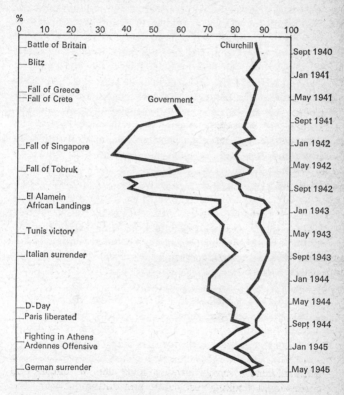

Popularity of the Coalition Government and Prime Minister
Percentage satisfied in reply to the question 'On the whole, in general, are you satisfied or dissatisfied with the Government's conduct of the war?'; and percentage approving in reply to the question 'On the whole, in general, do you approve or disapprove of Mr Churchill as Prime Minister?'
Figures by courtesy of The Gallup Poll

Labour Party was concerned, was that its leaders had been gradually schooled in the functions of government, so that when they came to power after having served in the Coalition, they arrived with a good knowledge of the Whitehall machine and of the reasons for existing policies. This made for efficiency; and it also nurtured a spirit of moderation in ideas and expectations. The five years of Coalition government had gone a long way to take the bitterness out of pre-war politics. They had done much to heal the scars of the 'class struggle'—to soften the harsh memories of the General Strike of 1926, the animosities aroused by the existence of mass unemployment, and the feeling shared by most Labour Party members that there had been something underhand or even unconstitutional about the way the National Government had come to power in 1931. Late in the war Attlee tried to express to Harold Laski, the Labour Party's leading intellectual of that time, how he personally felt that things had changed. He wrote that in discussion with colleagues of other parties he had found 'on many matters more agreement than you would expect.' But in any case there were 'limits to the extent to which the clock can be put forward or back.' As for the future:

> I have never suggested that we should drop our principles and programme, but it is, I suggest, better to argue from what has been done to what may be done rather than to suggest that very little has been accomplished.[29]

It was part of Attlee's case that during the war there had been a remarkable advance of opinion among politicians of all parties and even among leading officers of the armed forces, about such things as the need for planning and for full employment. Naturally there was some truth in this, though Attlee as a Coalition minister was obviously more

29. Attlee to Laski, 1 May, 1944, quoted Martin, *Laski*, p. 161.

willing to give his Conservative colleagues the benefit of the doubt than he had been as Leader of the Opposition.

The spread of collectivist ideas in the middle class was a feature of the war years: as we have seen, it found one striking manifestation in the Common Wealth movement. It was not, however, by any means all a result of wartime influences. It owed a great deal to the memory of interwar unemployment and the belief, reinforced by the percolation downwards of the ideas of J. M. Keynes, that something could and should be done to prevent its recurrence. Men who had at least grown up in the twentieth century, and had been profoundly influenced in their ideas by the experience of the First World War, were now assuming the positions of leadership in public opinion. Among them was William Temple, who became Archbishop of Canterbury in 1942: he had long been an advocate of the positive use of the powers of the state in social matters, but more attention was paid to him when he was at Canterbury than when he was at York. It was apparently he who coined the term 'Welfare State',[30] though it made little impact at the time and did not come into common use until it was employed, in a pejorative sense, by the American opponents of President Truman's domestic policies at the end of the decade.[31] Another important moulder of opinion in the latter part of the war was the new editor of *The Times*, R. M. Barrington Ward, who succeeded Geoffrey Dawson in 1941. He had long been something of a Tory Radical, and when he recruited E. H. Carr, the diplomatic historian and expert on Soviet Russia, to write leaders on foreign affairs, *The Times* began to be regarded in right-wing circles as 'the three-penny edition of the *Daily Worker*.' Yet if it had not been for the war, the impact of Barrington Ward's radicalism, at least, might have been felt somewhat earlier. Dawson's retirement from the editorship of *The Times* was put off

30. W. Temple, *Citizen and Churchman*, (1941), p. 35.
31. See, e.g., H. L. Marx, *The Welfare State* (New York, 1950).

for twenty-one months owing to the need for re-organization at Printing House Square at the beginning of the war.[32]

The war witnessed a formidable concentration of power in the hands of the government, and within the government in the hands of the Prime Minister and Minister of Defence. Churchill certainly by-passed the Cabinet a great deal by determining strategy with the Chiefs of Staff only: already by 1942 the Cabinet Secretary recorded that 'in recent months' the War Cabinet had rarely discussed general strategy.[33] On civil affairs the War Cabinet was more fully in charge, but Churchill here also developed a new practice by passing many of the papers to his personal advisers, Bracken, Beaverbrook and Cherwell, only one of whom was ever a member of the War Cabinet, and then only briefly. Oliver Lyttelton spoke of this group of Churchill's friends as a 'Palace Government', which ministers found it profitable to 'square' before submitting their papers for Cabinet approval.[34] Still, as it was the Labour ministers who most objected to this, there was not much prospect of it continuing in the same way after the war. There does not seem to have been much permanent increase in the power of the Prime Minister as a result of the war, although it is obvious that the long-term effect of modern mass communications has been to enhance his role as leader of a party. Churchill's broadcast speeches in 1940 were heard by as many as seven out of every ten people;[35] but it was the accident of personality as well as the nature of the political situation that prevented his predecessors, or for that matter his immediate successor, from making use of the same medium to a similar degree. Already before the war a Prime Minister had great power,

32. Wrench, *Dawson*, pp. 417, 440.
33. Ehrman, *Grand Strategy*, vi, 324.
34. Halifax Diary, 28 Mar., 1945, Hickleton Papers.
35. R. J. E. Silvey, 'Recent Trends in Listening', *BBC Yearbook*, 1946, p. 28.

and Chamberlain's relations with his Cabinet colleagues were such that one of them could later describe his government as a 'one-man band'.[36] Chamberlain certainly had more freedom in assigning ministers to particular posts, or in replacing them, than Churchill did: for Churchill had to discuss many of his appointments with Attlee and obtain his approval for them. The wartime innovations that increased the power of the Prime Minister—for instance, the No. 10 Office, forming a personal staff for him—did not make a great deal of difference. And from 1946 onwards the duties of Minister of Defence were taken off the Prime Minister's shoulders by the appointment of a separate minister. Since the separate departments—the Admiralty, the War Office, and the Air Ministry—still retained great power, the Minister of Defence once again experienced many of the difficulties in co-ordinating defence policy which had existed in the 1930s.

There was of course a danger that the growth of the government's power in wartime, and in particular the emergency regulations of 1939 and 1940, would damage the authority of Parliament and weaken the freedom of the press. In practice, however, the prestige of Parliament suffered less from this than from the electoral truce, which prolonged the life of the Commons far beyond the point where it could reasonably be said to represent public opinion. Churchill as Prime Minister with his great personal popularity might have been tempted to ignore the House, rather as Lloyd George had done for a time. Certainly Churchill showed signs of wanting to transcend the role of an ordinary Premier. When the tide turned in favour of Allied arms, he usually put on military uniform on visits to the troops abroad, and seemed to look more and more like an autocrat. This may, however, have had the effect of making some electors of limited political knowledge think that he was altogether above the electoral battle: and so may have reduced his influence in the course of the 1945 election campaign. It certainly threat-

36. Lord Swinton, *Sixty Years of Power* (1966), p. 116.

ened to eclipse the position of the King—a point well illustrated by their exchange of views on the question of whether either of them should go to Normandy with the troops on D-Day.[37] But Churchill had a profound respect for the traditional elements of the constitution, and this included both the Crown and Parliament. His experience, instinct and sense of gratitude all led him to treat the Commons as the main forum of his oratory: and although in January 1942 he tried to persuade the members to allow his major speeches to be electrically recorded in the House, so as to relieve him from the necessity of repeating them on the radio, he accepted their refusal without complaint.[38]

Freedom of debate in the Commons was likely to suffer much more from the fact of war itself, which imposed restrictions on the public discussion of many matters on the ground of security; and also from the existence of the Coalition, which made almost all of the MPs into supporters of the government. Lord Winterton complained in 1941 that under these conditions ministerial statements tended to be followed by 'votes of thanks' from across the floor.[39] But in spite of this, there were several major debates in both 1941 and 1942 which reflected the grave concern felt in the country about strategy and economic policy, and on these occasions the Commons was clearly maintaining its function as a forum for criticism and rebuttal on vital matters of the day. Nor did ministers or MPs have any doubt that the life of the ministry itself depended upon the voting at the end of the debate. The size of the majority in the government's favour on each occasion cleared the air, and gave it the authority that it required both at home and abroad. Towards the end of the war, however, MPs became a little too smug about their success as an instrument of government. It was unfortunate for the future that the principal decisions about the rebuilding of the Chamber of the House of Commons,

37. Wheeler-Bennett, *George VI*, pp. 601-3.
38. Churchill, *Second World War*, iv, 57.
39. *New Statesman*, 19 Apr., 1941.

which had been destroyed by a bomb, were taken before the 1945 election rather than after. In the atmosphere of mutual congratulation that prevailed, Churchill persuaded his fellow-members to reconstruct the Chamber almost exactly as it was when bombed. This meant that there were no additional facilities for the conduct of MPs constituency business—which was destined to grow rapidly in the post-war period in parallel with the growth of the power of the government departments.[40]

A large part of the responsibility for the maintenance of free discussion naturally still remained with the press. The BBC was not much of a forum for controversy even in peacetime, as Churchill himself had cause to know, having been prevented from broadcasting for years when he was a back-bencher. The most that could be expected from the BBC was that it should present the news that it received as honestly as possible, and, for the rest, should do the best it could in the way of popular entertainment. Its regular news bulletins, particularly those at 9 p.m., were in fact 'a succession of peaks in the daily curve of listening'; and after the first winter of the war the public largely gave up the practice of tuning in to 'Lord Haw-Haw' from Germany.[41] The fact that the BBC was never actually controlled by the government gave its presentation of news a certain detachment and a sense of reliability, although of course it could not be genuinely impartial. Its European services, by contrast with the radio propaganda of other countries, gained a remarkable reputation for trustworthiness.

The task of the newspapers and journals, therefore, was not so much to provide the news as to interpret and comment on it. This was rendered difficult, not only by the censorship of incoming news (the papers themselves were

40. For Churchill's speech, see Hansard 393, 403ff. (28 Oct., 1943). For a backbencher's view of the post-war expansion of constituency work, see C. Ponsonby, *Ponsonby Remembers* (Oxford, 1965), p. 111.

41. Silvey, *op. cit.*, p. 28. Cf. Allingham, *Oaken Heart*, pp. 138f.

not censored) but by Defence Regulation 2D of 1940, which empowered the government to suppress any organ which published matter 'calculated to foment opposition to the war.' Fortunately the government showed restraint in the exercise of its emergency powers; and it was greatly helped by the desire of the editors themselves to assist the war effort. The Communist *Daily Worker* was the only daily to fall a victim to Regulation 2D: it was banned from January 1941 to September 1942. In March 1942 the *Daily Mirror*, which had been voicing rank-and-file criticisms of red tape and army routine, received an official warning that it would be suppressed if it did not mend its ways.[42] In fact it did not mend its ways much, but after the victory of El Alamein later in the year the government became much less touchy about press criticism. Even in the dark days of 1941 a prominent American journalist had been able to describe the British press as 'not only free but amazingly virile and informative.'[43]

To some extent the war held up change in the structure of the newspaper industry. The *Mirror*'s circulation— perhaps more because of its strip cartoons than because of its radicalism—was rising more rapidly than that of any other daily: it reached 3.7 million copies in 1947, which was an increase of 1.3 million since 1937.[44] But there were no take-overs or mergers: nearly all the newspapers, including the more highbrow ones, were gaining readers rapidly in this period. Newsprint shortages reduced their size drastically—a state of affairs which lasted for some time after the war. For this reason people were often inclined to buy more than one paper; and the weeklies also markedly increased their readership. The *New Statesman*, the organ of the left-wing intelligentsia, trebled its circulation during the war.[45] In spite of wartime difficulties,

42. Cudlipp, *Publish and Be Damned!*, p. 178.

43. Laird and Graebner, *Hitler's Reich and Churchill's Britain*, p. 32.

44. 'Report of the Royal Commission on the Press, 1947-9' P.P. 1948-9, xx, 198.

therefore, the body of the press survived and even prospered, and the weaker brethren were protected from the cutting winds of peacetime competition.

The maintenance of the essential liberties of Parliament and the survival of a vigorous press did much to protect the freedom of the ordinary subject. This had certainly suffered some erosion from conscription and from the direction of labour, although as we have seen the arrangements for conscientious objection were not illiberal, and the Minister of Labour was extremely cautious in using his powers of direction. The greatest danger to free speech was from Defence Regulation 18B (first used in 1939 but extended in 1940) which empowered the Home Secretary to detain any person whom he had 'reasonable cause' to believe to be hostile to the state. The courts ruled, in the famous case of *Liversidge* v. *Anderson*, that 'reasonable cause' did not mean that the Minister had to have a cause which appeared reasonable to other people.[46] In the period of acute anxiety and alarm about an invasion— that is to say, in May and June 1940—a number of British subjects, many of them with Fascist associations, were arrested under this regulation and detained without trial. A considerably larger number of persons of enemy nationality were also interned, although many of them were refugees from the continental dictatorships. It was only after a vigorous press campaign and questions in Parliament that their individual cases were properly investigated —many of them being at once released. Before this process had taken place, some of them had been sent to Canada by sea, and a few were drowned when their ship was torpedoed. Of the British subjects there were still about 1250 in detention in December 1940;[47] and of them some, including Sir Oswald Mosley, were imprisoned for most of the war. But the government was not without popular sup-

45. Martin, *Editor*, p. 265.

46. HL[1942]AC 206. For relevant extracts see G. Le May (ed.), *British Government, 1914-53* (1955), pp. 329-333.

47. Hansard 367, 642 (5 Dec., 1940).

port in this matter; and when Mosley was released in 1943 owing to a serious illness, a considerable agitation took place against the decision. It was a misfortune that the National Council of Civil Liberties, which might have educated the public on the matter, was under strong Communist influence, and simply refused to take up cases of people whose politics it disapproved: it officially 'deplored' Mosley's release.[48] But Regulation 18B was extinguished, along with many other restrictions upon individual liberty, at the end of the war.

The great expansion of the Civil Service which took place during the war naturally led to many improvisations. It was thought that university dons would make good civil servants; and on the whole this proved to be so—some of them indeed such as Oliver Franks and Harold Wilson made their names in this way. Naturally also as in the First World War many business men were brought in. Partly because of this influx of new blood and partly because of the need for dealing with emergency situations, the Civil Service was loosened up and brought more fully to appreciate the popular reactions to government policy. There was also a considerable development in the use of public relations officers by government departments, to ensure that official policies were properly explained to the public. The public relations officers have become a permanent feature of Whitehall: the growth of the mass media, as well as the extension of government functions in peacetime, has seen to that.[49] But the pre-war rigidity of the system of employment and promotion of civil servants was restored after the war; and a Committee of Enquiry over twenty years later deplored the fact that there was no major reform of the Service at the end of the war, when the opportunity existed: 'In the 1950s the old

48. *Civil Liberty*, Dec., 1943.
49. Royal Institute of Public Administration, *The Government Explains* (1965), pp. 56-67.

ways re-asserted themselves. The nature of the task was changing and the Service was left behind.'[50]

The extension of state intervention in the course of the present century has been accompanied by a great development of co-operation between government and voluntary bodies—employers organizations, trade unions, professional associations, other interest groups and charities. This process has often enhanced the status of the voluntary bodies, but it has given them extra responsibilities. The war saw an immense development of this process, though it was already beginning beforehand. The trade unions, for instance, although they had been at odds with 'the state' in the 1920s, were already in the 1930s being invited to take part in state-sponsored activities such as the re-organization of the textile industry and the plans to assist the fishing industry. During the war, with one of their former leaders running the Ministry of Labour, and with the government in urgent need of trade-union co-operation in any case in order to preserve good industrial relations at a critical period, the trade unions were invited to help in the formulation of policy on almost every aspect of life on the home front, from the operation of the black-out to the treatment of conscientious objectors. Sir Walter Citrine, the TUC secretary, found himself serving on some thirty public or semi-public bodies.[51] At the end of the war he regarded this as a permanent change, and told Congress: 'We have passed from the era of propaganda to one of responsibility.'[52] To be sure, he was taking into account the fact that there was now a Labour Government in power, which the trade-union leaders felt had a special claim on their loyalties. But there was little change when the Conservatives returned to power in 1951.

But although the trade-union leaders enjoyed their new

50. *Report of the Committee on the Civil Service, 1966-68* (1969), Cmnd. 3638, p. 13.

51. W. Citrine, *Two Careers* (1967), p. 28.

52. TUC *Report*, 1946, p. 269.

status—as did the officers of other bodies representing previously rather downtrodden occupational groups, such as the National Farmers Union—they still saw their primary role as being the defence of the sectional interests of the members of their respective unions; and it is important to realize how little they gave away in this respect. The voluntary system of collective bargaining remained unaltered throughout the war. Strikes were formally prohibited under Order 1305 of 1940, which also set up a National Arbitration Tribunal as a final court of appeal in wage bargaining. But there was no way of preventing unofficial strikes, or of penalizing strikers, without doing serious damage to the process of production, as was shown in the course of the Betteshanger Colliery strike of January 1942.[53] Nor could anything be done in wartime to rationalize the pattern of trade-union structure. Union membership expanded considerably as a result of full employment; but this if anything only increased the danger of demarcation strikes within particular industries. It certainly might have been better for post-war industrial productivity if the trade unions had been destroyed during the war, as they had been in Germany, and had had to be reconstructed on the basis of the modern pattern of industry.

Nor was it only the trade unions which managed to safeguard their structure and independence during the war. The Law Society under the pressure of necessity agreed to introduce a system of cheap legal advice for the many people who suddenly found themselves faced with legal problems arising from the government's innumerable regulations or from other incidents of war. The Society also provided a Services Divorce Department, and a Poor Persons' Civilian Divorce Department, to cope with the increased demand for advice in matrimonial cases.[54] Solicitors and others who were engaged in this work realized

53. Bullock, *Bevin*, ii, 267f.; Parker, *Manpower*, pp. 460-2.
54. B. Abel-Smith and R. Stevens, *Lawyers and the Courts* (1967), pp. 316-19.

the need for permanent arrangements to enable the ordinary citizen of modest means to get legal advice without undue expense. The result of this was the Legal Aid Act, passed in 1948. But the scheme that the Act introduced was entirely administered by the Law Society, and the income limits that it laid down were, allowing for inflation, hardly more generous than those which had existed for free legal aid before the war. The principal burden of advising and assisting ordinary people on their rights was left to the Citizens' Advice Bureaux—the semi-official local centres established during the war by the National Council of Social Services, which was really a charity. The legal profession survived the war with its old-fashioned system of fees and services almost unaltered. At first it had to pay the price of seeing the courts increasingly by-passed by the expansion of administrative tribunals, which were set up by Parliament to undertake judicial functions under the legislation of the post-war period.[55] But as time went on, the lawyers moved into the administrative tribunals also.

Local government also changed comparatively little as a result of the war. This may be surprising, as the immediate impact of war was to impose on local authorities many extra functions—in particular, the tasks of organizing the evacuation or reception of mothers and children, air raid precautions, and the sustenance of families bombed out of their homes. All these functions clearly called for local initiative; and plenty of this was available, as was shown by the willingness of people to volunteer their services, often unpaid: indeed the Women's Voluntary Service, founded in 1938 with the problem of air raids in view, has become a permanent organization. But as Professor Titmuss has shown in his official history, it is difficult for local authorities, many of them of very limited size, to cope with a national emergency.[56] Under such circumstances a cheese-paring attitude on the part of the Treasury could

55. See, e.g., R. S. W. Pollard, *Administrative Tribunals at Work* (1950).
56. Titmuss, *Social Policy*, passim.

only result in extra suffering for the victims of a disaster. The government had established a series of Regional Commissioners, whose primary task it was to take over the functions of the central government if heavy bombing or an invasion prevented Whitehall from maintaining its control. The Regional Commissioners did not have to undertake this primary task, but they were able to provide valuable co-ordinating functions during heavy air raids in their respective regions. But this was a temporary service which did not last very long. In practice, most of the staffs which grew up around the offices of the Regional Commissioners were outposts of Whitehall departments, working under central control.[57] Many of these regional staffs remained after the war; but the Regional Commissioners were abolished, and the idea of regional government virtually disappeared until the 1960s. The local authorities resumed almost all their normal functions, including that of running the fire brigades, which had been nationalized at the height of the Blitz. To be sure, the postwar expansion of the social services caused some changes: the old local responsibility for poor relief and hospitals was ended, but on the other hand for some years the provision of new houses became an almost exclusive function of the local councils. The net result was that local government expenditure continued as a more or less constant percentage of the gross national product; but the proportion of local government revenue that came from exchequer grants, rather than from the local rates, continued to rise as it had done before the war.[58] All this indicates the growing importance, over the long term, of the central government as compared to the local authorities. The war seems to have made little difference to this tendency.

In the hectic days of 1940, it was quite common for people to suppose that the war was effecting a social

57. O'Brien, Civil Defence, pp. 175-9, 643f.
58. Peacock and Wiseman, op. cit., pp. 96ff.

revolution in Britain. Many of the wealthy thought so, and lamented that they had lived to go through such an experience. Their domestic servants had been taken from them by the demands of the factories, just at the moment when their pleasant houses in the country were being invaded by mothers and children from the slums. Now taxation had risen sharply, and the standard rate of income tax reached 10s in the pound, as against 5s in the peak period of the First World War. By 1941 Harold Nicolson was shocked to think that he would 'have to walk and live a Woolworth life hereafter.'[59] This was an absurd exaggeration, but undoubtedly he had to live a somewhat reduced existence. By contrast, the wages of nearly all manual workers rose faster than the cost of living, and with the advantages of overtime, opportunities for work by married women, and general full employment, their families were usually better off than before the war. Left-wing publicists like J. B. Priestley and Sir Richard Acland were glad to believe that social distinctions were being eroded, and argued that the process should be deliberately encouraged in order to 'release fresh stores of energy and enthusiasm' for the war.[60] But to Conservatives this argument seemed to be a case of the wish being father to the thought; and the government was mindful of the fact that Parliament still had a Conservative majority. The long-term effects of the war on the distribution of income in Britain are very difficult to measure. The economist H. F. Lydall has concluded that there was a modest reduction in social inequality in the twenty-year period 1938 to 1957, for in these years the share of total disposable income that went to the top one-hundredth of the population fell from 12 per cent to 5 per cent.[61] But this change may be related in large part to long-term tendencies which had

59. Nicolson, *Diaries*, ii, 170.

60. Priestley, *Out of the People*, p. 115.

61. H. F. Lydall, 'Long-term Trends in the Size Distribution of Incomes', *Journal of the Royal Statistical Society*, cxxii, Part 1 (1959).

little to do with the war, such as the growth of the white-collar class at the expense of the class of manual workers.

Undoubtedly the war brought into existence for a time a stronger sense of community throughout the country than normally existed in peacetime. Dunkirk, the Battle of Britain and the Blitz produced a 'backs-to-the-wall' solidarity that transcended class barriers and brought together all sorts of people in the Home Guard, Civil Defence, the air raid shelters and even to some extent the factories. There were frequent lapses of the customary unwillingness of the average middle-class Englishman to converse with strangers. The increased mobility of the population caused by the call-up, by evacuation and by changes in occupations tended to break down parochialism. In 1940 no less than 19 per cent of the population changed their residence at least to the extent of crossing a local government boundary: this was probably about four times the peacetime rate.[62] As Josiah Wedgwood said in a letter to Lothian in America, 'We all make new friends, as on a steamer voyage.'[63]

All this movement, combined with other wartime changes, had an immediate impact on intellectual life and the general appreciation of music and the arts. On the one hand, writers and artists found themselves separated from their peacetime livelihood, and either thrust into humbler occupations, or else obliged to seek some form of government patronage for their activities. On the other hand, a considerable body of serious readers and people with minority interests in art and music were starved of their usual cultural opportunities. It was to try to fill this gap that the Council for the Encouragement of Music and the Arts (CEMA) was founded at the beginning of the war, partly with government money, partly with the aid of a charity, the Pilgrim Trust. CEMA, although by no means well endowed, was able to sustain much cultural

62. *Report of the Royal Commission on Local Government, 1969-9* (1969), vol. iii, Cmnd. 4040 (II), p. 83.
63. J. Wedgwood to Lothian, 17 Sept., 1940, Lothian Papers.

activity which would otherwise have lapsed. It supported provincial orchestras and founded mobile drama companies. It encouraged tours by art exhibitions, including the work of artists such as Henry Moore, John Piper, Paul Nash and Graham Sutherland, all of whom had been appointed official war artists. It even made possible serious concerts in air raid shelters. Above all, it gave its backing to the Covent Garden Opera, the Sadlers Wells Ballet and the Old Vic, all of which attained new heights of achievement in the later war years. CEMA's work was warmly appreciated, and at the end of the war it became a permanent body with the new title of the Arts Council, and with an annual Treasury grant, fixed to begin with at £235,000.[64]

There was also a considerable amount of adult education going on during the war, and in some directions the need for it greatly expanded. The army arranged for lectures on current affairs to the troops, some by visiting civilian lecturers, but most by officers to their own units. For the guidance of the latter, two series of pamphlets were published, one on current affairs generally, one on the somewhat intangible subject of 'The British Way and Purpose'. Men and women on civil defence duties had time on their hands before and after the Blitz and took part in discussions and attended courses. They could call upon the intellectuals in their ranks for help in the instruction: Stephen Spender, for instance, was a member of the London firemen and became one of their discussion group leaders.[65] Prisoners of war on the Continent were able to read for degrees and other qualifications by post, and even to take examinations. One popular BBC innovation was the Brains Trust, on which pundits such as C. E. M. Joad and Julian Huxley discussed topics of intellectual concern. There was also a keen demand for new serious literature. Penguin Books were able to fill a good deal of the demand because the success of their 'Specials' on

64. Arts Council, *The First Ten Years* (1956), pp. 5-17.
65. S. Spender, *World Within World* (1951), p. 305.

current affairs just before the war entitled them to a very large paper ration—publishers' quotas being based on the size of their pre-war sales.[66] John Lehmann's *Penguin New Writing*, which appeared periodically throughout the middle and later stages of the war, enjoyed a steady sale of 80,000 for each issue and brought the latest poetry and short stories to a wide audience of new readers.[67]

But it would be a mistake to make too much of all this. Some of the interest in serious culture was quite fortuitous: that is to say, it arose out of the temporary absence of some of the lighter forms of entertainment. The BBC did not find, from its audience samples, that the market for serious music was expanding rapidly, but rather that it was growing slowly as it had done before the war.[68] Army education was not taken very seriously by unit commanders, and the ordinary soldier usually looked forward to the lectures only as an opportunity to relax for a time—perhaps to go to sleep. John Lehmann and Penguin Books Ltd found after the war that they had underestimated 'the ease with which the outer circle of those who had become readers . . . when there were few competitors for the occupation of their leisure hours, would slip away':[69] this led to the demise of *Penguin New Writing* in 1950. Finally, the Arts Council although a permanent organization has to do its work on what is no more than a shoe-string budget when compared with the lavish state encouragement of the arts which is characteristic of foreign countries.

Some people thought that the destruction of large parts of London and other cities in the air raids would provide a wonderful opportunity for planned reconstruction after the war, as had occurred in London after the Great Fire in 1666. The Ministry of Town and Country Planning, set up in 1944, was looked upon as the pioneer of a new and well-ordered world. But post-war achievement fell far

66. W. E. Williams, *The Penguin Story* (1956), p. 14.
67. Lehmann, *I Am My Brother*, p. 308.
68. Silvey, *op. cit.*, p. 29.
69. J. Lehmann, *The Ample Proposition* (1966), p. 70.

short of wartime hopes. The system of compensation for air raid damage forced many property owners to reconstruct their buildings exactly as they had been before. Reasons of economy prevented the fulfilment of plans for new public buildings, or for new vistas of old buildings, and in the City of London St Paul's Cathedral became hemmed in by office buildings as closely as ever. A few small successes—the new Coventry Cathedral, the replanning of the centre of Plymouth, London's Festival Hall— do not add up to a fulfilment of the promise that was offered by the opportunity. The shortage of land and the increased interest in town planning has led to the establishment and planned development of a number of new towns, many of them as satellites of London. But rigid economy, combined with certain errors of design, has prevented most of them from being very attractive.

Looking back on wartime cultural achievements, one is struck by the lack of original contributions to the arts. If there was a temporary renaissance of literature, music and the drama, it was almost entirely confined to the performance and appreciation of existing work. To take poetry as an example: in the Second World War there was no new composition of the quality of that of Rupert Brooke or Wilfred Owen in the First World War. Whether the Spanish Civil War had exhausted British talent, or whether the accident of battle killed off the more promising poets—for instance, Keith Douglas and Alun Lewis—there was not much to show for six years of war, and we are left with the despairing question posed by Roy Fuller, himself a poet of quality, in September 1944: 'Has there ever . . . been a period which has produced so much bad verse as the last five or six years?'[70]

The explanation of it all may lie in the fact that, in spite of the shocks of 1940, the Second World War made much less of an impact on the British mind than the First World War had done. In 1914 the country was not prepared men-

70. *Time and Tide,* 16 Sept., 1944.

tally for the trials that it had to undergo—the appalling suffering of the trenches and a rate of casualties never previously experienced. But in 1939 most people feared a repetition of the First World War, and so there was no psychological trauma resulting from the sacrifices that it eventually involved. The average Briton might be impressed, at least for two or three years, by what he took to be the exceptional military prowess of the Soviet Union, and wonder what the reason for it was; but the war did not really weaken his adherence to his own distinctive national institutions and customs. Parliament, the political parties, the Civil Service, local government, the press, the law, the trade unions—all emerged from the war with slightly different surface features, but basically unaltered. There had not been much of that 'inspection effect' which is supposed to be one of the by-products of war; or, if there had been, it had found most institutions not unsatisfactory, and so served to reinforce the view which so many people in Britain still retained: that somehow or other, things in their own country were arranged much better than elsewhere in the world—even if, in limited directions only, there might be some room for improvement.

# Unpublished Sources

The following unpublished sources have been cited in the footnotes:

A. V. ALEXANDER PAPERS. Diaries and papers of A. V. Alexander, later Lord Alexander of Hillsborough. At the Library of Churchill College, Cambridge.

ATTLEE PAPERS (C). Letters of C. R. Attlee, later Lord Attlee, to W. S. Churchill. At the Library of Churchill College, Cambridge.

ATTLEE PAPERS (U). Papers of C. R. Attlee, later Lord Attlee. At the Library of University College, Oxford.

BEVIN PAPERS. Papers of Ernest Bevin. At the Library of Churchill College, Cambridge.

BEVERIDGE PAPERS. Papers of Sir William Beveridge, later Lord Beveridge. At the British Library of Political and Economic Science, London.

CABINET MINUTES. Minutes of Cabinet Meetings. At the Public Record Office, London.

CABINET PAPERS. Papers circulated to Cabinet Ministers. At the Public Record Office, London.

CHERWELL PAPERS. Papers of Prof. F. A. Lindemann, later Lord Cherwell. At the Library of Nuffield College, Oxford.

DALTON PAPERS. Diaries and papers of Hugh Dalton, later Lord Dalton. At the British Library of Political and Economic Science, London.

HICKLETON PAPERS. Diaries of Lord Halifax. Consulted by arrangement at the City Library, York.

LEAHY DIARIES. Diaries of Admiral William D. Leahy, USN. At the Library of Congress, Washington DC, USA.

WENDELL PHILLIPS PAPERS. Diaries and papers of Wendell Phillips. At the Houghton Library, Harvard University, Cambridge, Mass., USA.

SAMUEL PAPERS. Papers of Lord Samuel. At the House of Lords Record Office, London.

TEMPLEWOOD PAPERS. Diaries and papers of Sir
Samuel Hoare, later Lord Templewood. At the Cambridge
University Library.

US ARMY, ETO Admin. Files. Administrative records of the
US Army, European Theater of Operations. At the Federal
Records Center, Suitland, Md, USA.

# Books for Further Reading

*Official History*

The British official histories of the Second World War, taken as a whole, probably constitute the best account of wartime administration that has ever been published. The six volumes of J. R. M. Butler, J. M. A. Gwyer and J. Ehrman, *Grand Strategy* (1956-64: two volumes still awaited) explain the conduct of strategy at the highest level. S. W. Roskill, *The War at Sea* (3 volumes, 1954-61) provides a clear and skilful narrative of naval operations. The story of land operations is necessarily more disjointed. T. K. Derry, *The Campaign in Norway* (1952) is, especially for its date of publication, frank and revealing. The other authors of studies of the land campaigns have conceived their task somewhat more narrowly. They are: L. F. Ellis, *The War in France and Flanders* (1953) and *Victory in the West* (2 vols., 1962-9); I. S. O. Playfair, *The Mediterranean and Middle East* (4 vols., 1954-66, the last one in collaboration with C. J. S. Molony); and S. Woodburn Kirby, *The War Against Japan* (5 vols., 1957-69). Air operations were dealt with in a brief, popular study by D. Richards and H. St G. Saunders, *Royal Air Force, 1939-45* (3 vols., 1953-4); but the work of Bomber Command has been subjected to exhaustive examination in the important study by C. K. Webster and N. Frankland, *The Strategic Air Offensive Against Germany, 1939-45* (4 vols., 1961). The Battle of Britain, the Blitz and the V.1 and V.2 offensives are described in B. Collier, *The Defence of the United Kingdom* (1957). The many volumes of the Medical History of the War, both military and civil, are summed up in A. S. MacNalty and W. F. Mellor, *Medical Services in War* (1968).

Of the civil histories, the most important single volume—a distinguished and comprehensive work—is W. K. Hancock and M. M. Gowing, *The British War Economy* (1949). Difficulties of administration in wartime are dealt with in masterly fashion by R. M. Titmuss in *Problems of Social Policy* (1950), and to this S. M. Ferguson and H. Fitzgerald, *Studies in the Social Services* (1952) forms a useful addendum. The bulk of the other volumes are studies of the work of particular ministries. The following have proved most useful for the present work: W. H. B. Court, *Coal* (1951), R. J. Hammond, *Food* (3 vols., 1951-62), E. L. Hargreaves and M. M. Gowing, *Civil Industry and Trade* (1952), P. Inman, *Labour in the Munition Industries* (1957), K. A. H. Murray, *Agriculture* (1955), T. H. O'Brien, *Civil Defence* (1955), H. M. D. Parker, *Manpower* (1957), M. M. Postan, *British War Production* (1952), and R. S. Sayers, *Financial Policy, 1939-1945* (1956). There is also a *Statistical Digest of the War* (1951), prepared by the Central Statistical Office, itself a product of the war. There is a rather dry narrative of foreign policy by E. L. Woodward, *British Foreign Policy in the Second World War* (1962). One interesting special study is J. W. Blake, *Northern Ireland in the Second World War* (Belfast, 1956). There is, regrettably, no official history of British prisoners of war, but a good substitute is provided by a volume in the New Zealand Official History, W. Wynne Mason, *Prisoners of War* (Wellington, NZ, 1954). There is no official history of the Ministry of Information or of the Board of Education, or of the Ministry of Reconstruction and the committees that preceded its formation. A start has been made on the study of the Special Operations Executive with the publication of M. R. D. Foot, *S.O.E. in France* (1966); but other secret intelligence work and operations remain secret. Yet the most deadly secret of all now has its official history—M. M. Gowing, *Britain and Atomic Energy, 1939-1945* (1964).

Several of the American official histories are valuable for British history or for joint strategy and operations. This is especially true of volumes published by the US Army, e.g. K. R. Greenfield (ed.), *Command Decisions* (Washington, DC, 1960), G. A. Harrison, *Cross-Channel Attack* (Washington, DC, 1951), M. Matloff and E. M. Snell, *Strategic Planning for Coalition Warfare, 1941-2* (Washington, DC, 1953), M. Matloff, *Strategic Planning for Coalition Warfare, 1943-4* (Washington, DC, 1959), and W. F. Craven and J. L. Cate (ed.), *The Army Air Forces in World War II* (7 vols., Chicago, Ill., 1948-58). For foreign policy, the series of volumes of documents called *Foreign Relations of the United States: Diplomatic Papers* (Washington DC, from 1956 for the war period) is illuminating. The Soviet Government has made one notable contribution in *Stalin's Correspondence with Churchill, Attlee, Roosevelt and Truman, 1941-1945*, (1958).

*Unofficial History*
Even the best official history may be disappointing to the general reader, because it refrains from assessing the contribution of individuals, tends to avoid party politics and controversy, and is

usually written at considerable length from a predominantly administrative point of view. But so far the absence of primary source material owing to the Thirty Year Rule for official documents has prevented other historians from examining the history of Britain during the war in any depth. A. J. P. Taylor, *England, 1914-1945* (Oxford, 1965) contains 163 pages directly on the war, and they are stimulating, if not infrequently inaccurate. W. N. Medlicott, *Contemporary England, 1914-1964* (1967) has 93 pages on pre-war diplomacy, which are valuable, but only a sketchy 54 pages on the war itself. The best introductory account of Britain's war effort—for all its natural bias, its omissions and its small errors—is Winston Churchill's *The Second World War* (6 vols., 1948-54). It also contains a good deal of documentation, largely in appendices. There are now also some important studies which lay the main emphasis on social history. Arthur Marwick, *Britain in the Century of Total War* (1968) has 70 pages directly on the Second World War, and is a pioneering attempt to assess the effect of war on social change —perhaps with some exaggeration. Angus Calder, *The People's War,* (1969) examines in great detail but with admirable lucidity the impact of the war on ordinary social life: and there is an excellent bibliography. Other books tend to be narrower in scope and can best be dealt with under specialised headings.

1. *Political and Administrative Studies.* There is a rather dry outline of the main changes in the structure of government in D. N. Chester and F. M. G. Willson, *Organisation of British Central Government, 1914-1956* (1957). J. W. Wheeler-Bennett, *King George VI,* (1958), gives a useful if as yet incomplete picture of the King's role and attitudes. There are no studies of the Conservative and Liberal Parties during the war, but G. D. H. Cole, *History of the Labour Party since 1914* (1948) and H. Pelling, *British Communist Party* (1958) contain chapters on the years 1939-45. R. B. McCallum and A. Readman, *The British General Election of 1945* (1947) the first of the Nuffield election surveys, contains much information but now seems unsophisticated and should be done again. There are many autobiographies and biographies, some of only marginal value. K. Feiling, *Life of Neville Chamberlain* (1946) contains important quotations from his letters and papers; there are a few more points in I. Macleod, *Neville Chamberlain* (1961). Some light on Churchill's way of life and thought is thrown by the work by his doctor, Lord Moran, *Winston Churchill: The Struggle for Survival, 1940-1965* (1966). Autobiographies or memoirs by former members of the War Cabinet are on the whole disappointing: C. R. Attlee, *As It Happened* (1954) reveals virtually nothing. Lord Avon (A. Eden), *Facing the*

*Dictators* (1962) and *The Reckoning* (1965) contain some fresh documentation, but appear to conceal a good deal behind a bland exterior. Lord Halifax, *Fulness of Days* (1957), H. Morrison, *Autobiography* (1960), and Lord Simon, *Retrospect* (1952) are all of very limited value. Lord Chandos (O. Lyttelton), *Memoirs* (1962) is enlivened by some gossip, and Lord Templewood (S. Hoare), *Nine Troubled Years* (1954) is a serious attempt to put the case for the appeasers. Books about Cabinet ministers are in most cases more helpful than their own memoirs. Attlee was somewhat more forthcoming in interview, as is shown by F. Williams, *A Prime Minister Remembers* (1961); and there is a valuable study by A. Bullock, *Life and Times of Ernest Bevin* (2 vols. so far, 1960 and 1967). Lord Birkenhead, *Halifax* (1965) contains extracts from Halifax's diaries, and K. Young, *Churchill and Beaverbrook* (1966) draws heavily on Beaverbrook's correspondence. J. W. Wheeler-Bennett, *John Anderson* (1962) contains some interesting material, though not a great deal; better is R. J. Minney, *Private Papers of Hore-Belisha* (1960). E. Estorick, *Stafford Cripps* (1949) has no original material for the war period.

Just below War Cabinet level was Hugh Dalton, whose account of wartime politics, *The Fateful Years* (1957) is much the best, spiced as it is with gossip and malice. Even so, it is only a small selection from his unpublished diaries. The third volume of L. S. Amery, *My Political Life* (1955) is of interest for its account of the growth of opposition to Chamberlain in the Conservative Party in 1938-40. Duff Cooper, *Old Men Forget* (1953) and Lord Reith, *Into the Wind* (1949) throw some light on the history of the Ministry of Information and on some other problems, including the failure of their authors to make more of a mark in wartime administration. Lord Birkenhead, *The Prof in Two Worlds* (1961) is a useful study of Lord Cherwell, based on his papers; R. F. Harrod, *The Prof* (1959) gives some idea of Cherwell's 'S-branch' from within. Autobiographical volumes by Lord Casey, *Personal Experience* (1962), by Harold Macmillan, *The Blast of War* (1967) and by Lord Swinton, *I Remember* (1949) are of more value for British policy in Africa and India than for home politics. The memoirs of the Conservative Chief Whip from 1941, Lord Stuart, *Within the Fringe* (1967) gives some idea of Churchill's relations with his party.

Some impression of the wider political scene may be obtained from R. Boothby, *I Fight to Live* (1947), which is interesting on Churchill's rise to power; R. Rhodes James (ed.), *Chips* (1967)—the diary of Henry Channon, a wealthy Chamberlainite; and Harold Nicolson, *Diaries and Letters* (3 vols., 1966-8), of which the second volume gives a fascinating and at times moving account of the war from the angle of a junior minister and back-bencher. The various attitudes of the Left may be traced in F. Brockway, *Outside the Right* (1963), the memoirs of a veteran pacifist; the first volume of Michael Foot, *Aneurin Bevan* (1962), which makes a good case for Churchill's most persistent Commons critic; Kingsley Martin, *Harold Laski* (1953) and Martin's own memoirs, *Editor* (1968). There is no good life of Lloyd George, but there is some material on the war period of his life in Frank Owen, *Tempestuous Journey* (1954) and in Frances Lloyd George, *The Years that are Past* (1967). G. M. Thomson, *Vote of Censure* (1968) describes the wave of criticism of government policy that developed in 1942. J. Eaves, *Emergency Powers and the Parliamentary Watchdog, 1939-1951* (1957) provides a lucid account of the relations of Parliament and the executive. D. Hayes, *Challenge of Conscience* (1949) outlines the story of the conscientious objectors; and R. C. D. Jasper, *George Bell, Bishop of Chichester* (1967) is the biography of Britain's leading critic of area bombing. For political opinion in the country at large, H. Cantril (ed.), *Public Opinion, 1935-46* (Princeton, NJ, 1951) contains a number of the more important results of the Gallup Polls.

2. *Studies of Social History*. The bibliography in Calder, *The People's War*, already mentioned, should be referred to. An interesting, if impressionistic, account of the early stages of the war as it affected the ordinary citizen is to be found in E. S. Turner, *The Phoney War on the Home Front* (1961). Life in a country village, coping with evacuees and later with the threat of invasion, is vividly depicted in Margery Allingham, *The Oaken Heart* (1941). R. Padley and M. Cole made a careful study of evacuation in *Evacuation Survey* (1940). Laurence Thompson's *1940* (1966) gives a good general account of events and reactions in Britain in the critical year. The best description in brief of the air raids of 1940-1 is probably that given by Constantine Fitzgibbon, *The Blitz* (1957). The reactions of the civilian population naturally attracted much attention from American journalists: Edward Murrow, *This is London* (1941) and Negley Farson, *Bomber's Moon* (1941) stand the test of time fairly well. There is some careful social observation in the work of two American journalists, S. Laird and W. Graebner, *Hitler's Reich and Churchill's Britain* (1942). John Strachey, *Post D* (1941) gives an idea of work in London civil defence during the Blitz; Sir Harold Scott, *Your Obedient Servant* describes the high-level administrative problems. Charles Graves, *Women in Green* (1948) is a brief account of the Women's Voluntary Service. Tom Harrisson and Charles Madge of Mass-Observation edited a study of popular behaviour at the beginning

of the war, *War Begins at Home* (1940); and throughout the war Mass-Observation produced a *Bulletin* which reported people's behaviour and feelings, and also undertook some special studies such as *War Factory* (1943). On the impact of the Beveridge Report, see Janet Beveridge, *Beveridge and His Plan* (1954). On the evolution of the National Health Service, H. Eckstein, *The English Health Service* (Cambridge, Mass., 1958) is probably the best account. The 1944 Education Act and its background as dealt with briefly in M. Cruickshank, *Church and State in English Education* (1963). Changing social conditions in the war period are discussed in B. Seebohm Rowntree and R. Lavers, *Poverty and the Welfare State* (1951) and the same authors' *English Life and Leisure* (1951).

3. *Studies in Economic History.* For an introduction see A. S. Milward, *Economic Effects of the World Wars in Britain* (1970) and S. Pollard, *Development of the British Economy, 1914-50* (1962). D. N. Chester (ed.), *Lessons of the British War Economy* (Cambridge, 1951) throws light on economic administration. R. F. Harrod, *Life of J. M. Keynes* (1951) is important for policy, but lacks full documentation. The closing stages of Lend-Lease and the American Loan negotiations are lucidly described by R. N. Gardner, *Sterling-Dollar Diplomacy* (Oxford, 1956). A. T. Peacock and J. Wiseman, *Growth of Public Expenditure in the United Kingdom* (Princeton, NJ, 1961) is important for the long term. On developments in trade unionism, see N. Barou, *British Trade Unions* (1947) and D. F. Macdonald, *The State and the Trade Unions* (1960).

4. *Press and Propaganda.* The Report of the Royal Commission on the Press, which is to be found in *Parliamentary Papers*, 1948-9, xx, gives a good deal of information on its structure and on changes effected by the war. For problems of editorial policy in wartime and before see J. E. Wrench, *Geoffrey Dawson and Our Times* (1955) and H. Cudlipp, *Publish and Be Damned!* (1953). R. Williams-Thompson, *Was I Really Necessary?* (1951) describes the work of a public relations officer. G. P. Thomson, *Blue-Pencil Admiral* (1947) is important and authoritative on the problems of censorship. The early days of the Ministry of Information are portrayed unkindly in N. Riley, *999 and All That* (1940). Lord Birkenhead, *Walter Monckton* (1969) gives some idea of a later and more stable era. For the work of the Political Warfare Executive see R. H. Bruce Lockhart, *Comes the Reckoning* (1947). Asa Briggs, *History of Broadcasting in the United Kingdom*, iii, (forthcoming) will cover the war years.

5. *Commonwealth and Empire.* The standard work is N. Mansergh, *Survey of British Commonwealth Affairs: Problems of*

*Wartime Co-operation and Post-War Change, 1939-1952* (Oxford, 1958); and to supplement this there is N. Mansergh (ed.), *Documents and Speeches on British Commonwealth Affairs* (2 vols., 1953). There is some fresh material in the same author's *Commonwealth Experience* (1969). J. W. Pickersgill (and D. F. Forster), *The Mackenzie King Record* (2 vols., Toronto, 1960, 1968) is revealing on Anglo-Canadian relations, as also is Vincent Massey, *Memoirs* (1963). On Australian attitudes, see R. G. Menzies, *Afternoon Light* (1967); on Smuts and South Africa, see W. K. Hancock, *Smuts: The Fields of Force, 1919-1950* (Cambridge, 1968). On India, P. Woodruff, *The Men who Ruled India*, ii (1954) and M. Edwardes, *The Last Years of British India* (1963) may be used for introductory purposes. On Burma, see H. Tinker, *The Union of Burma* (1957) and M. Collis, *Last and First in Burma* (1956). There is a useful article by R. von Albertini, 'The Impact of Two World Wars on the Decline of Colonialism', *Journal of Contemporary History*, iv (1969). J. M. Lee, *Colonial Development and Good Government* (Oxford, 1967) throws interesting light on the social background of changes in British colonial policy.

6. *Foreign Affairs and Allied Political Strategy.* The Churchillian view of the coming of the war, expounded not only in Churchill's *Second World War*, i, but also in the work of historians in the early post-war years—e.g. J. W. Wheeler-Bennett, *Munich: Prologue to Tragedy* (1948)—was seriously shaken by A. J. P. Taylor, *Origins of the Second World War* (1961). A new edition (1963) and a paper-back edition (1964) contain a Foreword of 'Second Thoughts'. But Mr Taylor's book, including the 'Second Thoughts', goes too far in re-interpretation. For a cogent criticism of his use of the evidence of German and Allied defence expenditure, see T. W. Mason, 'Some Origins of the Second World War', *Past and Present* no. 29 (1964). M. Gilbert and R. Gott, *The Appeasers* (1963) is a throw-back to the Churchillian standpoint; but M. Gilbert, *The Roots of Appeasement* (1966) shows more sympathy with its subject. I. Kirkpatrick, *The Inner Circle* (1959) are the memoirs of a diplomat closely involved in Anglo-German relations before and after the war. The fundamentals of the British strategic situation on the eve of the war are described in Royal Institute of International Affairs, *Political and Strategic Interests of the United Kingdom* (1939), and the relative strength of the powers is assessed in the Institute's survey, *The World in March 1939* (1952). W. L. Langer and S. E. Gleason, *The Challenge to Isolation* (1952) is a valuable account of the international scene from the American angle. I. Maisky, *Who Helped Hitler?* (1964) gives

an account from the Soviet point of view, of the negotiations for a military alliance between Britain, France and Russia in 1939.

For the period of the Anglo-French war, P. Reynaud, *Mémoires* (Paris, 1964) is useful. The crisis of May and June 1940 is dealt with vividly in E. Spears, *Assignment to Catastrophe* (2 vols., 1954). D. Thomson, *The Proposal for Anglo-French Union in 1940* (Oxford, 1966) is a brief but useful study. Paul Baudouin, *Private Diaries, March 1940—January 1941* (1948) throws light on the attitudes of French politicians in the critical year. Charles de Gaulle, *War Memoirs* (3 vols., 1955-60) is one of the most important works to have emerged from the war: it has interesting sidelights on Britain and her leaders. I. Maisky, *Memoirs of a Soviet Ambassador* (1967) is of some help on Anglo-Russian relations up to 1943.

The forging of the wartime alliance between Britain and the United States is largely the subject of J. R. M. Butler, *Lord Lothian* (1960) and R. A. Divine, *The Reluctant Belligerent* (New York, 1965). For the collaboration of the three major powers from 1941, see W. H. McNeill, *America, Britain and Russia,* 1941-6 (1953) and H. Feis, *Churchill, Roosevelt, Stalin* (Princeton, NJ, 1957). The best outline of American foreign policy in the war years is Gaddis Smith, *American Diplomacy during the Second World War, 1941-1945* (New York, 1965). Of memoirs, by far the best is R. E. Sherwood (ed.), *The White House Papers of Harry Hopkins* (2 vols., 1949). Cordell Hull's *Memoirs* (2 vols., New York, 1948) are of importance, though they try to conceal the weakness of the author's position as Secretary of State. J. M. Blum, *From the Morgenthau Diaries,* iii (Boston, 1967) throws light on Anglo-American relations in the diplomatic and financial spheres. For the events of 1945 and the beginnings of the Cold War, see E. R. Stettinius, *Roosevelt and the Russians* (1950); H. S. Truman, *Year of Decisions* (1955) and *Years of Trial and Hope* (1965); H. Feis, *The Atomic Bomb and the End of World War II* (Princeton, NJ, 1966); W. Millis (ed.), *The Forrestal Diaries* (1952); and M. F. Herz, *Beginnings of the Cold War* (Bloomington, Ind., 1966). There is a stimulating if unstructured discussion of the beginnings of the Cold War in P. Seabury *et al.*, 'Origins of the Post-war Crisis', *Journal of Contemporary History* iii (1968). A view more sympathetic to Russia may be found in G. Kolko, *The Politics of War* (1969), but the author exaggerates the consistency and skill of American policy-making in this period. P. Dixon, *Double Diploma* (1968) throws light on the Potsdam Conference, and R. Murphy, *Diplomat Among Warriors* (1964) and E. Monroe, *Britain's Moment in the Middle East, 1914-1956*

(1963) are useful for Anglo-American collaboration and disagreement in Africa.

7. *Military Strategy and Operations.* The most straightforward military narrative of the war, largely from the British point of view, is B. Collier, *Short History of the Second World War* (1967). For criticism of British strategy see B. H. Liddell Hart, 'The Second World War' in *New Cambridge Modern History*, xii (2nd. ed., Cambridge, 1968) and J. F. C. Fuller, *The Second World War, 1939-1945* (1948). The formation of British strategic policy is described in A. Bryant, *Turn of the Tide* (1957) and *Triumph in the West* (1959) which are based on the revealing diaries of the CIGS, General Sir Alan Brooke. Also of some interest for an earlier period is R. Macleod and D. Kelly (ed.), *The Ironside Diaries, 1937-40* (1962). High-level planning is discussed in Lord Ismay, *Memoirs* (1960), which is very loyal to Churchill, and in J. Leasor, *War at the Top* (1959) and B. Fergusson, *The Business of War* (1957) which are more critical. General Sir Frederick Morgan in his *Peace and War* (1961) criticizes the other generals also. E. J. Kingston-McCloughry, *The Direction of War* (1955) is interesting on aspects of air policy.

Anglo-American military strategy has been much debated. The American contribution to joint policy is discussed briefly in S. E. Morison, *American Contributions to the Strategy of World War II* (1958) and, more fully, in K. R. Greenfield, *American Strategy in World War II* (Baltimore, 1963). Some of the inter-allied disputes are mentioned in W. D. Leahy, *I Was There* (1950), but this is rather a dour chronicle. H. L. Stimson and McG. Bundy, *On Active Service in Peace and War* (New York, 1948) is the memoir of the able American Secretary of War. The merits of particular strategies are discussed in M. Howard, *The Mediterranean Strategy in the Second World War* (1968) and in R. M. Leighton, 'Overlord Revisited: an Interpretation of American Strategy in the European War, 1942-4', *American Historical Review*, lxviii (1963). Two harsh critics of British policy and performance are A. C. Wedemeyer, *Wedemeyer Reports!* (New York, 1958) and J. W. Stilwell, *The Stilwell Papers* (1949): both of these generals were involved in the China campaigns. D. D. Eisenhower, *Crusade in Europe* (1948) naturally contains no recriminations. H. C. Butcher, *Three Years with Eisenhower* (1946) and Omar Bradley, *A Soldier's Story* (New York, 1951) in different ways convey the story of the American command in the Mediterranean and European campaigns of 1942-5.

There are now two good studies of senior British commanders in the field: J. Connell's *Auchinleck* (1959) and *Wavell* (2 vols.,

1964-9). Christopher Sykes, *Orde Wingate* (1959) is a fair portrait of the most bizarre of war heroes. Of the generals' own memoirs, oustanding is W. Slim, *Defeat into Victory* (1956)—perhaps the best account of the Burma campaign and not less impressive because the author admits that he made mistakes. B. L. Montgomery, *Memoirs* (1958) are naturally important, though less revealing, except of the author's character. Naval biographies and memoirs do not compare very well, but Lord Cunningham, *A Sailor's Odyssey* (1951) and D. Macintyre, *Fighting Admiral* (1961), which is about Sir James Somerville, are of some value. The best of the air marshals' memoirs is Lord Tedder, *With Prejudice* (1966), which is certainly very critical of the soldiers, if not so much of fellow-airmen. J. Slessor, *The Central Blue* (1956) and Sholto Douglas, *Years of Command* (1966) contain useful information. R. Wright, *Dowding and the Battle of Britain* (1969) throws new light on the controversy about fighter tactics.

There are now many accounts of particular campaigns or operations, and the following is only a selection: P. Fleming, *Invasion 1940* (1957) which is about Hitler's projected invasion of Britain; B. Collier, *The Battle of Britain* (1962); C. Barnett, *The Desert Generals* (1960); M. Carver, *Tobruk* (1964) and *El Alamein* (1962); N. Barber, *Sinister Twilight* (1968) on the fall of Singapore; W. G. F. Jackson, *Battle for Italy* (1967); A. Moorehead, *Eclipse* (1949) on the campaigns of 1943-5 in Europe; C. Wilmot, *The Struggle for Europe* (1952), on the invasion and campaign of 1944-5; C. Hibbert, *The Battle of Arnhem* (1962); B. Fergusson, *Beyond the Chindwin* (1945) and *The Wild Green Earth* (1946) on the Chindits' exploits; and D. Irving, *The Destruction of Dresden* (1963). On naval operations, there are some attractive brief studies: D. Macintyre, *Battle of the Atlantic* (1961) and *Battle for the Mediterranean* (1964) and S. W. C. Pack, *Battle of Matapan* (1961). F. Pile, *Ack-Ack!* (1949) is the story of the rather neglected Anti-Aircraft Command, told by its commander. Questions of military morale are dealt with in R. H. Ahrenfeldt, *Psychiatry in the British Army in the Second World War* (1958). For an interim report on the Home Guard, see C. Graves, *The Home Guard of Britain* (1943).

Some light on the SOE is thrown by B. Sweet-Escott in his *Baker Street Irregular* (1965), an entertaining book, and by E. H. Cookridge in *Inside S.O.E.* (1966). Both have suffered from restrictions on publication, as has D. MacLachlan in telling the important story of naval intelligence in his *Room 39* (1968). Perhaps the best adventure story of the war is provided by an intelligence officer who stayed on in Malaya after the collapse: F. Spencer Chapman, *The Jungle is Neutral* (1949).

The German view of the war with Britain may be derived from Admiral Doenitz, *Memoirs* (1959), for naval operations; B. H. Liddell Hart (ed.), *The Rommel Papers* (1953) and *The Other Side of the Hill* (1951) for military operations; and A. Galland, *The First and the Last* (1955) and H. Rumpf, *The Bombing of Germany* (1963) for the air war. R. R. A. Wheatley, *Operation Sealion* (Oxford, 1958) tells the story of the projected invasion of Britain from the German side.

8. *Science in War.* M. M. Gowing, *Atomic Energy* and the biographies of Lord Cherwell have already been mentioned. Sir Solly Zuckerman, *Scientists and War* (1961) offers an authoritative view of the relationship between scientists and defence problems. R. W. Clark, *The Rise of the Boffins* (1962) is a popular but useful account of the work of scientists in the war. The same author's *Tizard* (1965) is the biography of one of the most important 'boffins'. C. P. Snow, *Science and Government* (1961) probably exaggerated the personal hostility between Cherwell and Tizard. A good deal about the British scientific contribution to allied victory can be gleaned from J. P. Baxter, *Scientists Against Time* (Boston, Mass., 1946) and R. G. Hewlett and O. E. Anderson, *The New World, 1939-1946* (University Park, Pa, 1962) which describe American scientific work for defence purposes. The official history of the medical services, already mentioned, includes information on the application of scientific advance.

9. *Literature and the Arts.* John Lehmann's autobiography of the war years, *I Am My Brother* (1960) is a good starting point for literary historians. I. Hamilton (ed.), *The Poetry of War* (1965), R. Skelton (ed.), *Poetry of the Forties* (1968) and R. Blythe, *Components of the Scene* (1966) provide some impression of the poetry of the war, but the reader may do better to turn up old copies of the periodicals *Horizon* and *Penguin New Writing* to see what was being published, and quite widely read, in both poetry and short stories. Richard Hillary, *The Last Enemy* (1942) and Keith Douglas, *Alamein to Zem-Zem* (1946) are two powerful narratives of war by young participants, both later killed. Novels which are set against the background of the war include Nigel Balchin, *The Small Back Room* (1943); Elizabeth Bowen, *The Heat of the Day* (1949); Henry Green, *Caught* (1943); Graham Greene, *Ministry of Fear* (1943); Gerald Kersh, *They Die with their Boots Clean* (1941); Colin MacInnes, *To the Victor the Spoils* (1950); and Evelyn Waugh's *Put Out More Flags* (1942) and the Sword of Honour Trilogy

(1952-61)—*Men at Arms, Officers and Gentlemen,* and *Unconditional Surrender*. G. W. Stonier's droll short stories, *Shaving Through the Blitz* (1943) must not be omitted. S. Orwell and I. Angus, *The Collected Essays, Journalism and Letters of George Orwell* (4 vols., 1968) contain much of interest to the political, social and literary historian. J. Maclaren Ross, *Memories of the Forties* (1965) is interesting both for sketches of army life and for impressions of literary personalities in wartime. For brief accounts of developments in ballet, the cinema, music and painting see A. L. Haskell, Dilys Powell, R. Myers and R. Ironside, *Since 1939* (1949).

# Index